RIPPER DIARY

THE INSIDE STORY

SETH LINDER, CAROLINE MORRIS
AND KEITH SKINNER

SUTTON PUBLISHING

First published in the United Kingdom in 2003 by
Sutton Publishing Limited · Phoenix Mill
Thrupp · Stroud · Gloucestershire · GL5 2BU

British Library Cataloguing in Publication Data
A catalogue record for this book is available from the British
Library.

ISBN 0-7509-2954-5

Dedicated to
Deirdre, Conor, Ciara and Saoirse
Butch and Carly
Michael and Jana

Typeset in 11/14.5 pt Sabon.
Typesetting and origination by
Sutton Publishing Limited.
Printed and bound in England by
J.H. Haynes & Co. Ltd, Sparkford.

Contents

Acknowledgements

The authors would like to thank the following: Paula Adamick, Andy Aliffe, Coral Atkins, Richard Bark-Jones, Michael Barrett, Paul Begg, Peter Birchwood, Harold Brough, Professor David Canter, Peter Cavanagh, Susie and Dougie Chandler, Ed W.G. Chick, Maurice Chittenden, Janet Dangar, Paul Daniel, Maggie Dawson, Paul Dodd, Ivor Edwards, Carol Emmas, Stewart P. Evans, Sally Evemy, Melvyn Fairclough, Paul H. Feldman, Martin Fido, Duncan Field, Mike Furlong, Christopher T. George, Anne Graham, Caroline Graham, Janet Graham, Alan Gray, Stephen Grey, Melvin Harris, Shirley Harrison, Richard Hollinshead, Mark Honigsbaum, Martin Howells, Albert and Valerie Johnson, Pinkie Kavanaugh, Michele Kimche, Loretta Lay, Mark Lea, Leslie Linder, Caroline Montgomery, Doreen Montgomery, Jenny Morrison, Richard Nicholas, Claudia Oliver, John Omlor, R.J. Palmer, Andy and Sue Parlour, Charlie Pulford, Sally Pybis, Norma Quine, Bill Renshaw, Frank 'Micky' Roach, Mary Roach, Bruce Robinson, Manon Rosat, Donald Rumbelow, Stephen Ryder, Dawn Shotter, Dr Diana Simpson, Robert Smith, Nancy Steele, Steve Swede, Nick Warren, Richard Whittington-Egan, Liz Winter, Eduardo Zinna.

Quotations from the original manuscript of the diary of Jack the Ripper, purporting to be by James Maybrick, are reproduced by kind permission of the copyright holder, Robert Smith.

Authors' Note

To avoid confusion, Anne Barrett (née Graham) is referred to throughout the text as 'Anne', Caroline Graham as 'Caroline' and Robbie Johnson, brother of Albert Johnson, as 'Robbie'. In all other cases we refer to people by their surnames.

Introduction

I live in hope that as the remaining slums of Whitechapel and Spitalfields are finally cleared, some hidden documentary evidence of the identity of Jack the Ripper will be found wedged behind a rafter. Or it may well be that, deposited with a solicitor or at a bank somewhere, there is a dusty tin box marked 'Not to be opened for one hundred years' and which contains a complete and evidential confession.

> JACK THE RIPPER: *One Hundred Years of Mystery*
> Peter Underwood, Blandford Press, 1987

A shadowy figure in hat and cloak moves stealthily through the gloomy, fog-shrouded lanes and alleyways of London's East End. There's the flash of a blade as he strikes, an ear-splitting scream slowly dying away, and then he is gone, disappearing into the anonymity of the covering night. One hundred and fifteen years since the discoveries of the mutilated bodies of five prostitutes shocked and terrified Victorian England, the popular image of Jack the Ripper still looms large in our minds.

Indeed, it is true to say that public interest in this most infamous of serial killers has never been greater. Every year many thousands of tourists retrace his footsteps through the streets of Whitechapel, visiting murder sites that are virtually unrecognisable from Victorian times. The Ripper is a favourite attraction at Madame Tussauds and the London Dungeon. On the page, his evil deeds are relived time and time again in best-selling books promoting yet another theory about his true identity, the latest of which is Patricia Cornwell's *Portrait of a Killer* (Little, Brown, 2002), benefiting from her reputation and 6 million dollars' worth of research. Hollywood blockbusters continue to exploit the sinister lure of his appeal. And over the last few years websites dedicated to the Ripper have proliferated on the internet. Some are among the internet's most-visited sites, sparking intense and often vituperative debate from Ripper experts and enthusiasts in countries around the world.

There is, arguably, just one piece of evidence that could finally prove, once and for all, who Jack the Ripper really was. It would be a document written by the murderer himself, a journal revealing his motives and his state of mind, and describing how he went about the murders. Perhaps obliquely contained within the journal we would at last find his true identity.

The final lines from the purported Diary of Jack the Ripper.

ONE

'You can almost feel the evil'

'I've got Jack the Ripper's diary, would you be interested in seeing it?' The man on the other end of the phone spoke quickly with a strong Liverpool accent but there was no disguising the import of his words. However extraordinary the notion might be of the world's most notorious serial killer keeping a journal, this did not appear to be a practical joke. Certainly the assistant at Rupert Crew, one of London's oldest literary agencies, was curious enough to ask the caller, a Mr Williams, to ring back when Doreen Montgomery, the joint managing director of the company, would be free. Once alerted, this also allowed Montgomery, an agent of forty years' experience, to prepare herself for the follow-up call.

At this time Montgomery's knowledge of Jack the Ripper extended only to the fact that his enduring fame was largely due to the combination of the gruesome murders he was alleged to have carried out in the Whitechapel area of east London in the late nineteenth century and the subsequent inability of the police to capture him. But she knew enough about the phenomenal global interest in the Ripper to be aware that should the Diary be genuine it would create one of the publishing sensations of the century. She decided to call Shirley Harrison, a client of hers for some years, a journalist and author with a number of well-received non-fiction titles behind her, to 'seek her immediate reaction to this unique call'. The response was positive. Harrison, 'ever the investigative writer, with a nose for a good story, was willing to join me in a voyage of exploration,' Montgomery recalls, 'should the Liverpool caller ring again'. Montgomery lists Harrison's tenacity and refusal to panic in the face of adversity as two of her key attributes. They would be needed. The Liverpool caller did ring again.

1

Over the course of two telephone conversations, on 9 and 10 March 1992, the caller, who gave his name as Michael Williams, described the dramatic effect the discovery of the Diary had already had on his life and that of his family, and his growing conviction, after some initial research, that it was the 'real thing'. Intrigued by the account but still cautious, Montgomery suggested that Williams and his wife Anne should come to her offices for a meeting, bringing the Diary with them for inspection. She also asked, and was given permission, to invite a fourth party to the meeting. Montgomery felt that Shirley Harrison's integrity and intuitive judgement would help provide a sound second opinion. Furthermore, should that opinion be positive, she would also make a suitable literary collaborator for Williams.

After the second call, on 10 March, Montgomery wrote to Williams, confirming that she and Harrison would look forward to meeting him and his wife, and seeing the Diary, in 'due course'. She also reassured him about the bona fides of the Rupert Crew Literary Agency, a highly respected company of many decades' standing, of which she was now deputy chairman and joint managing director. She confirmed the presence of Shirley Harrison, 'a writer of great flair and ability', at the meeting, and again suggested her as a potential literary collaborator. The die was cast.

In the event, it would not be until 13 April 1992 that the meeting, at the central London offices of Rupert Crew, would take place. It perhaps comes as no surprise in a story as full of intrigue, deceptions and half-truths as that of the Diary that even the name given by the Liverpool caller would, in the meantime, prove to be false. In a subsequent phone call to Montgomery, Michael Williams revealed that his real name was Michael Barrett. He had decided to conceal his true identity until he was sure his story would be taken seriously. At the time Barrett was forty years old, an unemployed ex-scrap metal dealer living in Goldie Street in the Anfield area of Liverpool, with his wife Anne and young daughter Caroline.

The day of the meeting arrived. Montgomery and Harrison waited in the office for the Barretts to arrive, plates of sandwiches already prepared for an early lunch. At 11.30 a.m., right on time and dressed, Montgomery recalls, in a smart new suit, Michael Barrett turned up alone. His wife Anne, he explained, was unable to make the trip owing to pressures of work. After the initial introductions, he produced from a briefcase held tightly under his arm a parcel wrapped in brown paper, which he laid gently on the table before tearing off its wrapping. There was a silence, Montgomery remembers, as she and Harrison took in their first impression of the document that would change their lives.

It was a scrapbook, approximately 11 by 8½ inches, hardbound in black cloth with black leather quarter binding, and with seven bands of gold foil across the 2-inch spine. The binding and paper were largely of good quality and well preserved, while the presence of some glue stains and the shape of the impressions on the flyleaf suggested it might once have been used for photographs. The first forty-eight pages had been cut and torn out, and there were seventeen blank pages, bound in at the end. But it was the other sixty-three pages, scrawled over in a handwriting whose style would vary at different stages through the document, that contained, Shirley Harrison says, 'the most sensational words we had ever read'.

The events, deeds and thoughts chronicled in these pages were some of the most violent, depraved and sickening ever committed to paper. Yet, at times, the writer could become tender, sentimental, despairing and even humble. His emotions, like his writing style, were capable of great swings, from arrogant and goading to furious and bloodthirsty to pathetic and helpless. The story that emerged was of a man who believed his wife was conducting an affair and who, as his conviction deepened, decided to enact revenge for her 'whorish' behaviour by killing and mutilating prostitutes. Emboldened by a growing dependence on arsenic, a not unusual addiction in Victorian England, he at first gloried in his bloodthirsty deeds, taunting the hapless London police force and, in particular, Chief Inspector Abberline with their failure to apprehend him, despite the clues he had left. Crudely rhymed pieces of doggerel, often, as with the rest of the Diary, with lines crossed out and rewritten, goaded the police and press, revealing an almost demented pride in the mayhem he was causing.

Through the course of the journal, which takes in just over a year of his life, he describes the murders of seven women. The first murder, in Manchester, and the last (an unspecified location, possibly in Manchester again) have never been identified. In between, the writer describes in chilling detail the murders and subsequent mutilation of the five prostitutes in the Whitechapel area of East London who are generally accepted by most experts as Jack the Ripper's victims. By the end, his health fatally weakened by his increasing dependence on arsenic, he is contrite and loving to his wife. In the last few lines he begs forgiveness of God, however little he deserves it, and concludes the document with a flourish aimed at posterity:

> I give my name that all know of me, so history do tell, what love can do to a gentle man born.
> Yours truly
> Jack the Ripper
> Dated this third day of May 1889.

As Montgomery and Harrison took turns to read through the document, Barrett talked them through the major events of his own life and explained how the Diary came to be in his hands. He told them he had spent all his life in Liverpool, apart from a few spells away when he was in the merchant navy and working on oil rigs. Having left school at the age of fifteen, he had worked largely in catering, on ships and in restaurants, and also as a barman. Most recently, until ill health forced him to retire, he had worked in the scrap metal business. He had met his wife, Anne Graham, in the summer of 1975, in Liverpool's Irish Centre, the couple marrying in December of that year. Their daughter Caroline was born in 1981.

Barrett's explanation as to how he obtained the Diary, however, would prove more controversial, and to this day remains one of the most important areas of conflict. Yet Shirley Harrison and Doreen Montgomery still believe that Barrett was telling them the truth. He claimed that he had received the Diary from a Liverpool man, Tony Devereux, with whom he had become friendly some time during

1989. Devereux, a former compositor at the *Liverpool Echo*, was fifty-eight years old. Divorced from his wife, he had three adult daughters, all of whom had left home. In an interview for a subsequent video about the Diary, conducted with writer/director Martin Howells in September 1993, Barrett expanded on the account he gave to Harrison and Montgomery. Although his story would change dramatically in later years, this account was substantially the same as the one he gave that day in the offices of Rupert Crew, some eighteen months earlier.

Barrett, who was on invalidity benefit, was a 'house husband' when he first met Devereux, his wife Anne supporting the family financially through her work as a secretary. It was around this time that Caroline started at a local school. Before collecting her from school each afternoon, Barrett says he fell into the habit of stopping off at the Saddle pub, across the road, for a quick pint. Here he struck up a friendship with the recently retired Devereux which, Barrett says, grew closer over the succeeding years. At Christmas 1990 Devereux slipped outside his front door and fractured his hip. For the next few months, according to Barrett, he used to run errands for his housebound friend, buying bread and milk, perhaps the odd bottle of beer or sherry. Although he can't recall the exact date – he can only say that it was in May or June 1991 – Barrett told Howells he had a clear recollection of the fateful day when he first saw the Diary. During one of his visits to Devereux, his friend, without preamble, presented him with a brown paper parcel, saying, 'Here, that's for you, Mick.' When Barrett asked what it was, Devereux said only 'Take it home and do something with it,' or so Barrett claimed.

Intrigued by the parcel and his friend's eccentric behaviour, Barrett told Howells that he returned to his house to investigate. 'So I come home that day and when I come home Caroline is in the room with me. And I skipped though the pages and I come to the last page, but it's not the last page, because there's no last page, you know, there's "Jack the Ripper", and I thought what the fucking hell are you playing at? So I phoned him [Devereux] immediately and said, "Come on Tony, tell me the truth, what are you playing at?"'

5

Devereux, according to Barrett, refused to elaborate either then or the next day, when Barrett confronted him at his house. Indeed, Barrett claims that on numerous occasions over the next few weeks he tried to press his friend for more details: 'I pressurised that man and asked him question after question after question and Tony would never give me an answer.'

As a provenance for what could be one of the most important historical finds of the twentieth century, it was hardly encouraging. Barrett, however, was adamant, and would remain so for over two more years, despite almost intolerable pressure, that this was exactly how he had obtained the Diary. Surely, Harrison asked, someone else must have had some information? Barrett told her that Devereux had lost his temper when he asked him who else knew about it – 'Absolutely no fucking bugger alive today,' was Devereux's graphic response. There would be no further chance to inquire into the Diary's immediate provenance, Barrett told them. Sadly, on Thursday 8 August 1991, just a matter of weeks after allegedly handing over the Diary, Tony Devereux had died, unexpectedly, of a massive heart attack in Walton hospital, Liverpool, aged sixty.

One crucial line of inquiry had been closed, but there were others. No one present at the meeting doubted that scientific testing would be able either to confirm the document's handwriting, paper and ink as contemporary with the Ripper murders in 1888 or to prove it a modern forgery. And there was another aspect of the Diary, Shirley Harrison knew, that could be investigated and was likely to cast some light on its true status. As Barrett himself had already discovered, there were clues within the Diary itself which pointed very clearly at the true identity of the writer. Furthermore, it materialised, his life and particularly his death, just a few months after the Ripper's murder of Mary Kelly in November 1888, had been subject to a very public scrutiny.

Barrett told Martin Howells that his first instinct was that the Diary was a fake. 'I honestly didn't believe it at the beginning but, then again, the more you read it the more you see there, and the more I began to really truly believe it.' As a consequence of this early scepticism, it was at least two months, Barrett claimed, before he began his own research into the Diary, searching Liverpool Central Library for books on Jack the Ripper. From August 1991, working on an Amstrad computer bought with money lent to him some years previously by his father-in-law, Barrett began to compile notes on the Ripper and the background to the Whitechapel murders gleaned from these books, notes he would later hand over to Shirley Harrison. Barrett told Howells that the purpose of these research notes was to give him a fuller understanding of the Diary's subject matter to better help him judge its authenticity. It was, he said, an analysis of what was in the Diary, rather than, as some maintain, the compilation of background material to enable him to forge it.

Piece by piece, Barrett says, he began to assemble biographical information on the five known Ripper victims: Mary Ann ('Polly') Nichols, Annie Chapman, Elizabeth Stride, Catherine Eddowes and Mary (Jane) Kelly. In often gory detail, using press or coroners' reports from the books he had read, he reproduced information on how they were murdered, where their bodies were discovered and what was found at the murder scenes. It was not until some weeks after this research began, Barrett told Martin Howells, that he took note of the mention early on in the Diary of 'Whitechapel Liverpool, Whitechapel London'. Then, he says, he started looking for books on Liverpool murders, eventually coming across *Tales of Liverpool – Murder, Mayhem and Mystery* by the distinguished crime historian Richard Whittington-Egan. Here was a vital clue, a reference to 'Battlecrease House, home of James and Florence Maybrick'. Finally Barrett had a connection. On the second page of the Diary were the following lines: 'I may return to Battlecrease and take the unfaithfull [*sic*] bitch. Two in a night, indeed pleasure.' As he learnt more about the Maybricks, it became clear to Barrett that here was the true author of the Diary. If it were genuine, Jack the Ripper finally had a name – James Maybrick. Barrett, he told Howells, was starting to be convinced.

James Maybrick, Barrett discovered, was a Liverpool cotton merchant, forty-nine years old at the time of the Ripper murders in 1888. It was early in that year that Maybrick, together with his young American wife Florence and their two children, six-year-old James (known as Bobo) and three-year-old Gladys, moved to Battlecrease House, which they rented, in the prosperous Liverpool suburb of Aigburth. Ripper or not, nothing more might ever have been known about James Maybrick were it not for the manner of his death in May 1889. The reason for the Maybricks' inclusion in *Murder, Mayhem and Mystery* was the trial and conviction in August 1889 of Florence Maybrick for the murder of her husband.

Barrett claimed to Howells that, in comparing the information he had researched on the murders with material from the Diary, everything seemed to tally. But he had little idea of how to proceed further. He decided to seek help. Looking on his bookshelves, he found a number of the books he owned were published by Pan Books. He called them up and told them of his discovery. They, in turn, advised him to seek out a literary agent and recommended Doreen Montgomery. Michael Barrett then made his fateful telephone call.

Barrett might have been convinced, but Harrison and Montgomery, despite the tangible presence of the Diary, were not so sure. 'We listened,' Shirley Harrison recalled in her book *The Diary of Jack the Ripper*, 'with a suppressed disbelief.' Unimpressed by the Diary's pedigree, Harrison immediately suggested taking the document to the British Museum, a short walk from the Rupert Crew offices, to see what the experts there had to say. Fortunately she and Michael Barrett were granted immediate access to the museum's curator of nineteenth-century manuscripts, Robert A.H. Smith. Clutching the Diary a little nervously, Barrett followed Harrison through the series of corridors that led to Smith's office. Smith's verdict did much to calm him. 'Fascinating,' the curator responded, after examining the Diary. 'Quite extraordinary. It looks authentic. But of course you will have to take it to a document examiner. We just don't have the facilities here.' Harrison's instinctive decision to show the manuscript to Brian Lake, owner of Jarndyce, an antiquarian bookshop opposite the museum, also elicited a positive response. Lake, a specialist on nineteenth-century literature, was enthusiastic but, like Smith, remarked that a precise date for the book's origin could only be given by a forensic scientist. It was far from conclusive proof, but Harrison now admits to 'a little surge of excitement that these men were not turning "my" Diary down out of hand'.

Two months later Shirley Harrison would receive written confirmation from both men of their initial reactions. 'From a limited look at the volume,' wrote Brian Lake on 5 June 1992, 'there is nothing to indicate that the "Jack the Ripper" diary is not of the 1880s and, in my view, the writing is of the same period.' Robert A.H. Smith saw 'nothing in it inconsistent with it being of a late nineteenth-century date'.

'It all seemed so easy in the beginning,' Harrison wrote in her book, but that impression would not survive many more weeks. In the meantime, however, Harrison and Montgomery decided that Robert Smith's positive if unscientific appraisal was encouragement enough to pursue the Diary further. Asked why the decision to press ahead was made prior to a forensic report on the Diary being completed, Harrison argues that the cost of such a report, which would have had to come out of her pocket, would have been prohibitive without a publishing contract first being guaranteed.

On 30 April 1992 Doreen Montgomery drew up an agreement of collaboration between Michael Barrett and Shirley Harrison, binding them to share the responsibilities, expenses and royalties from any future book. Both parties also signed confidentiality agreements, binding anyone with access to the Diary to secrecy. So sensational was the Diary's potential that a premature leak to the media could have serious implications for its eventual impact on an unsuspecting world. A week later, on 6 May 1992, Montgomery redrafted the collaboration agreement to include Barrett's wife Anne, something Montgomery and Barrett felt was 'desirable from every viewpoint'.

In a letter written soon after meeting Barrett, Shirley Harrison described him as 'out of his depth' and 'terrified'. His ordeal could only get worse. Patiently Doreen Montgomery tried to reassure him that she understood the tension he was experiencing and to prepare him for the next hurdle in the process. She now believed that the time was right to gauge interest in the Diary from the publishing world. On 3 June 1992 Barrett duly returned to London from Liverpool, accompanied by his daughter Caroline (Anne Barrett was, again, too busy at work to attend), for what amounted to a two-day auction for the publishing rights to the Diary. As well as having Barrett in attendance, to give his account of the Diary's provenance and the early research he had completed into the Ripper murders and James Maybrick, each representative from the publishers present was allowed a certain amount of time to study the Diary. Each one would be reminded in the strongest terms of the need for absolute confidentiality. Even at this stage the potential publishing impact of the Diary could not be jeopardised.

It was on the next day, 4 June, that Robert Smith (no relation to the British Museum curator), founder and managing director of the London-based publishers Smith Gryphon, visited the Rupert Crew offices to inspect the Diary. Smith, whose company had been in operation since 1990 and had published books on Princess Diana, Charlie Kray and Marilyn Monroe among others, brought along expert help. In 1987, while at publishers Sidgwick & Jackson, Smith had published *The Ripper Legacy* by Martin Howells (who would write and direct the video on the Diary) and Keith Skinner. Skinner, who had also co-authored *The Jack the Ripper A to Z* (with Paul Begg and Martin Fido), was an historical researcher specialising in crime. Both Smith and Skinner were intrigued by the Diary, taking far longer than anyone else to examine the document. Despite a few misgivings, Smith, a keen historian himself, had seen enough to make an offer of a £50,000 advance, based on the Diary being authentic.

That afternoon, Barrett and Caroline returned to Liverpool in good humour after the auction, soon striking up conversation with a man they encountered on the train, Phil Maddox, who was then, unknown to Barrett, the owner of a free Liverpool newspaper. Barrett, as Maddox later recounted to Harold Brough of the *Liverpool Daily Post*, was in a state of some excitement. 'He said he could show me something so valuable I would never see anything like it again. Then he pulled out this battered fibre case covered in plastic, a sort of overnight case, and inside was this book, about three-quarters of an inch thick, about A4 size.' 'You can almost feel the evil', Maddox recalls Barrett saying as he showed him some of the pages (thus, and not for the last time, breaking the confidentiality agreement).

Barrett told Maddox that he had spent the day with publishers and his agent and that the Diary had undergone checks to determine its authenticity. After telling Maddox that he had been left the Diary in the will of an elderly drinking partner in Liverpool, Barrett went back to the bar, taking the Diary with him and asking Maddox to keep an eye on his sleeping daughter. Unlike the Ripper, Maddox revealed, Barrett did leave one clue. He let slip that Caroline had played the Last Post on the bugle at a remembrance service for Second World War soldiers at a Liverpool church. Maddox did not press this potential story further, convinced he now had a way of tracing Barrett.

On 12 June 1992 Doreen Montgomery sent a fax to Robert Smith expressing her pleasure, and that of Harrison and Barrett, that he was the successful bidder. She detailed the arrangements concerning the £50,000 advance and royalties and looked forward to receiving a draft contract in due course. The agent, Rupert Crew Ltd, would receive the advance, which, after deduction of a 10 per cent commission, would be divided equally between Shirley Harrison and Michael Barrett (Barrett was to be named as co-author on the publishing agreement with Smith Gryphon). From her share Harrison would have to pay research costs (to which Barrett was expected to contribute equally), which included travel, accommodation and payment to her research partner, Sally Evemy (the two have a writing and research business called The Word Team). But the greatest cost of all would be the vital scientific testing of the document.

For an average non-fiction book £50,000 was a substantial advance, but for the diary of the world's most famous serial killer, if that is what it was, it did appear relatively modest. But here, of course, was the crux of the matter. Though all concerned believed that such proof would be forthcoming, it was too early to make more than an educated guess about the Diary's authenticity. Publishers still recalled the events of 1983, when the world had briefly been shaken by the apparent discovery of the Hitler diaries. The *Sunday Times*, advised by the distinguished historian Hugh Trevor Roper, had begun a serialisation of these world-shattering diaries, only to face humiliation when they were exposed as forgeries. The publishing world, already wary of the likelihood of the world's most infamous serial killer keeping a journal, would now be doubly suspicious. Robert Smith believed the Diary was likely to be genuine, and Keith Skinner could find nothing that directly contradicted the possibility that the Diary had been written by Jack the Ripper, but Smith was still wary: 'We knew we faced a possibility that the whole project could blow up in our faces at the first hurdle – what we naively imagined would be the definitive scientific test.' That test would take place soon, and it would substantially affect the amount of money Smith was prepared to advance.

So far, judgement about the authenticity of the Diary was largely subjective and, despite the doubts about Barrett's story of how he obtained it, Shirley Harrison felt that the balance of probability was that it was genuine. She had certainly been warned of the need to be careful with the Diary, particularly as her investigation took her northwards. 'I'm sure you'll take the greatest pains,' wrote BBC radio producer Roger Wilkes, 'to authenticate its provenance; Liverpool is full of rogues on the make!' Nevertheless, with a publishing offer tabled, she now felt it was time to move to the next step, even if it meant risking the entire publishing venture, with its prospect of massive sales, should the result be negative. Science, surely, could now provide the answer.

Dr David Baxendale had been a forensic document examiner for twenty-two years when Harrison brought the Diary to the offices of his company, Document Evidence Ltd, in Broad Street, Birmingham. An ex-Home Office scientist, Baxendale had, in his own words, 'examined thousands of documents involving handwriting, inks and paper of unknown or disputed origin and had given expert advice in court on hundreds of occasions'. He was certainly highly thought of, and Harrison believed he would be the perfect man to ascertain the crucial information she needed – the age of the ink and when it was put to paper. His first report, dated 1 July 1992, which he sent to Robert Smith, was not encouraging.

Baxendale did note that the paper, which was 'unbleached and contains no optical brighteners' and consisted mainly of cotton fibres (modern paper consists mainly of wood fibres), was broadly in keeping with its purported age. Having noted that approximately twenty-four sheets (i.e. forty-eight sides) had been torn out from the beginning of the book and a fragment of what he believed to be the 'torn edge of a small photograph' was lodged in the binding, he concluded that the pages which had been torn out had had smaller articles, possibly photographs, attached to them with glue. More worryingly, Baxendale believed that the ink was probably not iron-based, iron being a necessary constituent, he believed, of late Victorian ink. He also noted that, unlike most late nineteenth-century inks, which change to a brown colour with age, this ink had not browned. He felt the free-flowing nature of the ink was also unusual for the period. Most unconvincing of all was the handwriting. Mostly it was in a looped, cursive style, he noted, where letters are connected to each other and have prominent loops. But he also isolated a number of instances of script-style writing, where plain letters were written separately. The disconnected script style only became common in the middle of the twentieth century, he wrote. 'I therefore,' he concluded, 'regard the handwriting in this book with suspicion.'

It was a major disappointment but worse was to follow. Robert Smith and Shirley Harrison immediately asked for a more detailed account of his reasoning. When this arrived, a week later, it was damning. Using the technique known as Thin Layer Chromatography (TLC) to examine the ink, Baxendale reported the discovery of a synthetic dye called nigrosine, a complex mix of substances which, he said, had only been in use since the 1940s. Again, he stated, he found nothing to suggest the presence of iron. He summarised the results as follows: 'The ink of the Diary is 1/ freely soluble and 2/ gives a chromatogram characteristic of a synthetic dye. Synthetic dyes did not become common until after the Second World War. They may have been used earlier (reliable information on this is scarce), but not before the First World War.' Both these features, he believed, pointed to an origin much later than 1889. 'My opinion therefore,' he concluded, 'is that the ink does not date from 1889. An exact time of origin cannot be established, but I consider it likely that it has originated since 1945.'

It was a huge setback to hopes that the Diary was genuine. But Shirley Harrison was about to discover that forensic examination is not the precise and objective science most of us assume it to be. Harrison and Smith now turned for a second opinion to a forensic document examiner who enjoyed a reputation equal to that of Baxendale, albeit in a slightly different field. Dr Nicholas Eastaugh was primarily a specialist in identifying and dating materials used on Old Masters and manuscripts and had worked for the Museum of London, the National and Tate Galleries and Christie's. At this stage though, as Harrison wrote to Eastaugh on 20 July 1992, there was a significant problem: 'The money at the table at the beginning will just about cover our basic research expenses and will not allow for Sally and me to pursue additional specialist areas.' Documents would be made available to Eastaugh if he would enjoy pursuing any particular area but financial remuneration appeared to be some way off. 'If eventually we have a winner,' Harrison concluded, 'I believe that the team which finally locks up "you-know-who" would benefit professionally and we would, of course, not forget our friends financially . . . It's a gamble. We shall regret, but understand, if you aren't tempted.'

Should Eastaugh be tempted to get involved on this basis, he would not be the only expert to do so. Forensic handwriting examiner Sue Iremonger had been so fascinated by what she had seen of the Diary, Harrison wrote to Robert Smith on 2 July 1992, that she had offered her services gratis.

Perhaps the most surprising information that emerged at this time came from Shirley Harrison's own research. From the Science Library in London she discovered Baxendale's assertion that nigrosine was not available until the 1940s was wrong. In fact, it was commercially patented in 1867 and was in general use in writing inks by the 1870s.

Baxendale's report would later have far-reaching consequences for the Diary's reception into the wider world. As far as Shirley Harrison's budget for research and scientific testing was concerned, it also had a more immediate and no less serious consequence. Robert Smith informed Harrison and Montgomery that the report had dramatically heightened the publishing risk involved and wrecked the market value of the book. 'One option was clearly to withdraw my offer entirely,' he says now, 'but relying on a gut instinct that the Diary was a very old document, I decided to proceed, though at a much lower level of investment. On a company level, I had to be sure that I was not so committed financially that I could not abort the project without serious financial damage to Smith Gryphon, if significant evidence were to emerge to back Baxendale's opinion.' Smith insisted that a special clause was to be inserted to cover this latter option. As to financial commitment, he withdrew the advance and offered instead the sum of £15,000. To support the research costs, £10,000 of this amount was payable on signature of the agreement, £4,000 on delivery and acceptance of the text and £1,000 on publication (typically, advances are paid in three equal amounts). It was a huge blow, with disturbing implications for the amount of scientific testing Harrison could now commission. But, in the prevailing climate, and in the absence of a better offer, she had no option but to accept, albeit reluctantly.

On 29 July 1992, less than five months since Michael Barrett had first called Doreen Montgomery, he and Harrison signed the publishing contract with Smith Gryphon. The book was due for publication in October 1993 with a copy deadline of 28 February. Given the volume of research to be undertaken on both Jack the Ripper and the lives of James and Florence Maybrick, as well as the supporting scientific tests, it would be a tough deadline to meet. Nor was there now much money to help undertake the work. If Michael Barrett were a forger aiming for a big pay day, the early indications of reward could not have been promising. The first of these arrived the very next day, 30 July, when the Rupert Crew agency sent

Barrett his first cheque. It was for £2,206.25. The same amount was sent to Shirley Harrison.

The results of the budget cut were soon apparent. Concerned that 'we still have no positive forensic evidence', Harrison wrote to Robert Smith on 13 August 1992, passing on Eastaugh's estimation that 'for a trumpet-blazing fanfare (which could prove negative) we might have to spend over £1,000'. She suggested a letter be sent to Dr Baxendale, explaining the decision to take a second professional opinion and, in the light of the information that nigrosine was available by the 1870s, asking him to reconsider his verdict that the Diary was 'suspicious'.

Baxendale duly wrote back. On 20 August there arrived a further report from him that was considerably more open-minded about the Diary's status. On the matter of paper and binding Baxendale wrote: 'The results of my examinations are all in keeping with the book itself being manufactured in the late nineteenth century.' As for his position on the ink used, it was now a little more cautious:

The ink of the handwriting in the Diary contains materials which have been widely used in the recent past but which I now understand were available in the late nineteenth century. As previously reported, the ink was found to be freely soluble, and I would have expected an ink applied to paper about a hundred years ago to be far less soluble, due to the effects of slow oxidation and other long-term chemical reactions. However, if an ink known to have been applied to a document about a hundred years ago were found to have a similar solubility, then there would appear to be nothing in the chemical properties of the ink in the Diary to preclude it being of similar age.

No such comparison was made at the time, though in Nicholas Eastaugh's report of 18 June 1993 he would write that, during the tests he conducted on the Diary, 'it was clear that the solubility of the ink was similar to the Victorian reference material and unlike the modern inks dried out for reference'. Also, Baxendale's finding that the ink was easily soluble would be contested by Leeds University in

November 1994. It was not quite the end of Baxendale's link with the Diary though. Writing to Robert Smith on 28 September 1992, Baxendale suggested that, as the contracted authors were unhappy with his report, he was prepared to waive his fee, in order to 'avoid the protracted correspondence you so subtly allude to'. Standing by the fairness of his assessment of all the evidence available, Baxendale asked for one proviso to this agreement: that Smith, Harrison and any other parties involved should give a written undertaking to the following effect: '1/ Not to use any part of my report for any purposes whatsoever. 2/ Not to mention my name or that of Document Evidence Ltd in any publication concerning "The Victorian Diary".' Otherwise the fee of £300 plus VAT remained payable in full. Smith duly gave his signed undertaking to the agreement.

Nicholas Eastaugh, however, was now on board. Like Baxendale, Dr Eastaugh, who examined the Diary at his studio in Teddington in south-west London, tried to ascertain the age of the ink and when, approximately, it was put to paper. He conducted two examinations of the Diary, as described in his main report of 2 October 1992. The first tested the ink with a view to establishing its chemical composition, as well as commenting on Baxendale's study. In the second phase he examined the elemental composition of the ink and also analysed some black powder that had been found embedded in the channel between the Diary pages.

Dr Eastaugh used a proton microprobe to carry out the main tests. This, he explained to Harrison, was a 'non-destructive method of exciting atoms in a small target area on a page with an accelerated beam of protons, in order to detect, to the parts per million, what chemicals are present in inks, papers, parchments and pigments tested'. A series of samples was also used for comparison, including a scrapbook which contained writing from 1871 to 1915 and other written documents with dates ranging from 1880 to 1907. Harrison eagerly awaited Eastaugh's conclusions. They were considerably more positive than those of his predecessor.

Several samples of ink from the Diary were taken and tested, and Eastaugh concluded, unlike Baxendale, that the ink was *not* based on a synthetic dyestuff (though he accepted that his means of testing might not reveal low levels). However, ink in some of the comparison samples, such as one 1907 postcard, did prove to be based on synthetic dyestuffs. Not only did Eastaugh conclude that the Diary ink did not 'appear to be substantially synthetic', as previously suggested, but he noted the presence of iron in clearly measurable amounts. Two of Baxendale's main concerns about the Diary ink had been contradicted. Moreover, Eastaugh felt that his identification of synthetic dyestuffs in the 1907 postcard suggested this would not have been a problem for the Diary anyway, particularly as 'the dye Nigrosin [*sic*] mentioned as being present in the ink of the Diary was first synthesised prior to the supposed date of the Diary'. Eastaugh also concluded that the black powder he found might be based on bone black, a purified animal charcoal used in the nineteenth century as a drying agent, but as yet no other examiner has confirmed the identification of this substance, a small portion of which still remains in the Diary.

'The results of various analyses of ink and paper in the Diary performed so far,' Eastaugh summarised, 'have not given rise to any conflict with the date of 1888/9. If the Diary is a forgery then it has "passed" a range of tests which would have shown up many materials now used in ink and paper manufacture. However,' he warned, 'we must be aware that we cannot as yet wholly rule out on the evidence as it stands a sophisticated modern forgery: although it is very specialist knowledge, someone just might have been able to synthesise a convincing ink or located a bottle of ink of sufficient age that was still usable (though these seem to be quite rare).' Accepting that historical document analysis 'is a field where much work remains to be done', Eastaugh was also anxious that further examination was needed to comprehensively establish the truth. That, however, was something Harrison's dwindling budget could not sustain.

Confidentiality had been an essential part of the strategy so far, but the media were beginning to sniff a story. On 5 September 1992 the first of what would be hundreds of newspaper articles on the Diary was published in the *Liverpool Echo*. An investigator, the paper reported, calling herself Sally McDonald (actually Sally Evemy), was trying to solve the mystery of a journal believed to belong to James Maybrick. In fact, the article, which featured printed textual extracts from the Diary, had been carefully planted by Evemy and Harrison in the hope they could tap into the collective knowledge of the *Post*'s readership and find some answers to questions raised in the Diary. The identity of the mysterious Mrs Hammersmith and the whereabouts of the missing pages were just two of the many questions they were hoping to have answered. The link with the Ripper wasn't mentioned but a few weeks later, on 9 October 1992, the *East London Advertiser*, circulating in the heart of Ripper territory, announced, in a story followed up a week later by the national newspaper *Today*, that newly found diaries said to have been penned by Jack the Ripper threatened to overturn all previous theories about the identity of the mass murderer. His true identity, they said, was being kept under wraps by Rupert Crew until at least the spring, though they understood that handwriting experts believed it was in an educated hand. It was just as well for the Diary team that few readers were in a position to link the two stories together.

News of the Diary was also now beginning to create waves among Ripperologists, a term coined by Colin Wilson, a highly respected crime writer, for the ever-growing band of people fascinated by Jack the Ripper. Prominent among them was Nick Warren, a London-based surgeon, whose quarterly magazine *Ripperana* covered a wide range of Ripper-related and general crime topics. Warren wrote to Doreen Montgomery on 10 November 1992 asking for details of the Diary, whose existence Montgomery confirmed in a letter two days later. Keeping the Diary under wraps would not be easy.

On the recommendation of Robert Smith, Shirley Harrison had decided to commission Keith Skinner to help her with research. By August 1992 Skinner, whose opinion had been a key consideration in Smith Gryphon's decision to publish the Diary, had brought in his collaborators on *The Jack the Ripper A to Z*, Paul Begg and Martin Fido. Although none of these three leading authorities on the Ripper was convinced of the authenticity of the Diary (indeed, Martin Fido categorically dismissed it as a fake), their view that nothing in the Diary fatally contradicted the known facts of the Ripper case was of great value to Shirley Harrison and Robert Smith – and to another central figure in these dramatic early months, a man whose influence on the evolution of the Diary story would be impossible to overstate.

In the light of ensuing events, it is ironic to consider now that London businessman Paul Feldman had actually identified another suspect, Montague John Druitt, as the main subject for his planned video about Jack the Ripper. The story of the Diary would have been very different had Feldman stayed with his original hunch. As it was, the appearance, usually heralded by a cloud of cigar smoke, of this relentlessly driven human dynamo into the arena would drastically change the atmosphere surrounding the alleged Maybrick journal, heightening the pitch of animosity between the pro- and anti-Diary camps which lasts to this day. Feldman himself, his obsessive energy and financial resources finally exhausted, has now retired from the fray, but his legacy is significant. He has left behind a voluminous mound of research concerning Jack the Ripper, James and Florence Maybrick and their relatives, and the England of that time, and, most notably, the culmination of his extraordinary pursuit, a book, titled with characteristic confidence *Jack the Ripper, the Final Chapter* (published in 1997 by Virgin).

By this time Feldman had already notched up a number of successful business ventures, starting with numerous menswear, photography and record shops. He had also built up a company called Hollywood Nights which had been bought out by Parkfield, a division of which, Parkfield Entertainments, he had run for some time. In the late 1980s and early 1990s Feldman had created the highly successful *Pathe News Year to Remember* video series. He had also made a number of sports videos and was a prime mover in the feature film, *The Krays*. By the summer of 1992, around the time that Shirley Harrison was embarking on the research for *The Diary of Jack the Ripper*, Feldman, having experienced some financial setbacks, was in the market for new projects. Long fascinated by the various theories about Jack the

Ripper, not least those with royal and masonic connections, and aware of the paucity of good videos on the subject, he wanted to consult with as many Ripper experts as possible before deciding whether to go ahead.

The first authority he contacted was Donald Rumbelow, whose book *The Complete Jack the Ripper* is considered a standard of the genre. Rumbelow, in turn, advised Feldman to seek out Keith Skinner, Paul Begg and Martin Fido, 'the new experts' as he termed them. And so it transpired that on 30 October 1992 Begg and Skinner (Martin Fido could not make it), over a long-drawn-out meal in a Chinese restaurant in London's Baker Street, gave Feldman and his business partner Gary Wickes the benefit of their extensive research into the Ripper. At the end of the meal, in which various suspects were debated, almost as an aside Feldman mentioned that Rumbelow had told him of a diary, allegedly that of Jack the Ripper, that had been found in Liverpool. Rumbelow had been dismissive, but what did Skinner and Begg think? Bound by a letter of confidentiality to Robert Smith (Begg had seen the Diary, and Skinner was already working on research around it for Shirley Harrison), neither could expand, though both felt that Feldman's projected video, which would look at several major Ripper suspects, would not be affected by it. However, so that Feldman's video would be totally up to date, they suggested he contact Robert Smith if he wanted to include the Diary. Martin Fido, whom Feldman met on 3 November, was more direct. The Diary, he believed, was worthless. 'Don't waste your time on it,' he advised.

So, following this advice and assuming, wrongly, that all three men believed the Diary to be a fake, Feldman discounted it and commissioned Paul Begg to advise him during the preliminary research into his favoured suspect, Druitt. Then, during a conversation on other matters with Paul Begg, who was bound by his letter of confidentiality to Robert Smith, Feldman was alerted by Begg's comment that he ought not to 'dismiss the Diary out of hand'. Intrigued, Feldman immediately called Robert Smith, who he now knew was the publisher of the Diary, and arranged a meeting with himself and Gary Wickes, who already knew Smith, at Smith's offices near Kings Cross. There Feldman expressed an interest in buying the video rights to the Diary, so he could refer to it in his video. Smith refused, and would not name the purported author of the Diary. The meeting ended with Smith telling Feldman that he would not consider the sale of any rights until after the book was published.

Feldman returned home determined to discover the identity of the alleged author. According to the account given in his book, he took out his complete set of the *Marshall Cavendish Murder Casebook* part work and 'slammed them on my desk'. It is a large series and it took Feldman some time to complete the search. He found nothing and started again. This time Feldman came across a photo of James Maybrick. 'It made me shiver,' he recalls, ten years later when speaking to the authors, 'it literally made me shiver. Then I read the story that went with it. I had it – here was the Liverpool connection, it was the right year. I don't think I've ever been so excited.' Feldman rang Begg to test his find. 'Would springtime for building be a good clue?' he asked. In his foreword to Feldman's book Begg described that telephone call. 'Paul didn't introduce himself or engage in any preliminary chit-chat. He just gruffly said "Spring is a good time for building houses" (or some such phrase). I thought I had a nutter on the line. Then I realised it was Paul and he explained what he meant – springtime equals May. Building houses equals bricks. I laughed.' Feldman interpreted Paul Begg's reaction as confirmation that he was right, although Begg had only been laughing at Feldman's well-meaning effort to be subtle and cryptic. 'I was just tickled by Paul converting May and brick into spring building and I laughed,' Begg explains ten years on. 'I'd have laughed at that even if the Diary author was someone else, and, of course, had it been someone else then Paul would have gone off barking up the wrong tree . . . Paul's not an arrogant man, but once he's reached a decision he never doubts it's the right one, and he'll gamble his soul on it being right.'

When Feldman next met Smith, this time at Feldman's office in Baker Street, on 17 November 1992, he had a huge advantage in negotiations. 'I was the only one outside the circle who knew who it was and hadn't signed the confidentiality agreement,' Feldman says. 'Boy did I have power and he [Robert Smith] knew it and I wasn't frightened to pretend I would use it.' According to Feldman, he now offered a £10,000 advance for the video rights for the Diary, telling Smith that he had a picture of the man who wrote the Diary on his desk. 'When I leave the room pick this up and have a look and if I'm right, shake hands now on a deal. If I'm wrong, I'll walk away.' He was right. 'I had little choice,' Smith recalls, 'but to consider negotiating a licensing agreement with him. We could not risk him revealing Maybrick's name to the press before the serious research had begun.'

On 4 December 1992 Smith drew up a contract with Feldman's company, Duocrave, selling them video rights, which Feldman made subject to validation by his own expert. Now he signed a confidentiality agreement himself and was allowed to view the Diary as Smith gave him an account of how it had made its entry into the public domain. Oddly, this first encounter with the journal that was to play such a huge role in his life for the next five years made little impression on Feldman. At this stage, he maintains, he was an agnostic in terms of judging its authenticity. His main interest in the Diary lay in the fact that Begg, Fido and Skinner, he claimed, continued to assure him they 'could not shake it'.

On the advice of his old friend Michael Marx, then finance director of the Heron Corporation, Feldman now identified the expert he needed. Anna Koren is a graphologist (someone who analyses personality from handwriting) who had occasionally worked for the Israeli Defence Ministry, Police and Defence Force and had given evidence in many fraud trials in Europe. Marx, who had employed Koren before, informed Feldman that she had never yet been proved wrong. If anyone could prove the Diary to be a fake, Feldman believed, it was Koren. According to Feldman, he was instructed by Marx to tell her nothing about the Diary before she examined it other than it was written by a male. She did not even know the nature of Feldman's own involvement, he claims, until afterwards.

Feldman arranged to fly Koren from Israel to London. On 23 December 1992 Robert Smith brought the Diary to Feldman's Baker Street office where Sally Evemy, Shirley Harrison and Doreen Montgomery, as well as an intrigued Michael Marx, were also present.

Koren, delayed by an hour, was still too early for Keith Skinner, who missed her analysis by minutes. It did not last long. Whatever the assembled onlookers might have thought of graphology before Koren's examination, Feldman recalls with amusement that all present turned over their notepads as Koren walked in. Flicking through the Diary, occasionally stroking the surface of the pages, she arrived at her conclusions in less than fifteen minutes. Graphologists base their analysis not on the meaning of words but on the construction of letters. Koren, Feldman maintains, did not read the words, but merely observed the way they were written. Speaking in her strong Israeli accent (she has a limited understanding of English), Koren talked about the fluctuating self-esteem of the author, his disturbed nature, sexual problems, multiple personality, neuroses and much else that corresponded with the analysis of Maybrick as a potential serial killer. For Feldman, who was convinced she had not read the last page with its famous signature, this was compelling evidence. He asked for her answer to the key question, 'Could it have been forged?' 'Impossible!' came the fierce reply. Feldman had the subject of his video, and would swiftly sign the agreement to buy the video rights for the Diary, with an option on the film rights, from Robert Smith.

Life for those directly involved with the Diary, not least Feldman himself, would never be the same again. From now on there would be not one but two teams working feverishly to unlock the secret of the Diary, both researching into the world of James Maybrick and the man he might have been – Jack the Ripper. It would not always be a mutually beneficial arrangement either, with a growing level of mistrust between Paul Feldman on the one hand and Robert Smith, Doreen Montgomery and Shirley Harrison on the other. Doreen Montgomery had also been 'riveted' by Koren's analysis. Now that Paul Feldman was involved, she wrote to him that same day, saying she believed there must be 'a great deal of communion' between all concerned for the future. It was a forlorn hope. Within just a few weeks of receiving her letter, Feldman's solicitors would serve notice of legal action on Smith and Harrison if they didn't immediately surrender every piece of information as it was discovered during the course of researching and writing the book. It did not augur well for the future.

TWO

'Dead men don't tell lies'

As the cast list of the Diary investigators was coming to life, so too was the cast of the Diary itself. Assisted by Keith Skinner and Sally Evemy in London and Michael Barrett in Liverpool, Shirley Harrison was making good headway in her research into the world of the Maybricks, gradually building up a picture of James Maybrick, his personality, habits, domestic and business life. Nothing, so far, of his known movements directly contradicted what was in the Diary.

On 28 June 1992 Harrison paid her first visit to the twenty-roomed Battlecrease House, finding much still intact from late Victorian times. Maybrick himself, she discovered, had been born on 24 October 1838 into a respectable, church-going family (his grandfather was succeeded as parish clerk by his father) resident in the centre of Liverpool. Of his surviving brothers, the younger three, Edwin, Thomas and Michael, all gain mentions in the Diary. Michael, with whom, according to the Diary, James stayed in London prior to one of the murders, was by some distance the most successful of the brothers. An accomplished opera singer, he had become by 1888 the most popular composer in England under the stage name Stephen Adams, his most famous song, 'The Holy City', written in 1892, remaining popular to this day.

Maybrick's career path was charted, taking him from commercial clerk to the position he held in 1889 as head of Maybrick & Company Cotton Merchants, by which time brother Edwin was a junior partner. Evidence was uncovered of James's frequent voyages to Norfolk, Virginia, where he opened a branch office of his cotton company and where, significantly, his addiction to arsenic was first noted by the owner of the local brothel that he regularly attended.

In 1880, at the age of forty-one, Maybrick first met Florence (Florie) Chandler, on board the transatlantic steamer SS *Baltic*, returning to Liverpool from New York. The vivacious seventeen-year-old southern girl, under the care of her formidable and well-connected mother Baroness Von Roques, clearly made a great impact. By the end of the voyage Maybrick had proposed and they would be married within a year; their son James Chandler (known as Bobo) was born in March 1882, their daughter Gladys Evelyn arriving in July 1886.

As more details of Maybrick's career, social life and fluctuating fortunes emerged, so too did crucial information about his growing dependency on arsenic, a vital element of his degenerating psychological state if we are to believe the analysis of him as a serial killer. Another key element of the Diary, Florie's alleged adultery with 'the whoremaster', could possibly have dated back to the winter months of 1887, with the appearance in the Maybricks' lives of Alfred Brierley, a fellow Liverpool cotton broker. Certainly James Maybrick's act of striking his wife after the Grand National meeting of 1889, during which Brierley publicly walked off with Florie, was attested to by servants. Florie was also rumoured to have had an affair with Maybrick's brother Edwin. Maybrick himself, it appears, had and continued to enjoy a string of affairs, but, if the Diary was to be believed, he now began to suspect his young wife of cheating too. From the great mass of information and new evidence that Harrison was compiling, nothing had yet emerged to discount the notion that Maybrick could be the Ripper. Clearly, the forger, if the Diary were not genuine, had enjoyed a large slice of luck.

Doreen Montgomery had hoped for a 'great deal of communion' between all concerned, now that Paul Feldman and his team had joined the investigation into the Diary. It was not to be. On the evening of 13 January 1993, with signs of a rift between the two teams becoming apparent, a meeting was held at Feldman's office to establish some kind of *modus operandi* for their respective work on the book and the video. With Paul Feldman came two men who would form part of his team, Martin Howells (who had just flown in from New Zealand to write the script of the video) and Melvyn

Fairclough, the author of *The Ripper and the Royals*. From the other team came Shirley Harrison, Sally Evemy, Doreen Montgomery and Robert Smith. Also present were the three authors of *The Jack the Ripper A to Z*, Paul Begg, Martin Fido and Keith Skinner.

Skinner, who at this stage had no contract with Feldman, recalls 'a stormy meeting'. In the end no financial or practical decisions were made; instead the meeting was dominated by Feldman's passionate belief that the Diary clearly solved the Jack the Ripper mystery, and his often perplexing theories as to why. At one stage, Skinner recalls, Doreen Montgomery inquired as to whether there was an agenda. There wasn't. Skinner described the meeting in his notes as 'a testing ground held under laboratory conditions'. If that were the case, it was a failure. Crucially no attempt was made to forge a working relationship between the two teams and nothing was organised to promote the dissemination of research material.

Within a few weeks this had become a major problem. Feldman was incensed at the lack of research and materials heading his way. Indeed, it appeared that Sally Evemy, in particular, was initially reluctant to supply details of research conducted into the Maybricks that she felt should be the preserve of the book. Feldman decided that drastic measures were necessary. On 10 February 1993 his solicitors, Gold, Mann & Co. wrote to Smith Gryphon in reference to the agreement made between the publishers and Feldman's company, Duocrave Ltd, on 23 December 1992. Referring to Smith Gryphon's undertaking to 'furnish and give complete and uninterrupted access to all research and other documents created or commissioned' by them, the solicitors believed that Smith Gryphon were in clear breach of that agreement. Unless the desired material was delivered within seven days, 'immediate and effective action will be taken against your company', they warned Robert Smith. Within days, Feldman would get the material he sought but relations between the two teams were soured and would never recover.

In the middle of all this, appearing increasingly beleaguered and bewildered, was the figure of Michael Barrett. Physically and psychologically he did not appear able, to those working on the

Diary, to withstand the pressures. Doreen Montgomery, in a letter to Paul Feldman dated 9 February 1993, expressed her mounting concern. Allowing that Paul Feldman was entitled to have access to Barrett, she urged him to consider Barrett's health. 'Mike suffers from renal failure,' she wrote, 'and has an invalidity pension. Stress and strain and anxiety will not help his condition.' Having tried to protect Barrett over the months since the project began, both for his sake and that of his wife and daughter, Montgomery would value Feldman's consideration and help in this respect. As for the wife, for whose sake she wished Barrett to be protected, Anne Barrett would, within little more than a year, take on a much more significant role in the Diary story than Montgomery could possibly have imagined. For now, however, Anne Barrett was keeping a very low profile.

Paul Feldman was getting some encouraging news, though. Leading crime writer Colin Wilson had been favourably impressed with the Diary. Indeed, as he wrote to Feldman on 4 March 1993, if the handwriting, paper and ink testing checked out, he could see no reason 'why your material should not constitute the genuine "final solution" of the Ripper case, and I'll be glad to say so on film'. It was a big if. Having talked to Donald Rumbelow, who felt the same way, Wilson was anxious to see some reports on these matters as 'we'd hate to be in the position of Trevor Roper with the Hitler Diaries'. In a further letter he also pointed Feldman towards an expert who might be able to date the Diary to within a year. Rod McNeil and his 'scanning augur' microscope might provide the answer, he believed.

If the Diary were the work of Jack the Ripper, and could be proved to be so, it was, unquestionably, worth a huge amount of money. If it were a recent forgery, and could be proved to be so, it was worth precisely nothing. Despite the latter possibility, someone was clearly willing to take a risk on it. On 19 March 1993 Michael Barrett was sent a letter from the solicitors Bloom Camillin. They had been instructed by a party who wished to remain anonymous for the time being to make an offer of £15,000 for the document penned by the person who might have been Jack the Ripper. The unnamed party appeared to have already made their mind up on the

28

truth about the Diary. 'Our client,' they wrote, 'does not propose to require authentication . . .'. There was a very good reason for this. The client, though Barrett would not discover it, was Paul Feldman.

It wasn't the first time that Feldman had tried to buy the Diary from Barrett. At their very first meeting, in February 1993, Feldman had arrived in Liverpool with Martin Howells, Paul Begg and £5,000 in cash stuffed into a briefcase. Aware that the money looked even more than it was worth, Feldman showed the case to Barrett and offered it all in exchange for a half share in the Diary. According to Feldman, Barrett had wanted to draw up a contract there and then but was persuaded by Feldman, who doubted whether such a contract would stand up in a court of law, to think about it overnight and get in touch if he was still interested. If he didn't have access to a solicitor, Feldman told him he would arrange independent legal advice. Two days later, Feldman says, Barrett got as far as ringing from Lime Street station to say he was on the way. Feldman told him to get a cab to his office in Baker Street from Euston station, for which he would pay. Barrett did not arrive. The next day, according to Feldman, he received a call from Barrett blaming an IRA bomb scare for delaying the train until it was too late to feasibly make the return journey. Feldman to this day remains convinced that Barrett changed his mind after being talked out of the sale by his wife Anne. Barrett himself resolutely maintains that he spent all morning at Lime Street waiting for train services to resume.

The deal might not have been done then but the letter from Bloom Camillin would set alarm bells ringing. Robert Smith, who had been informed of the offer by Barrett, was horrified. 'If he [Barrett] had sold it to a third party,' Smith says today, 'then the third party could have held Smith Gryphon, Mike and Shirley to ransom over the use of the diary in Shirley's book. It would also have put Mike and Shirley in breach of the Author Agreement, as they were contracted to deliver the diary to Smith Gryphon as part of the manuscript and illustrations.' Smith says that Barrett had already told him that he wanted to sell the Diary to him, to avoid the temptation of selling it elsewhere. The letter from Bloom Camillin, he claims, propelled him into 'immediate defensive action to protect my investment'.

On 23 March 1993, just four days after the Bloom Camillin letter was sent, an agreement was drawn up transferring ownership of the Diary from Michael Barrett to Smith Gryphon Ltd for the nominal figure of £1. The next day Smith travelled to Liverpool with three copies of the agreement. Though the wording had already been approved by Barrett (along with Shirley Harrison and Doreen Montgomery), he was to meet resistance. Anne Barrett, as she would later confirm, was not happy with the agreement and insisted Smith meet her and her husband at the latter's solicitors, Morecroft, Dawson & Garnetts in Dale Street near the centre of Liverpool. There Liz Winter, assistant to Barrett's solicitor Richard Bark-Jones (who was away in London), advised him not to sign. According to Smith, Barrett became angry with the delay and walked out to Rigby's pub, just across the road. Anne and Smith followed shortly afterwards, the latter bringing the three copies of the agreement with him. Anne says that, despite her reluctance to sign, her husband, who had been drinking, would not be dissuaded so the two Barretts and Smith duly signed. Michael Barrett had turned down £15,000. Now, he had sold the alleged diary of Jack the Ripper for the princely sum of £1.

All those working on the Diary, from either the Harrison or the Feldman camps, had signed a confidentiality agreement not to disclose information about it. But a diary allegedly written by Jack the Ripper was not an easy subject to keep quiet. The national press were getting closer and closer. On 24 March 1993 the *Guardian* triggered a series of national newspaper articles under the headline 'Explosive diary to uncloak Ripper'. According to the publishers of the forthcoming book *The Diary of Jack the Ripper*, the paper announced, the killer was about to be unmasked. Not in the *Guardian*, though. Neither Paul Feldman nor Robert Smith was giving much away, though the latter informed the paper that more than a dozen experts had been consulted to verify the Diary's authenticity. 'We don't want another Hitler's Diaries on our hands,' he told the *Guardian*. 'And we're sure we haven't. None of the tests we have had done has thrown the slightest doubt on the Diary's authenticity.' Feldman mentioned a three-hour dramatised

30

documentary for television that he was co-producing, but kept the identities of the cast secret. 'They know how explosive this story is, and have asked us to protect them from the Press,' he explained.

Nick Warren, for one, was not impressed, writing to Paul Feldman soon after, to make it clear that *Ripperana* 'quite understandably, wishes to disassociate itself as far as possible from your project of mental disorder'. However, Warren concluded, should Feldman and company wish to drop their blanket of silence and submit these documents to expert scrutiny, he offered his services as an independent consultant.

Two days later, on 26 March 1993, an article in the *Daily Mail* actually included some tantalising extracts from the Diary, which Smith Gryphon and Feldman's company, Duocrave, had released, plus the news that the US book publication rights had been sold to Warner (with the UK paperback rights to Simon & Schuster). Rather curiously, as a direct result of this article, the unnamed client of Bloom Camillin solicitors decided that very same day to withdraw his offer to buy the Diary. Apologising for any inconvenience, the solicitors informed Barrett that their client believed the article was 'potentially damaging' and that he now had 'grave concerns over the value of the document'. Given that the unnamed client was Paul Feldman this would have been an extraordinary development had it been true. In fact, as Feldman would later reveal, the *Mail* article had provided him with a way of extricating himself from an offer that was no longer viable.

While the tussle over ownership of the physical Diary appeared to be over, investigation into its contents continued apace. The latest to join the fray was document examiner Sue Iremonger, whose preliminary findings were sent to Shirley Harrison on 29 March 1993. She had reached these findings from studying a list of documents which included the Diary, James Maybrick's will of 25 April 1889, the 'Dear Boss' letter (the anonymous letter dated 25 September 1888, written in red ink and sent to the Central News Agency, the signature on which gave Jack the Ripper his name) and other alleged Ripper letters plus examples of handwriting from Michael Maybrick and Florie. Her conclusions were not good news.

The writing in the Diary, she believed, clearly did not match that of the will. Nor was the handwriting in the 'Dear Boss' letter the same as that in the Diary, despite the fact that the writer of the former clearly used the same kind of language. Perhaps the one positive note was that she saw a similarity between Michael Maybrick's handwriting and that in the will. Had Michael written his brother's will, she asked.

Despite increased media speculation, the connection between Maybrick and the Ripper had not yet been made but another journalist, much closer to home than Fleet Street, was getting nearer and nearer the real story. Soon after the article in the *Daily Mail*, Harold Brough of the *Liverpool Daily Post* received a call from a journalist who had an interesting story to relate. The journalist was Phil Maddox – the man who had encountered Michael Barrett on the London to Liverpool train in June 1992, when Barrett was returning from the publishing rights auction. According to Maddox, Barrett had boasted of having the diary of Jack the Ripper. Maddox suggested that if Brough wanted to follow up the story he should try to trace Barrett through his daughter Caroline, who, Barrett had let slip, had played the Last Post at a remembrance service held in a Liverpool church the previous year.

Intrigued, Brough set to work. He began by making enquiries at various Liverpool church associations to find the girl who had played the Last Post. Step by step, Brough was led to the British Legion club which had organised the service and from there he was directed to Caroline's maternal grandfather, Billy Graham. Brough visited Graham at his sheltered-accommodation flat in the Anfield area, but though the Second World War veteran, now approaching eighty, was polite, he was unable to help. He did, at least, confirm Maddox's recollection that Michael Barrett had talked of receiving the Diary from an elderly friend. 'Agents, and even people from America', Graham told Brough, were now chasing his son-in-law. Having failed to find Barrett at 12 Goldie Street, Brough was pleased to get a telephone call from him that afternoon and told him he would like to question him about the Ripper Diary. 'I don't know what you are talking about,' Brough recalls Barrett as saying. 'I have no knowledge of the fact whatsoever and please, never bother my father-in-law again. You don't involve my family. Good afternoon. Goodbye.' But Brough now had enough for his article, which appeared in the Wednesday 21 April 1993 edition of the *Liverpool Daily Post*, telling 'of a mysterious encounter with the man who may – or may not – own the most sensational document in British criminal history'.

The day the story appeared Brough received a telephone call from Paul Dodd, a teacher in Liverpool and the current owner of Battlecrease House. Dodd told Brough that he had been visited by Shirley Harrison, who had been researching the diary of James Maybrick, which, she said, had been found by a Liverpool man. Two different diaries found by two different Liverpool men was a coincidence too far. Brough took the Maybrick file out of the paper's archives and discovered that Maybrick had died just months after the last Ripper murder. Now he realised that the two diaries were one and the same, and that the forthcoming book would assert that local man James Maybrick was Jack the Ripper. Brough went quickly to work. Michael Barrett now admitted that he did own the Diary. Brough tracked down Paul Feldman, who, without admitting the identity of the purported author of the Diary, affirmed its existence and informed the journalist that it was not written by one of the known Ripper suspects. Neither Paul Begg nor Shirley Harrison would name Maybrick but Harrison acknowledged 'you are the first to track me down'.

The next day, 22 April, Brough published his findings under the heading 'Book Claims Solution to Riddle of "Real" Ripper'. The link between Maybrick and the Ripper had finally been made. Harold Brough had won the media race to name the suspect. It wouldn't take long for Fleet Street to catch up. That very afternoon, the *London Evening Standard* leapt into the fray with an article naming James Maybrick as the latest Ripper suspect and crediting the *Liverpool Daily Post* with blowing the secret. Though the article claimed that experts were convinced there would be no rerun of the Hitler Diaries fiasco, it highlighted one potential hole in the argument – 'no one had proved where the diary had been since

1888'. The paper, however, did quote Paul Feldman's own rather mysterious answer to this puzzle. 'It was hidden in the man's home and came to light when something was touched that had not been touched for 105 years.'

The following day the story was also revealed in *Today* and revisited in the *Guardian*, which quoted a distraught Doreen Montgomery as groaning, 'we have all been sworn to secrecy on this'. The *Daily Mail* too was on to the story. The *Liverpool Daily Post* could not contain its delight at the scoop. 'Newsroom telephones were red hot,' it reported on the 23rd, 'as every national newspaper wanted to know more about our astounding exclusive.' An interview with Paul Dodd in the *Post* also revealed that a succession of researchers had been visiting Battlecrease House but none had mentioned anything about Jack the Ripper to him. One researcher had told him that 'new material' about the case had been found during renovation work on the house. He had even been recently visited by a nun in her nineties, who he believed was a niece of James Maybrick.

With even members of the Diary teams doubting the alleged provenance of the journal, that Michael Barrett had received it from Tony Devereux, it was thought that Battlecrease, the home of James Maybrick, might hold a better one. Indeed, a number of papers had assumed this to be the case already. Harold Brough was quick to pick up on the possibility, as he wrote in the *Post* of 24 April 1993. Extensive rewiring had begun in the house in 1990, he reported, though neither Paul Dodd nor Colin Rhodes, the managing director of the company which had carried out the work, had any knowledge of any documents being recovered. On 21 April Rhodes had received a call from a man claiming to own the Diary but as this man would not divulge his own address or telephone number, Rhodes refused to give him any information on his employees who had worked at Battlecrease.

Perhaps it was to dampen speculation about a Battlecrease provenance that, on 26 April 1993, Michael Barrett decided to swear an affidavit that he had received the Diary straight from Tony Devereux. This was more or less the same account he had given

Shirley Harrison and Doreen Montgomery and would, a few months later, give to Martin Howells. It described how he first met Tony Devereux at the Saddle and how their friendship developed, particularly after Devereux fractured his hip just before Christmas 1990, after which Barrett said he would call with groceries each school day. After recovering from a hip replacement operation in March 1991, Devereux had become mobile enough to walk to the Saddle, with the help of sticks, for a drink. It was during this period, Barrett said, that he first met the three Devereux daughters. One afternoon, which Barrett now places in the beginning of July 1991, he called round and was told by Devereux that he had something to give him, which turned out to be a brown paper parcel. Barrett recalled his words, almost verbatim: 'This is for you because you are the only fucking one who has not asked for anything in the time I have known you.'

Barrett describes returning home after collecting Caroline from school and opening the parcel to find a handwritten ledger. He began trying to read it, which he found difficult owing to the handwriting, and turned to the last page and laughed 'as it was signed, "yours truly, Jack the Ripper"'. According to Barrett, he then rang Devereux straight away and said, 'Who are you trying to kid?' Barrett then describes badgering Devereux several times in person at his house the next day until he was told that he was 'getting on my fucking nerves'. Devereux's last words on the subject, Barrett maintains, were, 'I have given it to you because you are my only mate and I know that you will do something with it.' Despite several more requests, Devereux would offer no more enlightenment on the Diary, Barrett claimed, and just two months later he died of a heart attack in hospital. Intriguingly, on a copy of the affidavit Barrett had written: 'Dead men don't tell lies. Tonys words. A fact, simple as that. And I go to my grave stating it. Mike.'

Thus far, press coverage, while not invited, had been largely supportive of the Diary. An article in the *Observer* on Sunday 25 April 1993 gave a more realistic indication of what was to come. Written by Brian McConnell (coincidentally a relative of a junior counsel for the prosecution at the trial of Florence Maybrick), it *from Sally - 23·1·1997.*

him one more question before he lost his patience with me and that was "who else knows about it?". He told me: "Absolutely no fucking bugger alive today".

9. Tony died two months later in Fazakerley Hospital following a massive heart attack. Although I had asked him on several occasions where he had got the diary from, he always refused to tell me, without giving any reason.

SWORN at Liverpool in the)
County of Merseyside this)
26th April day of)M Barrett.
1993)

Before me,

D.A. Walker

Solicitor/Commissioner for Oaths

NOTE: DEAD MEN DON'T TELL LIES. TONYS WORDS. A FACT, SIMPLE AS THAT. AND I GO TO MY GRAVE STATING IT.

Mike

Michael Barrett's affidavit of 26 April 1993, stating that he had been given the Diary by Tony Devereux. The handwriting is Michael Barrett's.

suggested that the Diary was a hoax and that James Maybrick was 'alive and not well, 200 miles away in Liverpool at the time the murders were committed in London'. Nick Warren and another noted Ripper historian, Stewart Evans, were both quoted as stating the Diary was a hoax, with Warren making the point that it contained 'no material about the case which was not known before'.

Stewart Evans would prove to be one of the Diary's most dismissive critics. A Suffolk police officer, he had recently begun researching, with colleague Paul Gainey, the American doctor Francis Tumblety (a named Ripper suspect). Evans, whose book (co-written with Gainey) would be published two years later, would continue to denounce the Diary as a hoax. The comments of Evans and Warren also made the *Liverpool Daily Post* the next day, though Paul Begg, who had seen the Diary, warned against hasty and ill-informed speculation. 'They are commenting on something they have not seen,' he said. 'All tests which might reasonably be expected to have been made have been made and the document has not been shown to be a forgery.'

The article also carried an angry statement from one of Tony Devereux's daughters: 'My father had nothing to do with this. It is a total mystery to us. He was never in possession of any diary and anyone who says otherwise is a liar.' On the same day Nancy Steele, one of Devereux's three daughters, wrote to Shirley Harrison on behalf of herself and her two sisters, expressing their 'deep distress to learn from the papers of the connection between James Maybrick and Jack the Ripper', a connection Shirley Harrison had been unable to make clear to them before, owing to the confidentiality agreement.

Reiterating a previous demand that the book should not be dedicated to their father, as Barrett had requested, the sisters maintained 'that there has never been any connection between our father and this Diary. Therefore, unless Mr Barrett can prove his story we feel that our father's name should not be mentioned.' Michael Barrett's actions, they felt, 'have not been those of a "so called" friend'. Some months later, in September 1993, when interviewed by Martin Howells for Paul Feldman's video on the

Diary, the sisters would also give a rather different perspective of Michael Barrett's friendship with their father from that given by Barrett himself.

On 9 June 1993 Smith Gryphon entered into an option agreement with Times Newspapers Ltd to serialise the Diary in the *Sunday Times*. It was an agreement that would have huge consequences for the Diary and all involved with it. Even the choice of the *Sunday Times* was controversial, as the paper had not enjoyed the best of experiences with diaries in the past. In 1967 the *Sunday Times* had shown interest in diaries allegedly written by the Italian dictator Benito Mussolini, which were proven to be fakes before any money had changed hands. In 1983 they had actually published the first instalment of the notorious Hitler Diaries before it was discovered that the paper they were written on contained a whitening ingredient not in use until well after Hitler's death. The paper had been able to reclaim its £3 million outlay but, given the humiliation it had experienced, seemed an unlikely candidate for Smith's approach. But this is precisely why, according to Robert Smith, he did approach it, believing that, because of the previous experiences, it would have given extra credence to the Diary if the paper accepted it as authentic. (Later Smith would describe his action as naive, saying of the *Sunday Times* that 'it was journalistically much safer and more sensational to brand it a fake'.)

Robert Smith had initially met with a representative of the *Sunday Times*, Susan Douglas, on 7 April 1993, when he informed her that he had acquired the rights to the Diary of Jack the Ripper. After a series of further meetings and an exchange of letters, the paper agreed with Smith Gryphon an option arrangement for serialisation of the Diary, with a down payment of £5,000 and a final purchase price of £75,000 if they decided to proceed with serialisation. The *Sunday Times* was also asked to sign a confidentiality agreement, part of which gave the paper the right, in the event that it decided not to purchase the serialisation rights, to explain why it had come to that decision. However, such an explanation could only be made after the commencement of the serialisation by another paper or on the publication of the work. In the light of subsequent events this would prove to be a highly significant clause.

It was around the time that two journalists from the *Sunday Times* Insight team, Maurice Chittenden and Christopher Lloyd, were beginning their investigation into the Diary that a startling new development threatened to destabilise the whole Diary project. On 3 June 1993, just two months before the hardback edition of *The Diary of Jack the Ripper* was due at the printers, Robert Smith received a telephone call from a man with a Liverpool accent. Though the caller was different, there was an uncanny echo of the call received by Doreen Montgomery over a year previously that had begun the whole story. 'I think I've got James Maybrick's watch,' said the voice on the other end of the phone. The next day Smith received a letter from the caller, Albert Johnson, who lived in the Merseyside suburb of Wallasey, describing the watch in his possession, an 18-carat gold Lancaster Verity hallmarked 1846, which he claimed to have bought eleven months previously. Johnson also included a very rough drawing of the watch's inside cover, highlighting a series of scratches. These included a signature, 'J Maybrick', and the chilling boast 'I am Jack'. Johnson believed there were seven sets of initials.

These scratches, decipherable only with a magnifying glass, had been examined under a microscope at the college in Wirral where Johnson worked part-time as a security guard. Johnson wrote that he was 'looking further into the background of the watch but would be a great help if you could compare signature in watch to any signature of J. Maybrick to verify if genuine'. He continued: 'I am sure if it proved genuine it would help the sale of your forthcoming book. Before finding all this out in the last week or so, I was quite happy with my watch, now I do not feel so good with it in case someone so evil owned it. I hope you can help me in proving one way or other of the authenticity of the watch, if James Maybrick was Jack the Ripper.'

Despite its potential to cement claims that Maybrick was the Ripper, the arrival of the watch was viewed by some in the Diary camp almost as if it were a ticking time bomb. Even a few months after the news, Shirley Harrison was writing to warn Robert Smith about the dangers of mentioning it in her book. 'It is such an extraordinarily suspect item,' she wrote, 'which could be used mercilessly against us.'

Albert Johnson, then in his late fifties, was living in semi-retirement with his wife Valerie. In dealings with either Shirley Harrison's or Paul Feldman's teams, both of whom would speedily descend on him, the quiet and self-effacing Johnson would nearly always be accompanied by his extrovert younger brother Robbie. Albert, who was interviewed by Martin Howells in September 1993 for the video on the Diary, remained resolute about how he obtained the watch. Unlike Michael Barrett, he has never deviated in any detail from this account. And, unlike Barrett, his story could be proved.

Johnson had bought the watch from Stewarts the Jewellers in Liskard, Wallasey, on 14 July 1992 for £225, after a successful horse-racing bet, as an investment for his young granddaughter because he felt that in a few years' time it would be worth 'quite a bit more money than I paid for it'. Having left it in a drawer for ten months, he says he didn't retrieve it until mentioning it to colleagues at work during a discussion about watches, when he promised to bring it in. As Johnson showed his colleagues how to open the back and front, he told Howells, the light from the window highlighted the scratches inside the back. It was the first time he had noticed them. Out of curiosity Johnson and his colleagues took the watch to the college's science and maths building and asked a technician to look at it under a microscope. 'At first we found "I am Jack" and "J Maybrick" underneath and a couple of initials on the lower part of the watch.' The words meant nothing at the time, but later that day a colleague of Johnson's, John White, revealed he had read about Maybrick and the Diary in the *Liverpool Echo*. He mistakenly informed Johnson that Maybrick had buried his wife and two children under the floorboards of his house in Liverpool, and more accurately mentioned the Ripper connection. Johnson immediately returned to the science and maths building and a larger microscope was found. This time they found other scratches and, according to Johnson's account, were able to make out M.K. and a couple of other initials. In the library, after vainly searching for a book on Maybrick, Johnson found one on Jack the Ripper. 'We found the initials in it were actually inside the watch.'

After ringing the *Echo* to inform the editor of his discovery, Johnson was redirected to its sister paper, the *Liverpool Post*, in which, it transpired, White had actually read the article. The *Post* sent a journalist round to interview Johnson and examine the watch, a young woman whom Johnson recalls was highly sceptical. In the archives section of the newspaper office Johnson finally found the article John White had read. After speaking to Harold Brough, who had conducted the investigation into the Diary for the *Post*, Johnson was given the name of the Diary's publishers, Smith Gryphon, and made his call to its managing director, Robert Smith.

From Albert Johnson's point of view, everything would now happen very quickly. On Monday 14 June 1993 Albert and Robbie Johnson brought the watch to the Islington offices of Robert Smith. After examining the watch for over two hours and a half and discussing its significance, Smith told them that the scratches in the watch did indeed match up to the content of the Diary. What Smith also noticed, but did not mention at the time, was that the signature on the watch, J. Maybrick, was very similar to James Maybrick's known signature, in stark contrast to the writing in the Diary.

Soon after, the brothers decided that they would need legal representation and duly contacted local solicitor Richard Nicholas. A few days later, on 26 June, Robert Smith received a written statement from Suzanne Murphy of Stewarts the Jewellers, confirming that the watch Johnson had bought from them had been in the Murphy family for the last five years. Unlike the Diary, the recent provenance of the watch was not proving a problem.

But how would the watch fare in the next and even more important stage? Like the Diary, scientific testing would be needed. On a visit to Liverpool on 27 June 1993, Robert Smith offered to fund the necessary research in return for a 25 per cent share in the watch and even went so far as to draw up a draft agreement on 1 July, but Albert Johnson decided he would prefer to fund the research himself. (On 27 August 1993 an agreement would be signed between Smith Gryphon on behalf of Shirley Harrison and Michael Barrett, and Richard Nicholas on behalf of Albert and Robbie Johnson, which licensed the two authors to reproduce photographs of the watch and the story of its discovery and authentication in the hardback edition.)

At the suggestion of the Johnsons' solicitor Richard Nicholas, the watch was taken for examination to expert Dr Stephen Turgoose. Nicholas had made enquiries with a number of laboratories which had reported that they did not believe that scratches in metal could be dated accurately, if at all. In August 1993 he contacted Dr Turgoose of the Corrosion and Protection Centre at the University of Manchester Institute of Science and Technology (UMIST), believing the department, according to Johnson, 'to be the best in the country on metal fatigue and metal awareness'. Contrary to Shirley Harrison's initial fears, Turgoose's assessment, using a scanning electron microscope to examine the inside of the watch, was positive. 'The wear apparent on many of the engravings,' he reported on 10 August 1993, 'evidenced by the rounded edges of the markings and the "polishing out" in places, would indicate a substantial age for the engravings. The actual age would depend on the cleaning or polishing regime employed, and any definition of number of years has a great degree of uncertainty and, to some extent, must remain speculation. Given these qualifications, I would be of the opinion that the engravings are likely to date back more than tens of years and possibly much longer.'

Dr Turgoose also revealed some interesting details to Johnson, such as the fact that every initial on the watch had been put on with a different implement, while 'I am Jack' and 'J Maybrick', the earliest of the engravings, he believed, were scratched with the same implement. Moreover, in the 'M.K.' initial, a piece of the implement, he believed, had broken off and, now corroded, was still in place, suggesting an age considerably greater than just a few years.

Could it have been a recent forgery? Turgoose saw no evidence but did not rule out the possibility, especially as he could not conclusively prove the age of the engravings. They could have been produced recently, he said, and 'deliberately artificially aged by polishing, but this would have been a complex multi-stage process, using a variety of different tools, with intermediate polishing or artificial wearing stages'. The forger would also have had to anticipate the unique ability of the scanning electron microscope to observe some of these features, 'indicating a considerable skill and scientific awareness'. Richard Nicholas told Martin Howells that he was not surprised, insisting that he would not have agreed to represent the Johnsons if he had had any suspicion they had 'manufactured a hoax'. Unless very sure of his work, he pointed out, it would be a brave act for a forger to pay out £400, as Albert Johnson had, for tests that would in all probability expose the scratches as a recent hoax.

Intrigued by the possibility that the watch might be Maybrick's, Albert Johnson had several times returned to the jewellers who had sold him the watch, asking questions as to where it came from. It emerged that the watch had been given to the owners of the shop, Suzanne and Ron Murphy, by Suzanne's father, Mr Stewart, as he was clearing out stock from his antique shop in Lancaster, prior to retirement. This was roughly two years before the Murphys had sold it to Johnson in July 1992. Albert Johnson contacted Stewart by phone but the now elderly man, battling with the onset of Alzheimer's Disease, could only recall that he had bought the watch between ten and fifteen years previously from a man who had come into his shop.

Johnson's account was expanded by Ron Murphy's, when he too was interviewed by Martin Howells in September 1993: 'My father-in-law can't remember how long he had the watch, he kept no records of purchase.' He told Howells that it wasn't working at the time, 'so we just stored it away . . . about a year later . . . about 1990/91, we had the watch overhauled and we put it in the window with a resale price of £295 or £275'. Crucially, Murphy did recall some scratches inside it, 'but I didn't notice anything out of the ordinary'. More would emerge about the watch later. James Maybrick's motto was 'Tempus Omnia Revelat' ('Time reveals all') – a significant choice according to some. But would it?

The watch was now part of the story of the Diary, but were the two truly connected? If it were a hoax, then the numbers of conspirators involved in the whole operation was now rising sharply. If it were genuine, it was much-needed good news for the Diary at a time when that commodity was in short supply. As the succeeding weeks would demonstrate, the core of the problems encountered by the Diary team would revolve around the claims made for its authenticity.

By early June 1993 Shirley Harrison, still busily researching the book, was becoming increasingly anxious about claiming too much on the Diary's behalf. 'An honest line', she wrote to Doreen Montgomery, 'would have just as strong a story and would whip up masses of interest instead of laying ourselves open to accusations of doctoring evidence in our favour'. Harrison believed the Diary was genuine but accepted that 'it is a belief and not a proven fact'. Should they be proved wrong after publication, 'it is then no worse than an honest mistake. Not a lie manufactured for commercial interests. The problem is that Robert [Smith] has already said it has been proved . . . we must try and set this right in the book.'

Commercial interests, however, were becoming ever more important. By this stage Paul Feldman had been busy in America pitching the story of the Diary to a number of Hollywood film companies and getting one or two encouraging bites in return. Hollywood meant serious money, but it also created serious difficulties. Just how far would Feldman have to go to convince potential backers that the story he was touting was legitimate? The first test came with MGM who expressed real interest in the story, but needed to know the Diary was genuine. This created a problem back home. How could Feldman give such an assurance, particularly at this relatively early stage of his research?

By 16 June 1993 the other parties involved were beginning to become concerned. Writing to Robert Smith, Michael Barrett's solicitor Richard Bark-Jones pointed out that a statement signed by his client two days previously for MGM was 'seriously defective in two respects'. First, there was no evidence for the claim that the Diary is 'now known' to be the original Diary of Jack the Ripper. This could, after all, be construed as 'a warrant of its authenticity'. Relating to the film offer, the second objection was that the agreement Barrett had entered into with Harrison and Montgomery referred to the book specifically but not to the Diary, 'all rights in which are retained by our client'.

Doreen Montgomery, Barrett's agent, agreed with these concerns and the revised statement Bark-Jones had supplied. She was determined to protect Barrett from any dangers that could ensue from this kind of exaggeration. The revised statement was considerably more guarded, describing the Diary as 'believed after extensive investigation to be the original diary of Jack the Ripper written in 1888 and 1889'. Barrett also noted that he and Anne had granted 'world publishing, film, tv and other visual rights in the book to Smith Gryphon Limited'. Not long afterwards, in July 1993, Anne too would sign a statement for the benefit of MGM, confirming she was the co-owner of the Diary with her husband.

Meanwhile, the *Sunday Times* investigation was continuing, but not quite along the lines envisaged by Robert Smith. Shirley Harrison had been contacted by the two journalists from the Insight team with a request to interview her and also to contact the Devereux sisters. As far as Harrison was concerned, this went well beyond the agreement with the *Sunday Times* which gave its journalists the right to read the text and Diary and to speak to the experts involved in testing its authenticity. The Devereux sisters, who believed the Diary somehow involved the besmirching of the family name, knew nothing about it and could hardly be described as expert witnesses, she said. Nor would Doreen Montgomery consent to the *Sunday Times* interviewing either Shirley Harrison or Michael Barrett until it had taken up its option right, lest it print a bona fide interview while the Diary was serialised in another paper.

Paul Feldman's team was also busy researching the Diary and by 19 June 1993, when he wrote to broadcaster and author Melvin

Harris, the production of the documentary video was already well under way. Harris, described in *The Jack the Ripper A to Z* as 'a noted and respected investigator of mysteries of all types, and a distinguished debunker', had made his name with a series of hoax-busting books and was regarded as one of the main authorities on the Ripper, about whom he had written two books already and was currently writing a third. Feldman, who had decided to consult Harris on the advice of Paul Begg, reminded him that he had promised his comments on the Diary some weeks previously but had still not delivered them. Feldman would already have a shrewd idea that Harris's views on the Diary would not tally with his own but he told Harris that he was anxious to receive his input in the near future as 'it is necessary for us to investigate not just the positive aspects of this but also the negative ones'.

Harris would indeed write back, though not until 23 July 1993. 'I'm sorry to tell you,' he began, 'that the account is a hoax and a recent hoax at that. Of this there is no doubt whatsoever.' The remainder of the letter made no better reading for Feldman. It would have been possible for the hoaxer, Harris believed, to have created the text using just two books, though he didn't, at this stage, name them. The hoax was a cunning one but its chief cunning, he felt, lay in its sheer emptiness. 'Its lack of content, its vague hints, have misled you into creating a story around it,' Harris warned. Crucially, in the light of being able to prove the matter scientifically, he stated that there was no way of dating a Victorian-style ink, unless the manuscript was examined within twelve months after the ink had dried, and less in the case of certain inks such as logwood. Asking Feldman to note that the writing in James Maybrick's will *did* belong to him, Harris warned him that, as the Diary was a modern hoax, Smith Gryphon did not legally own the copyright in the text. That would remain with the writer, whoever he was. Feldman, he suggested, was probably entitled to a refund. 'Integrity above all things,' he concluded.

As if life were not complicated enough for those involved in investigating the Diary's authenticity, the *Liverpool Daily Post* raised the possibility, in an article published on 24 June 1993, that even its ownership was now open to legal challenge. The good news was that a more plausible provenance might be in the offing. The bad news was that Paul Dodd, the owner of Battlecrease, whose family had owned the house since 1946, believed he might have a better claim to the Diary than Michael Barrett. One theory of how the Diary had surfaced after all these years was that it had been found during extensive rewiring of the house during 1991 or 1992. The *Post* had traced three electricians who had worked on the house and all three denied finding the Diary. However, Dodd's lawyer had written to Smith Gryphon, asking them to halt publication until the question of ownership had been resolved. Dodd himself told the *Post* that he was not doing it for money: 'I am doing it because I would like to establish the truth,' he said. 'It must be certainly possible, if not probable, that the Diary did come from the house.' Feldman claims he now approached Paul Dodd. Should this account be true, he believed that legally Dodd would have a claim to the Diary. Would Dodd, he says he asked, be prepared to come to a deal with Michael Barrett as regards ownership? Dodd indicated he would and an offer was made to Barrett. For a 5 per cent stake, Dodd would forgo the possibility of legal action. Barrett's reply was to the point: 'Tell him to fuck off. The Diary never came from the house.' In truth, the legal basis for any such deal was dubious, particularly as neither co-owner of the Diary, Robert Smith or Shirley Harrison, who received 50 per cent of the royalties, was involved. Even so, Barrett had turned down a golden opportunity to take on a decent provenance for the Diary. Or was he telling the truth about Devereux?

By the beginning of July 1993 the *Sunday Times* option agreement on serialising the Diary was on the point of lapsing and the paper showed no sign of taking it up. Robert Smith wrote to Tony Rennell, Associate Editor of the *Sunday Times*, to point this out. The reply was devastating. As a result of rigorous inquiries into the text and after calling in outside experts, Rennell replied, the paper had 'come to the conclusion that the Diary is a fake and we will not therefore be exercising the option to purchase serial rights'. Not only that but

Rennell suggested that any attempt by Smith Gryphon to sell serial rights elsewhere, or to publish a book claiming the Diary to be authentic, would be 'very seriously misleading'.

Before deciding what to do about warning other interested parties that the Diary was a fake, the paper would give Smith the opportunity to show them his experts' reports and answer their own expert's deep-seated concerns. It appeared that there were four main sticking points for the *Sunday Times*. One was the handwriting on James Maybrick's marriage certificate, signed in 1881, which they claimed was identical to the will and which, like the will, bore 'no resemblance to the handwriting in the diary'. The others were their expert's belief that the handwriting in the Diary used character forms associated with twentieth-century teaching; that Nicholas Eastaugh had told them that he examined paintings and drawings principally, rather than text, that he would not describe himself as a forensic scientist, and was 'concerned that his report is being used by you to authenticate the Diary'; and that there were two linguistic anachronisms, of which 'one off instance' had not been recorded before 1934 and 'top myself' before 1958.

The paper also had other concerns, such as the 'significant discrepancies between the Diary and the known Ripper facts', and the fact that Florence Maybrick had kept quiet in prison, 'rather than unmask her husband for the murderer he was'. They were also worried about the provenance of the Diary and the roles of Tony Devereux and Michael Barrett. When Smith responded to the four main questions, the paper would then decide what was in the public interest and how to prevent third parties being misled into believing the Diary was authentic.

Shirley Harrison immediately faxed her own response to Robert Smith, including her belief that 'topped is very old indeed'. She wrote: 'What a bunch of free-loading bully boys looking for a cheap story. I am more than ever glad that we finally managed to swing the message of the book from "This is *it*" to "I believe this is it". They could have justification in attacking the first claim but not the second. The book is now honest and open and admits problems where there are some.'

Harrison signalled her intent by asking Robert Smith if the report she had commissioned from handwriting expert Sue Iremonger could be included in the book. Readers would want to know if she had commissioned a handwriting report, she told him. 'We have, and we should have the guts to say so, even though it was not in our favour. We have a very strong counter-argument in the multi-personality handwriting examples (from Anna Koren).'

Meanwhile, Robert Smith and Tony Rennell of the *Sunday Times* continued to exchange very different views on the authenticity of the Diary while their respective lawyers communicated on contractual matters. One major area of contention was the Baxendale report, which the *Sunday Times* journalists believed had been hidden away from them because it undermined the Diary. Smith responded that in fact he had been unable to release the report owing to an obligation placed on him in an agreement with Dr Baxendale to keep the report confidential. He had, however, advised the *Sunday Times* journalists to approach Baxendale directly to see if he would supply the report to them, together with his further report of 20 August 1992, which significantly modified the reports of 1 and 9 July. In a letter dated 9 July 1993 Smith accused Rennell of ignoring the serious flaws in Baxendale's report, which, he claimed, was based on 'fundamentally wrong assumptions'. Baxendale, Smith said, had been wrong in stating that synthetic dyes were not in use before the First World War; that nigrosine was not in use before the 1940s; that there was nothing in the ink to show the presence of iron; and that Victorians always used the formal copperplate style of writing.

Smith was also critical that no one had examined the Diary apart from the paper's own forensic document examiner, Audrey Giles, who had only 'looked through it for a few minutes in my office while she briefly talked to me'. Other meetings at which Smith had agreed to present the Diary for scientific testing at her premises had been cancelled by her or the paper.

Smith argued that, until a piece of Maybrick's informal writing style could be found, it would be hard to form an opinion as to whether Maybrick's will is genuine. Signatures are a 'notoriously' unreliable source for handwriting comparisons and therefore the signature on Maybrick's marriage certificate could not be compared with the writing in his will. Smith had never claimed that Dr Eastaugh had written a forensic report, he said, but he had conducted a series of scientific tests and had reported that he found no ingredient in the ink or paper inconsistent with an 1888 date. Smith could not believe the paper's language expert couldn't trace the phrase 'to top' in the sense of to kill before 1958. According to him, the Oxford English Dictionary (second edition) gives a date of 1718.

Rennell did not wait long to reply. Among a host of issues which both men saw differently was Smith's alleged claim that he had expert evidence proving the Diary was authentic, evidence that Rennell now concluded did not exist. Acknowledging that David Baxendale's report was flawed, in that he had not realised nigrosine was available in the nineteenth century, Rennell believed, however, that there were other questions raised in his report which remained valid and had yet to be addressed by Smith. Both Martin Fido and Donald Rumbelow, Rennell claimed, had supplied the paper with 'specific instances' where the Diary was at odds with known facts about the Ripper. He also disputed the use of 'to top myself', as in commit suicide, before 1958, claiming its earlier use was only 'to top' as in to hang. To Smith's assertion that Audrey Giles, the handwriting expert employed by the *Sunday Times*, only observed the Diary for a few minutes, he replied that Smith had refused to allow her to remove a page of the Diary for an ESDA test. 'There being no other recognised method of dating the moment when pen touched paper, so further forensic tests were meaningless,' Rennell maintained. 'We reserve the right to take whatever action we think necessary now,' he concluded, in his letter of 14 July 1993.

There was, Shirley Harrison wrote to Robert Smith a few days later, a good reason (apart from the fact that a page would need to be torn from the Diary) why no ESDA test had been commissioned. She had been told by Nicholas Eastaugh that such a test would be totally inappropriate. An ESDA test is used to reveal indentations caused by pen on paper, such as biros on thin notebooks, which produce an indentation from one page to another. 'It would be useless for the Diary because a fountain pen was used, the paper is thick and it is a bound notebook.' She had just spoken to Dr Eastaugh who said the *Sunday Times* statement showed 'total ignorance' and he had given them the telephone number of an ESDA man who told them exactly the same.

But these were only details. Both Harrison and Doreen Montgomery believed the crux of the matter was whether or not Robert Smith had claimed to the paper that the Diary was genuine. Harrison, who believed the paper had shot itself in the foot by claiming the Diary could not be proved either way, had always said it would be wrong to say 'we have proved it is genuine'. 'Our experts', she said, 'are totally agnostic. Our Ripperologists have only a personal and equally unprovable stance.' As long as Robert Smith had not claimed anything other than that he *believed* the Diary to be genuine throughout his correspondence with the *Sunday Times*, Montgomery agreed, then the paper hadn't a leg to stand on. If he had said more, then she and Harrison must be told.

Shirley Harrison told Doreen Montgomery that a meeting with Smith should be arranged as quickly as possible. Earlier mistakes must not be repeated as the publication date drew nearer. The Diary had proved a hugely stressful and difficult book to research and write, and Harrison had a number of major concerns about the way things had been done. She had been hampered from the beginning by contracts which left her inadequately funded and with an unrealistic timescale. No one had realised 'what a bottomless research pit' the project would present, or anticipated the flood of contradictory material constantly thrown into the arena to disrupt the creative writing process. In fact, it had been less of a literary inspiration than a 'construction-kit creation', with Harrison and Evemy gluing it all together, only for it to be dismantled by someone else. To make matters worse, the latest version of the book which she had sent to Robert Smith had been accepted as a final draft. 'Now we have the proofs and I remain disappointed.' The proofs had arrived without warning and with the request that they be returned within five days. It was both 'impossible' and 'very dangerous', she maintained.

It was nowhere near as dangerous as the deteriorating relationship between Robert Smith and the *Sunday Times*, however. On 14 July 1993 the Times Newspapers' solicitor, Alastair J. Brett, wrote to Mishcon de Reya, the legal firm representing Smith Gryphon, to give formal notice that 'in the light of your clients' bad faith and continued bad faith, the *Sunday Times* will be publishing the evidence that it has amassed showing that the Diary is not genuine and could not possibly have been written by James Maybrick'. Mishcon de Reya were invited to petition the court for relief should they believe that the *Sunday Times* was in any way constrained by its option agreement for the serial rights. The paper was also considering a claim for the return of its £5,000 advance. Angered that Smith Gryphon should consider selling the serialisation rights to another party 'when it is quite clear that the diary is a fake', Brett repeated the paper's intention to 'discover whether Barrett or Smith Gryphon were behind what appears to be a sophisticated "con" job'. A follow-up letter, written on 22 July, was even more specific: 'If your clients fail to concede that the book and the theory behind it is based on a fake, albeit a good fake, they will dig their own graves and should expect a court case in which they will be accused in open court of gross deceit and seeking to exploit a fake when any reasonable man must have known and appreciated that it was a fake.'

So far, the sum result of all the expert analysis commissioned on the Diary had hardly painted a conclusive, or even a coherent, picture. For those who believed the Diary was a hoax, there was, however, one vital piece of evidence. The handwriting in the Diary was incontestably different from the writing and signatures in James Maybrick's will. The *Sunday Times* believed the signatures in the latter were clearly written by the same hand that signed Maybrick's marriage certificate, thus rendering ludicrous the accusations that his will was forged. Unconvinced, Paul Feldman had commissioned American graphologist Reed Hayes to compare Maybrick's two-page will, his marriage certificate and the signature of Edwin Maybrick, James's youngest brother.

Acknowledging that his opinion was based on an 'inadequate number of comparable standards', poor photocopies and the difficulty of comparing writing created by wide-nibbed and italic pens, Hayes nevertheless delivered his opinion that 'it is highly probable' that the signatures on James Maybrick's will were *not* written by the same hand that signed his marriage certificate. 'It should also be noted,' he continued, 'that the writing and signatures appearing on the Will have a distinctly contrived look. In my opinion there is an effort to disguise the author's handwriting.' Hayes also noted similarities between Edwin Maybrick's signature and the handwriting in the will but felt there was not enough conclusive evidence to say whether or not he wrote the will or the signatures on it.

One of the great advantages in publishing a book on Jack the Ripper is the world's continuing obsession with him. In no other country outside the UK is that interest greater than in the US. With the deteriorating relationship with the *Sunday Times* creating problems on the domestic front, the last thing Robert Smith needed to hear was any ripple of discontent from abroad. Unfortunately for Smith, the US tide was also beginning to turn against the Diary. On 30 July 1993 the *Washington Post* ran a highly damaging article, as a result of which the prospective US publishers, Warner, decided that they would have to launch their own investigation and promised to cancel the book if doubts as to its legitimacy were not resolved. While acknowledging that, if genuine, the Diary would be the historical find of the century, the writer of the article clearly had his doubts. Melvin Harris had none. 'Are you good at spelling? It's C-R-A-P,' he was quoted as saying. 'An obvious hoax,' added Nick Warren. More damaging, because they came from a man who had provided one of the central scientific reports that were positive to the Diary, were the comments of Nicholas Eastaugh. Far more circumspect than in his report, Eastaugh was quoted as saying, 'with the current state of the testing, we can't distinguish between it being a document from 1889 and something much more recent – say, five to ten years old'. He also told the *Post* journalist that he had been saying 'for some time' that more tests were needed, but that none had been ordered. 'I'm not happy with the current state of investigation,' he concluded. According to Harrison, who was quickly in touch with Eastaugh, he accepted he had spoken to the journalist but claimed he had been caught unaware. Believing, Harrison said in a memo to Robert Smith, that he had been misquoted out of context, he repeated his statement that even lengthy research would not necessarily produce a conclusion. Warner now had little time to set up and conclude their investigation before the proposed publication date. Consequently, on 20 August 1993 Robert Smith set off for Chicago with the Diary and some key documents concerning Maybrick and the Ripper to deliver to their investigative team. The stakes could not be higher. Should their investigation prove the Diary a forgery Warner would, despite advance orders of over 200,000 copies from US booksellers, withdraw from publishing Shirley Harrison's book.

The team assembled by Warner to examine the Diary and other documents brought over by Smith looked formidable. Headed by Kenneth Rendell, whose gallery sold historical letters and documents from ancient to modern times, and who had played a part in the exposure of the Hitler Diaries a decade earlier, it also featured a number of experts in their field: Dr Joe Nickell, who had worked on and written about the Shroud of Turin; Rod McNeil, whose ion migration test, he claimed, could date when ink was put to paper to within ten years, and had been used, so Rendell said in his report, for the FBI and the US Secret Service; Robert Kuranz, a research ink chemist; and Maureen Casey Owens, an expert in forensic handwriting. It was, on paper, a team that packed a truly heavyweight punch – one they would duly deliver. Coincidentally, Rod McNeil had also been recommended to Paul Feldman by Colin Wilson.

On the first day of September 1993, a day that would see a flurry of activity concerning the Diary, Robert Smith received the first blow. A fax from Kenneth Rendell confirmed that his report, the final version of which would reach Time-Warner two days later, would clearly state 'that James Maybrick did not write the Diary'. There were a number of problems, Rendell said, including a large amount of non-handwriting evidence against authenticity, but the major obstacle to the Diary being genuine was the disparity between the handwriting in the Diary and Maybrick's will. 'We all discovered, quite surprisingly,' Rendell wrote, 'that the Maybrick Will is definitely signed by him and is completely in his handwriting. It does not compare favourably with the Diary.'

Smith's response was immediate. 'I thought we already had an agreement' (whereby Warner would release the Rendell report to Smith before it went public), he faxed back to Warner Books regarding the report, 'which you signed on 19th August before I came to Chicago.' Smith informed the publishers of Reed Hayes's findings on the will and marriage certificate and the report by Dr Turgoose on the watch, suggesting that he and Warner exchange all reports on the basis that 'we do not release them to anyone without mutual permission'. He also attached a copy of Michael Barrett's handwriting, 'as requested'. The same day Smith faxed another letter to Warner to inform them that the *Sunday Times* had persuaded a judge to agree a trial for 28 September in the UK (in the event it would be earlier). 'Unless we can get rid of it the book's contents will become public knowledge from that date.' As a consequence, Smith suggested, serialisations and a projected *60 Minutes* feature should run on or after 26 September rather than 3 October.

A letter was faxed back by Warner the same day, 1 September, defending their actions: 'You represented all along that the Diary was created contemporaneously with the crimes of Jack the Ripper and is authentic; we therefore asked you for all your reports, which you agreed to provide to us.' As a result of the *Washington Post* article, Warner had decided to engage Rendell's services. Asking to see Hayes's report and any other information suggesting the will was a fake, Warner promised to release Rendell's report to Smith as soon as it was publicly released.

Shirley Harrison heard the news the same day. Far from being depressed about Rendell's report, she felt sure it was 'another step on the ladder to a runaway success'. 'We have an on-going, possibly insoluble, teaser,' she wrote to Smith. 'That is excellent for promotion. Let's use the latest "onslaught" to stimulate public interest. Be honest.' She was not prepared to throw in the towel because one – or even several – 'experts' had produced difficult reports: 'When they give me scientific proof I will accept it. Until then, I fight.'

Harrison, as she wrote to Doreen Montgomery, also on 1 September 1993, was perplexed by Rendell's conclusion. How had he discovered that James Maybrick's will was in his handwriting? 'The problem of the will has been openly confronted in my book and has been known to exist for some time.' She also pointed out that Reed Hayes had reached a very different conclusion from Sue Iremonger on the will and marriage certificate signatures. Nor did she believe that Rendell could dismiss the work of twelve months after a mere two weeks of testing on the basis of such controversial science. What was Rendell's non-handwriting evidence, she asked, when none of the Ripper specialists consulted by her had found 'one single hard fact against it'. Where, she demanded, 'is the PROOF that this diary was not written in 1889?' The next day, she wrote to Robert Smith regarding one piece of evidence held against the Diary. According to Dr Tony Deeson of the Institute of Mechanical Engineers, the phrase 'one-off' appeared in the records of builders Trayners of Kent in 1860 (though, to date, Harrison has not seen the record herself).

No amount of argument from Robert Smith or Shirley Harrison could sway Warner. On 3 September 1993 Time Inc (Warner's parent company) faxed Smith to inform him that, as a result of Kenneth Rendell's report, they were pulling out of US publication. Smith, who had still not seen the report, was furious, faxing back immediately that their behaviour was 'professionally and contractually unacceptable'. Why were they so reluctant to show him a report they had promised to send him at the same time as Warner? In order to travel to Chicago, Smith had left his wife on their wedding anniversary and just one day after her father had died of cancer. 'And now you say you will only show me the results at the same time that you publicly announce them.' The report, he told them, must be shared immediately so it could be evaluated and publication plans reviewed. 'Considered, rather than dramatic, action is called for now.'

It was to no avail. On 7 September, along with the rest of the public, Smith and Harrison were at last able to see Rendell's report. It would do little to dilute their anger. Criticising Shirley Harrison's own research into the Diary as lacking in scepticism, Rendell and his team dismissed the Diary on virtually all possible grounds. In his damning summary, Rendell listed a number of key points that had persuaded them that the Diary was not the work of James Maybrick. 'The style of the handwriting', he wrote, 'is not Victorian.' Echoing Dr Baxendale's previous report, he continued that it was 'indicative of the early to mid-twentieth century at the earliest'. Furthermore, 'the layout, pen pressure and ink distribution suggested that many entries were written at one time', a feature that reminded Rendell of the Hitler Diaries.

The fact that the Diary was in a scrapbook and not a diary book also made Rendell's team suspicious. Why had a wealthy man such as Maybrick not bought a new diary rather than using an old scrapbook and removing used pages, as he seemed to have done. Surely this was the work of a forger buying an old scrapbook and taking out the incriminating used pages before filling in the Diary. The language of the Diary was questioned too. Rendell made the accusation that 'one-off' was a post-Victorian phrase. The Diary contained, the report said, a number of phrases and expressions that were also to be found in the famous 'Dear Boss' letter (now actually believed by many Ripper experts to have been a hoax, written by a journalist) that first gave the world the name Jack the Ripper. 'The Diary,' the report said, 'is inexorably linked to that letter. All comparisons of the two handwritings conclude they are written by different people.'

Finally came the results of Rod McNeil's ion migration test. This, Rendell stated, had pinpointed a date of 1921, plus or minus twelve years. 'There is no credible evidence whatsoever,' the summary concluded, 'that this Diary is genuine. Every area of analysis proves or indicates the Jack the Ripper Diary is a hoax.'

The Diary team prepared to fight back, but would soon be overwhelmed by press reaction from around the world. Ripper expert Martin Fido agreed to send Shirley Harrison a statement that the Diary could not have been written in 1921 and also pledged his willingness to go to court to vouch for Robert Smith's constant efforts to authenticate the Diary. Paul Begg offered the observation that no other Ripper document had undergone such scrutiny. On 9 September 1993, when the news broke, the papers had a field day. Accusing the *Sunday Times* of achieving the amazing distinction of a gullibility hat-trick (after the Mussolini and Hitler Diaries), the *Daily Mail* reported that Warner Books' winning bid for the Diary was said to have been a record. Now the massive international advertising campaign which was to have promoted the publication date of 7 October as 'the day the world's greatest murder mystery will be SOLVED' had gone sour and Warner would have to pulp the 200,000 copies of the Diary they had branded a hoax (in truth, not a single copy had been printed). Robert Smith was quoted as saying he intended to press ahead and had not been impressed with Rendell's report. He was, he informed the *Mail*, 'amazed rather than annoyed' at America's perception of a hoax and he urged *Mail* readers to judge for themselves, claiming thirty other experts had given the Diary their approval.

The *Daily Express* quoted Kenneth Rendell. 'The English attitude has been: "Prove it's a fake." They should prove it's real.' Robert Smith, however, was taking a positive, if not mathematically correct, line in the Press. 'The report swept away my last doubts. Rendell says the Diary was written in 1921, plus or minus twelve years. But another test says plus or minus thirty years. That takes us back to 1881 [*sic*]. We believe that when you read this book you will be convinced.' The argument was carried into the *Independent on Sunday*, in which Smith announced he had a 'startling new piece of authenticated evidence . . . which will put the matter beyond dispute' that the Diary was not a fake. Though Smith would not elaborate, the paper believed this proof was in the form of a Victorian pocketwatch supposedly engraved with the Ripper's real name, Maybrick, and the initials of his victims.

Finally, on 15 September 1993, came better news with a letter from Hyperion, a publishing company then owned by the Disney Corporation, which outlined a deal to transfer the US rights on the

Diary from Warner to them. An advance of $50,000, plus another $10,000 for permission to publish the Rendell report, payable directly from Hyperion to Warner was agreed, with a further $10,000 from Hyperion payable to Smith Gryphon for production materials.

When the US edition was eventually published, its preface contained a summary of Rendell's report and a lengthy rebuttal of it by Smith, who described it as 'fundamentally flawed, inaccurate and unreliable'. Comparing the two weeks Rendell was given to compile his report with the fifteen months which Shirley Harrison and her experts had spent researching the Diary, Smith listed a number of key points where he felt Rendell had erred. Rod McNeil had given a median year of 1921 as the likely date when ink was put to paper. Why had Rendell not given details of McNeil's test, and if it was not believed to be a modern forgery, why did he not investigate the implications of this? According to Ripper expert Martin Fido, Smith reported, the suggested date 'is the most insane worst possibility – science dates the document to a historically impossible period'. How, for instance, had a forger of that time known that there was an empty tin matchbox near the body of Catherine Eddowes when that information was not released until 1984 and not in a published book until 1987? Similarly, it was believed until the 1950s, Smith claimed, that the Ripper had been responsible for seven Whitechapel murders. How had a 1920s forger known there were only five?

Probably the most crucial conclusion of the Rendell report had been the clear discrepancy between the handwriting in Maybrick's will and that in the Diary. But why, Smith asked, had not Rendell seriously investigated the possibility that the will was forged? The will, dated 25 April 1889, Smith believed, was probably not written by James Maybrick. 'There is evidence recorded for the trial of Mrs Maybrick for the murder of her husband, which clearly shows that Maybrick was under pressure from his sinister brothers to sign a new will, when it became obvious he was going to die. A witness saw two of the brothers going into Maybrick's room with papers the night before his death, on May 11, 1889, and heard James Maybrick complaining about the duress.'

Could the dying Maybrick, Smith asked, largely paralysed by the effects of chronic arsenic and strychnine poisoning, write in so precise a hand during the last days of his life? Would he really twice misspell his own daughter's name, Evelyn as Eveleyn? 'There are also,' Smith wrote, 'many differences between the words in the "will" as it appears in a transcript taken down by a lawyer, Alexander MacDougall, soon after Maybrick's death, and published in his book of 1891 [*Treatise on the Maybrick Case*], and the "will" that exists in Somerset House today.' According to American document examiner Reed Hayes, the signatures on the will and the marriage certificate were not even similar. The controversy over the will would continue.

Eleven days after Warner had come to their decision, the controversy shifted back to England. On 19 September 1993 the *Sunday Times*, under a headline that screamed 'Fake', launched the result of its own investigation into the Diary, conducted by associate news editor Maurice Chittenden and journalist Christopher Lloyd. Still reeling from the Rendell report, the Diary camp now faced another highly damaging critique.

However, by this stage it was not unexpected. During the previous weeks both sides had been preparing for and engaging in a very costly legal battle, in which the paper, having decided not to take up the option agreement on serialisation, was aiming to withdraw from the confidentiality agreement that bound it from commenting on the Diary before the publication date or the commencement of serialisation by another paper.

In his defence Robert Smith had vigorously contested the paper's justifications for having this agreement set aside, claiming that any statement he made regarding the Diary's authenticity was an expression of opinion, and that the purpose of the agreement was to give the paper the opportunity for a thorough investigation of the Diary. At various meetings through April, May and June, Smith admitted to saying that he believed the paper would 'be completely convinced of the Diary's authenticity' and that it was an important historical document; that he claimed the publishers could prove the Diary genuine 'beyond reasonable doubt' and that 'historically, the diary gets it right every time'. He also denied being under any obligation to disclose the Document Evidence report written by Dr Baxendale, pointing out that, on the contrary, Baxendale had required him to make a written undertaking 'not to use any part of my [Baxendale's] report for any purposes whatsoever' and 'not to mention my [Baxendale's] name or that of Document Evidence Ltd in any publication concerning the "Victorian Diary".' Smith also denied there were significant factual errors in the Diary or that representations were made fraudulently. Nor did the reports by Dr Eastaugh and by Dr David Forshaw (a forensic psychiatrist, who had compiled a detailed psychological profile of the Diary author) contain any serious doubts about the Diary, he said.

Smith was now counter-claiming to prevent the *Sunday Times* publishing the results of its investigation into the Diary ahead of publication. But on 15 September 1993 came notice that he had failed, ironically just days before the paper would, in any event, be released from the obligation by the commencement of serialisation of the Diary in the *Liverpool Post*. The verdict went with the *Sunday Times*, with Smith Gryphon agreeing to pay the paper £6,500 (the return of the £5,000 option money plus nominal damages of £1,500) and releasing it and its experts from their confidentiality agreement. The paper was free to publish its own verdict.

It was, yet again, a highly damaging one. The Diary, the article claimed, was either the publishing coup of the decade or the biggest hoax since the Hitler Diaries (for which, the paper reported, it and the German magazine *Stern* had paid a whopping £2.5 million). Needless to say, the article came down heavily in favour of the second possibility. Much of the reasoning reflected the concerns of the Rendell report, putting forward the same doubts about the use of a scrapbook and the alleged post-Victorian handwriting style. The article also objected to the use of two expressions ('top myself' and 'one-off') which had concerned Rendell and which, the article said, originated in post-Victorian times. Its experts – forensic document examiner Audrey Giles; lecturer in Victorian and modern English literature at Oxford University Dr Kate Flint; and Ripper writer Tom Cullen – were united in condemnation.

There were other accusations too. The *Sunday Times*, while accepting Dr Eastaugh's report, had received the permission of Smith and Dr Baxendale to be provided with a copy of Document Evidence's report. It was particularly struck by Baxendale's observation that the scrapbook may have contained photographs of a size that was popular between the two world wars, creating the bizarre possibility that someone had used the scrapbook as a photograph album at least thirty years after the Ripper had supposedly used it as a diary. The paper also claimed that Smith had told them that the only proven example of Maybrick's handwriting in existence was the signature on his will, but it failed to mention that Shirley Harrison's manuscript, supplied to it by Smith, had openly disclosed the existence of Maybrick's signature on his marriage certificate. The handwriting in both these examples, the paper claimed, was identical, and vastly different from the handwriting in the Diary. There was no question, the article made abundantly clear, that the Diary of Jack the Ripper was a fake. Perhaps more disturbing for Robert Smith, the article revealed that on 29 July the paper had reported the matter, and sent key documents, to Scotland Yard, which was now considering its own investigation.

Combined with the Rendell report, the impact of the article was devastating. Smith's published rebuttal lay in the future. Frustrated by remaining silent, Shirley Harrison wrote to Smith, expressing her wish to defend the Diary and the publisher/author relationship against the article, which 'has so many flaws itself'. Its six main reasons why the Diary was a fake could, she said, be easily rebutted on each count. A call from Brian Lake, the antiquarian bookdealer to whom Harrison had taken the Diary on the day Michael Barrett first brought it to London, suggested that she move the argument away from detailed analysis of the Diary to the idea that the document is 'of quite exceptional interest'. It cannot be dismissed, he said, as the paper had done, without further research. There was a danger, he said, of them 'being made to wriggle on the end of the *Sunday Times*'s hook'.

To the casual observer, it must have seemed as if the Diary was a shabby fake which would now disappear from public view for good. But was it so simple? Three weeks later, on 4 October 1993, the hardback version of Shirley Harrison's *The Diary of Jack the Ripper* was published in Britain. Without the negative publicity, the combined sales of the hardback and paperback versions might have run into millions. As it was, the book in its various editions would still achieve sales figures of over half a million around the world; ironically, it reached number 6 in the *Sunday Times*'s own bestseller list. The pendulum, which at the time of publication was swinging so sharply towards the anti-Diary camp, would in time swing back the other way. The surface had only just been scratched. The drama had barely started.

THREE

'The writer of the Diary is still alive'

The press launch of a book is normally a fairly straightforward affair; a short speech from the author or publisher is usually followed by a few polite questions from the assembled journalists. To nobody's surprise, the press launch of *The Diary of Jack the Ripper* on 4 October 1993 was a little more dramatic than that. It was held in the august surroundings of the Arts Club in Mayfair and an element of theatre was evident from the moment guests entered the billiards room where the event was staged. There, on a side table, like exhibits in a court case, in full view of the Press and beneath the steely gaze of a uniformed security guard, lay the Diary and watch, side by side.

Stung by the negative publicity of the previous few weeks, the Diary team was determined to reclaim some ground and give the book the impetus it would need for healthy sales. But, as more than one journalist noted, the combined effect of the Rendell report and the *Sunday Times* article was clearly evident on the copies of the book that were made available to the press. Peeling off the sticker on the book's cover that read 'Is It Genuine? Read the evidence, then judge for yourself' revealed a rather bolder claim underneath: 'The Discovery, The Investigation, The Authentication.' 'The change', Robert Smith told reporters with some understatement, 'was due to doubts being voiced in the press.'

Doubts were being expressed at the packed launch too, where the publishers had promised that detailed questions could be asked of the author and experts. While representatives of the media, including international television and newspapers, questioned the panel of Robert Smith and Shirley Harrison, present in the audience (along with Michael and Anne Barrett) were a number of Ripper experts keen to provide their own opinions on the Diary. Paul Begg, who had 'sat on the fence so long I'm in danger of getting piles', represented a small group of neutrals. Most, like Donald Rumbelow, believed the Diary was a hoax. But it was another noted Ripperologist who stole the limelight. Melvin Harris, who had written two books on the Ripper and was in the process of writing another, had already been quoted in a number of newspaper articles denouncing the Diary as a fake, including the *Washington Post* article that had triggered the Rendell report and the *Sunday Times* article. As the question time drew to a close, to the delight of the assembled journalists Harris rose from his seat at the back of the room to challenge Robert Smith.

Pointing at the Diary, Harris shouted out, 'This is a fake. It is a modern fake, most likely by someone who was schooled in the 1930s.' One of the major reasons Harris had decided it was a fake was the clear difference between the handwriting in the Diary and the writing in James Maybrick's will, made just days before his death, a point of considerable difficulty for those who believed the Diary was genuine. Both Shirley Harrison and Robert Smith had put forward the possibility that the will might not have been written in Maybrick's hand, a claim which did not wash with Melvin Harris. In an appendix to his book *The True Face of Jack the Ripper*, Harris gave his own version of the encounter. 'I uncoiled myself from my back seat and made two very basic requests. "Where", I asked, "is the expert who will put his reputation on the line and state that this Diary is an authentic document written by James Maybrick in 1888 and 1889? And where is there another expert also prepared to put his reputation on the line and state that James Maybrick's will is a forgery?" The silence was uncanny. Mr Smith was left alone at the bridge of the *Titanic*. His experts had either deserted him or they had never existed.'

Robert Smith, according to Harris, answered by referring to the disputing of the authenticity of the will in 1891 in Alexander MacDougall's book about the trial of Florence Maybrick written soon after the event. An account which, Harris rebutted, was inaccurate and contradictory. As the temperature rose, the

Liverpool Daily Post reported, Smith went on to question Harris's apparent role as self-appointed critic-in-chief of the Diary. 'Melvin Harris's name occurs,' he said, 'in almost every article that has been printed. I wonder why he is so interested in doing this Diary down.' 'You know why,' Harris interrupted angrily. 'I have a reputation at stake. I will not endorse this thing. I have no ulterior motive. It's not money.' Smith begged to differ, suggesting that the forthcoming publication of *The True Face of Jack the Ripper* (due to be published in spring 1994), which named another suspect, Roslyn D'Onston Stephenson, was motivation enough for Harris's campaign.

Harris did not just believe that the Diary was a modern forgery, he appeared confident that he knew who was behind it. Back on 18 September 1993 he had given Paul Feldman 'the following forecasts: the writing in the diary is not Victorian, but was written by a man schooled in Liverpool in the 1930s; this hoax was not a lone venture; the writer of the diary is still alive and is a man never once mentioned by you; though he penned the text he did not conceive the text – that was provided by someone else'. On 27 September Feldman wrote back to inform Harris that he had been aware for some time of his theory that the Diary was dictated by Tony Devereux and actually written by a Mr Kane who 'vanished' at the time the report on the Diary appeared in the Liverpool papers. 'We have, of course, investigated this,' Feldman claimed.

Unfortunately, Harris's theories would not be aired on Paul Feldman's video about the Diary. As he explained to Feldman in a letter written the next day, it was against his union's rules not to work at proper professional rates and he insisted that his name was not to be used in connection with the video. He also referred Feldman to the Rendell report's analysis and comparison of James Maybrick's will and Diary, which 'conclusively shows they were written by two different people'. Having spoken to Joe Nickell and other examiners in the USA, and gleaned a great deal more from Rendell himself, Harris felt 'this whole affair has a very unpleasant odour about it'. He did not, however, confirm or deny Feldman's identification of his suspects.

Hardly had the dust settled from the launch when Robert Smith found himself the subject of a more serious examination, a Scotland Yard investigation instigated by the *Sunday Times*. After receiving documents from the paper, the Yard had dispatched two detectives from its Organised Crime Squad, who arrived in Liverpool on 20 October 1993 to interview a number of people connected with the Diary. The investigation was trailed in the *Daily Express* of 5 October by journalist Stephen Grey, who reported that at the launch Melvin Harris had claimed the diary was 'an audacious fraud'. Grey would continue to monitor the story.

Scotland Yard's task was concerned with deciding whether Robert Smith, as the publisher, had attempted knowingly to pass off a fake document as genuine. It was yet another serious blow to the Diary's credibility, this time with possible consequences that went far beyond a negative impact on book sales. Were Smith to be found guilty a custodial sentence was not beyond the bounds of possibility.

For Michael and Anne Barrett, whose lives had already been turned upside down by the events of the past eighteen months, it would ratchet up still further the huge degree of pressure they faced. Barrett, in particular, had not been bearing up very well. Harold Brough, who had first contacted him back in April, had seen a dramatic change, as he reported in the *Liverpool Daily Post* of 28 September 1993. Only forty-one, Barrett had aged visibly over the last few months and now walked slowly with a stick, the result, he told Brough, of a stroke which had left him with limited use of his right side and which he blamed on the stresses and strains involved in living with the Ripper story. 'Nothing can bring back my health,' he said. 'My life is in total turmoil. I wish I could turn the clock back, that I had never been given that brown paper parcel.' It did not help the Barretts that neither was aware who the real subject of the investigation was. According to Anne, when the two detectives visited, Barrett, 'slipped out of the room once or twice and I was sure he was taking a drink into the bathroom with him. I was under the impression that they were investigating Mike as they thought he had forged the Diary.' Only later did Anne discover their visit had formed part of the investigation into Robert Smith's role. Barrett was under the same impression. It was, Anne told Shirley Harrison, 'the worst day of my life'. By ill chance, 22 October, the day of the interview, was also their daughter Caroline's twelfth birthday (Anne's was the next day).

Crucially, during the three-hour interview Barrett denied to the police that he possessed a word processor. It was a puzzling decision. In the just-published first edition of her book, Shirley Harrison had already dealt with Barrett's purchase of a word processor and described how he claimed to have used it to type up research notes on the Diary. Barrett was also asked if he knew the whereabouts of his copy of *Murder, Mayhem and Mystery* by Richard Whittington-Egan. He replied that he had given it to someone, but could not recall whom. In fact it was in the boot of the detectives' car outside, having been given to the two men by one of Tony Devereux's daughters. Without a solicitor present, Barrett refused to sign his statement. Towards the end of the interview Anne's father, Billy Graham, arrived in a taxi but at Anne's request he was not told who the detectives were in case it upset him.

The Barretts were not the only Liverpudlians to be visited by Scotland Yard. Detective Sergeant Thomas, known as 'Bonesy' to his colleagues, who was leading the investigation, also visited Tony Devereux's three daughters; Harold Brough; the landlord of the Saddle pub, where Devereux and Barrett first met; Paul Dodd, the owner of Battlecrease House; and several electricians who had worked on the house's rewiring. Even Gerard Kane, the witness to Devereux's will, who, Paul Feldman alleged, was Melvin Harris's main suspect for penman, received a visit. However, Kane, while happy to answer questions and confirming that he had been a friend of Tony Devereux's, did not appear to recognise Michael Barrett's name. Robert Smith himself was finally interviewed by DS Thomas at Belgravia police station on 19 November 1993. 'It was a perfectly civilised occasion,' Smith recalled later, 'and it was quite clear to me that the police were satisfied that the *Sunday Times* complaint was going nowhere. In the end it was all about the *Sunday Times* getting a front-page story.'

Just a few weeks after Scotland Yard had concluded its investigation, Shirley Harrison was sent to the US to participate in a coast-to-coast promotional tour for the book. She soon found herself being interviewed on the highly popular Larry King show along with Kenneth Rendell. The man whose report had so wounded the status of the Diary had another blow to deliver. He had, he told Harrison on air, just heard of a 'sinister development' from the UK. A word processor had been found, he told Harrison, with a transcript of the Diary on disc. Rendell had been told this news by Scotland Yard, Harrison understood, though the detectives had not found (nor even searched for) Barrett's word processor during their interview with him.

Barrett, as Harrison explained to Rendell on air, had his own explanation for the disc. Back in March 1992, when he was due to take the Diary to Doreen Montgomery, he claimed he had decided that it would be a good idea to type out a transcript of the Diary which would be easier to read. His own attempt at typing was so poor that it was eventually typed by Anne, a secretary by profession, while Barrett dictated. For the sceptics, whose numbers had grown considerably by this time, this was yet more proof that the Diary was a fake. For many, the question was no longer whether it was a forgery, but who forged it? Kenneth Rendell offered hope that a solution was close at hand. Replying to a letter from American Ripperologist Chris George on 4 November 1993, he suggested that George contact Melvin Harris: 'I do know that Melvin Harris is writing a book on this subject, and he is very far along in identifying who actually forged the book.' These were anxious weeks for Robert Smith and for Shirley Harrison's and Paul Feldman's teams. Nor did it help that, as Scotland Yard was not communicating directly with them, they had to wait on Press reports for news of the investigation.

The next revelation from that quarter was not hopeful. Barely a month after the investigation was launched, an article in the *Liverpool Daily Post* announced that Scotland Yard had sent a report to the Crown Prosecution Service, claiming that the Diary was written post-1987 by an unknown hoaxer in Liverpool.

According to the *Post*, the Yard officers had based their report on the findings of Kenneth Rendell and his team, focusing specifically on the discrepancy between the handwriting in the Diary and Maybrick's will; on the two phrases believed to be post-Victorian ('one-off' and 'top myself') and on the fact that large sections of the Diary appear to have been written in one go. 'The Diary appears to have been cobbled together from three other books on the Ripper,' a police spokesman was quoted as saying. 'The only mystery is who wrote the thing.' Sadly, the report gave no indication of any desire to solve the mystery. It was a disappointing conclusion, both for those who believed in the Diary and for the sceptics. Rather than revealing new information on potential forgers, the detectives, it seemed, had simply reproduced existing arguments against the Diary's authenticity. The Diary was further tarnished, but still no forger had been named. But would there be enough evidence for a conviction?

In all the commotion about the Diary, Shirley Harrison had not forgotten the watch. At the outset the watch had seemed a potential embarrassment, now it was beginning to look like a major plank in the campaign to reinstate the Diary as a genuine document. Having already featured a positive report on the watch by Dr Turgoose, Harrison suggested that Albert Johnson submit it for another inspection. This time the examination, at a cost of £587.50, paid for by Johnson, would be carried out by metallurgist Dr Robert Wild of the Interface Analysis Centre at Bristol University. Under an electron microscope, using a technique of scanning auger microscopy combined with argon ion depth profiling, his conclusions, produced on 31 January 1994, were very welcome for the Diary team after the events of the previous few months. The report read:

The particles embedded in the base of the engraving are brass from the engraving tool (ref Turgoose, 1993). The particle investigated is very heavily contaminated and appears to have been considerably corroded. In this investigation the etching process, which was continued for some 45 minutes, only began to reveal zinc oxide. This suggests that the particle has been embedded in the surface for some considerable time.

The changes observed here would then indicate that the engravings were of some considerable age. Provided the watch has remained in a normal environment, it would seem likely that the engravings were at least of several tens of years age. This would agree with the findings of Dr Turgoose (1993) and in my opinion it is unlikely that anyone would have sufficient expertise to implant aged, brass particles into the base of the engravings.

Privately, according to Robert Smith, Dr Wild was even more encouraging, telling him that it was possible that the scratches could date to 1888 or 1889. There was a very important proviso, however, with Dr Wild stressing the need for much more lengthy work to pinpoint the precise age of the scratches. It was a familiar story.

On 15 November 1993, less than six weeks after the publication of Shirley Harrison's book, Paul Feldman's video about the Diary, subtitled 'Beyond Reasonable Doubt?', was released. Written by Martin Howells and directed by him and Chris Short, it was presented by the flamboyant film director Michael Winner. Culled from many hours of interviews with key personnel involved in the Diary story and that of the watch, it ran for a brisk sixty-five minutes. As might be expected, the video painted a persuasive case for the likelihood of Maybrick being the Ripper; while critics might accuse it of selectivity, it provided a compelling and dramatic, if somewhat confusing, story.

Several Ripperologists, including Martin Fido, Paul Begg, Donald Rumbelow, Colin Wilson and Melvyn Fairclough, were filmed discussing the pros and cons of the Diary and its provenance, which Fido, for one, found impossible to believe. A weary, rather haunted-looking Michael Barrett again defended his story to camera. Despite the onslaught of doubt he knew would prevail for years to come, Barrett repeated his mantra. 'I will never change my story,' he said, 'because when you're telling the truth, you're telling the truth.'

There were interesting cameo appearances too. Forensic psychiatrist David Forshaw, then a specialist consultant in addiction at the Maudsley psychiatric hospital in south London, saw the journal as Maybrick's means of coping with his world and with his feelings. He had an explanation for the missing pages too, suggesting that it might have been a normal journal which Maybrick had used to record happier times with his wife and family. As his attitude towards his wife changed so violently, Forshaw reasoned, the earlier jottings clashed so much with his mood that he removed them.

Anna Koren also had an answer for another aspect of the Diary which caused strong problems for believers, namely the clear link with the 'Dear Boss' letter. The handwriting in this letter, which many Ripperologists anyway believed was a fake, was starkly different from that in the Diary. Anna Koren had an explanation. Clearly, she said, the writing was a copy of an original, a copy in which the writer had, for obvious reasons, disguised his handwriting.

There was another significant contribution too, that didn't cast such a positive light on Michael Barrett's story. In September 1993, while conducting a number of interviews in Liverpool for the video, writer Martin Howells had also spoken to the three daughters of Tony Devereux. This interview was not included in the video, much to the chagrin of the sisters (though it would be shown in the version that was screened on television in February 1996). The three sisters, Nancy, Janet and Caroline, had been anxious about the Diary project from the first and had written to Shirley Harrison in dismay when they first learnt of the connection between James Maybrick and Jack the Ripper. They were adamant that their father could not have been involved in the manner that Barrett suggested. Indeed, they claimed, Barrett was not even a particularly close friend of their father's, who, they insisted, had family and plenty of other friends to look after him when he became housebound.

Nor did they accept Michael Barrett's account that he was a regular visitor to their father's house, though they acknowledged that he did run occasional errands for him, such as placing bets. According to their account, Barrett had told them that their father had given him the parcel for being so good to him while he was housebound. Why would he give it to a 'relative stranger', they asked, when there were family and closer friends looking after him? Had he not wanted to give it to his daughters because of the subject matter, they speculated, then it was far more likely that he would have given it to one of his brothers rather than Barrett. But such a possibility was remote anyway, they claimed. It was 'extremely unlikely' that their father would not have mentioned something as significant as the Diary to them. 'He told you everything that had happened to him since the last time you'd been, 'cos he loved to talk because he was living on his own, lack of company.'

And what of the rumours, already beginning to circulate, that Tony Devereux was part of a conspiracy to forge the Diary, perhaps even the forger himself. This, the sisters said, was impossible. 'No, no, no, he wasn't capable, he wasn't a great writer, he wasn't a great reader . . . he used to block print everything, he wasn't a great handwriter, you can see in his will – it's in block print. . . . I don't think he was capable of doing something like that. I mean he wasn't a stupid man but he didn't have the intelligence, the capability to do something like that.' But, Howells persisted, he worked as a printer at the *Liverpool Post*, could there not have been a connection, perhaps with a journalist there? 'No . . . I mean when we say he was a printer, he wasn't . . . it was the big sheets of metal he used to handle, I don't know exactly what a printer does but he wasn't a printer in the sense of the word.' (In fact, Devereux was a compositor, who had the job of typesetting the pages.)

What, asked Howells, of the possibility that their father was involved with somebody at the Saddle pub, where Devereux and Barrett used to drink? That the Diary had been stolen from Battlecrease by an electrician (a possibility that Paul Feldman would later investigate) who also drank at the Saddle and who handed it over to Tony Devereux? Again, came the reply from the Devereux sisters, their father told them everything, and he would hardly leave out such a significant event. 'If something like that happened at the Saddle, which would be an unusual occurrence, he would have told us.'

Could Devereux have had the Diary in his possession for a period of time without the sisters knowing? 'Well, if me dad had it the chance of him having it hidden in the house for years are so slim, you know, without any of us knowing . . . there were no secrets in the house. His army documents, things like that, he kept, we all knew where they were, insurance documents and things like that. Once he died, we just knew straight away they were kept in a box in the wardrobe. He was not secretive.'

There was something else. They recalled seeing a copy of Richard Whittington-Egan's *Murder, Mayhem and Mystery* sometime in 1991 at their father's house and asking to borrow it. 'Only if you bring it back', they remember their father replying, as the book belonged to Michael Barrett. This was the book that Barrett said had steered him towards identifying the writer of the Diary as James Maybrick, yet he had claimed that he did not come across it until well after he began his research on the Diary, which he said he embarked on at least two months after being given the Diary in late May or June 1991. Devereux had died that August. Barrett had last seen him in late July. It didn't add up.

The sisters' verdict on Barrett, at least at this point, was damning. Howells asked if they thought their father was being used as a patsy by Barrett. 'Oh definitely, definitely. He's making money out of a dead man's name as far as I'm concerned. I'm not saying that he's the only one involved because I think there's other people involved as well, but I don't know who they'd be. Possibly they knew me dad as well.'

On 21 September 1993, a few weeks before the video was launched, the sisters had also touched on their anger towards Barrett in a letter to Shirley Harrison. They were furious that, because of local gossip about the Diary, a prospective buyer of their father's house had dropped out of the sale, thinking Devereux must have been a 'psycho' who had kept the Diary hidden for years, along with goodness knows what other horrific secrets. 'She told us she had heard about Mike bragging in a local pub that he had got the diary off Tony Devereux and [was] making a fortune out of them.' They wanted their father to be remembered by his friends and the local community as 'the decent, respectable man he was, not the strange man who gave away Jack the Ripper's diary'.

The video revived interest in the Diary, but the impact of this too, like Shirley Harrison's book, was greatly reduced by the prevailing sense of scepticism that had surrounded the Diary since Rendell and the *Sunday Times* had denounced it as a fake back in September. The Diary would sell more than respectably (by January 1994 the hardback edition had sold more than 50,000 copies worldwide), but far less than would have been expected had its claim to authenticity not been contested. The video (which would be first screened on national television on 20 February 1996) would sell around 20,000 copies. It was a sizeable figure, but again compared to what might have been it was trifling.

On 26 November 1993 came the next development in the Scotland Yard investigation. Under the heading 'Ripper Diaries are a Fake', journalist Stephen Grey announced in the *Daily Express* that the detectives would soon report to the Crown Prosecution Service that the Diary was 'almost certainly bogus. The Yard view emerged after detectives interviewed top forensic and Ripper experts – including Kenneth Rendell, the man who exposed the Hitler Diaries as a fake.' In fact, the paper reported, the detectives believed the Diary was penned in Liverpool in the last decade, though the identity of the forger was still not revealed. Interestingly, the paper estimated that world rights for the Diary could have been worth more than £4 million were it not for the press investigations.

Hot on the heels of Grey's revelations, Paul Feldman and Robert Smith were equally damning in their assessment of the Scotland Yard report. The detectives, they told the *Liverpool Post* on 27 November 1993, had not seen the original Diary and had based their conclusions on the Rendell report. Feldman claimed to have ten facts that disproved Rendell's findings. Robert Smith had gained the impression from talking to the police that they had 'no new evidence to suggest the diary is a fake'. As for Michael Barrett, he had no doubts. 'To suggest that the diary was forged is clear nonsense,' he said. 'No one has been able to show it is a forgery.'

Whether he was telling the truth or not, Michael Barrett had stuck to his story through thick and thin. But the pressure was clearly telling. Indeed, according to the account Barrett gave Shirley

Harrison for her book, the problems had started from the moment the Diary arrived in his house. 'I haven't had a proper night's sleep from that day to this. I've eaten and drunk the Diary. It virtually destroyed my life and my marriage, though thank goodness, Anne has the patience of a saint and she has seen me through it.'

It was becoming abundantly clear to Shirley Harrison's and Paul Feldman's teams that Barrett was not handling the situation well. He was likeable and engaging when sober, but another side would emerge when he was drinking, a circumstance that was occurring with increasing frequency. But it was behind the scenes that the real damage was being done. By the turn of the year it had all become too much for Anne. Having struggled with what she claimed had been a failing marriage for some years, it seemed that the furore around the Diary had propelled Barrett's behaviour beyond a level she could tolerate. On 2 January 1994 Anne left him, taking Caroline with her. The marriage was over. It was a personal tragedy but one with wider implications too. The consequences for those involved with the Diary would be immense.

A week after leaving Barrett, Anne and Caroline moved into a flat in the Sefton Park area of Liverpool. As Shirley Harrison recalls, Barrett's already fragile state of mind now seemed to deteriorate rapidly. 'Michael responded by telephoning all of us, at any time of the day or night, sometimes using up an entire tape on the answerphone. Those calls were heartbreaking. He repeatedly said he was dying and wouldn't last the night. He was lonely, hurt and desperate to see his daughter. We all felt anguish for him. But it was clear that when he drank he lost his grasp on reality.' Barrett's behaviour was becoming more and more unpredictable.

Writing some eighteen months later, Anne described the circumstances that brought her to her decision:

When I eventually left my husband in the January of 1994, after eighteen years of marriage, I told Michael within weeks that I had every intention of applying for a divorce. I also told my friends and family and anyone who was prepared to listen. This had nothing to do with the Diary but was due to the fact that for the last few years of our married life I had endured both physical and mental abuse, due for the most part to my husband's alcoholism.

Within the last year, the physical abuse had increased to the extent that on the 2nd of January 1994, after an argument which rendered me unconscious, I left the marital home with my daughter and never returned. Unfortunately, Michael refused to accept that I had no intention of returning and after my daughter and I moved into a flat he would not leave us alone. We were continually harassed by him both by day and night.

Every day I either received a letter or visit, sometimes he came five or six times in 24 hours, anytime of the day or night. One morning I received eight telemessages, one of which announced that he had died in the night. My friends, family, the school, and the family of my daughter's friends were constantly being telephoned by him demanding my telephone number. The wife of Caroline's music teacher was actually on the verge of a nervous break-down due to his continuing harassment.

On 15 January 1994 came some relief for the Diary team when the *Liverpool Daily Post* announced that the Crown Prosecution Service would be taking no further action against Robert Smith. 'We have now decided against a prosecution,' a spokesperson told the paper, 'because there is not enough evidence to have a realistic prospect of getting a conviction.' Robert Smith saw this as vindication of the Diary: 'The Yard went to Liverpool and made a very thorough investigation into the origins of the Diary. I am not surprised they found no evidence to suggest the Diary is anything other than genuine.' Others felt, and would maintain, that proving the identity of the forgers was not an important consideration; the onus lay on the Diary team to prove authenticity, not on sceptics to prove who the forgers were.

It was unquestionably, though, a missed opportunity to bury the Diary once and for all, if modern fake it was. Given that the detectives clearly had strong suspicions of at least one culprit, could it have been that difficult to prove his guilt? Who was the forger they hinted at? Later in the year, on 16 July, Shirley Harrison wrote to the officer in charge of the case, Detective Sergeant Thomas, in regard to a letter which Michael Barrett had received from Nick Warren. In the letter Warren had written:

I understand that you were investigated by SOI at New Scotland Yard. I further understand that they concluded: 1/ The Diary was a forgery dating from post 1987 and run up in Liverpool. 2/ That they knew who precisely forged the Diary since he had lied to them. 3/ That the liar was unable to produce his own copy of a book (which he denied lending to a third party). Scotland Yard had already obtained such a copy from the party concerned so that they were able to deduce he was a liar.

Presuming the book was *Murder, Mayhem and Mystery*, Shirley Harrison wanted DS Thomas to let her know if the book had any distinguishing marks as she believed it may not have belonged to Michael Barrett.

Allegations of forgery had been levelled at the watch too, but this did not prevent interest in it from all over the world. Early in January 1994 Albert Johnson's solicitor Richard Nicholas had received a letter from Robert E. Davis, in Waco, Texas, who was hoping to add the watch to a collection of historical artefacts that included guns used by Bonnie and Clyde and Billy the Kid. Despite a considerable offer, the Johnson brothers, it seemed, were not tempted, at least not yet, as a letter written by Davis to Nicholas on 20 January 1994 reveals: 'I would be very interested in working out some arrangement to purchase the watch for my collection but after our conversation it was apparent that your clients place a much greater value on the watch than I feel it is worth.'

For an artefact that Davis pointed out had not been proved beyond question, the (unquoted) figure the Johnsons had in mind was clearly well beyond his own estimation. However, his interest remained: 'If, at some time in the future, they decide to place a positive price on the watch . . . somewhere in the range of $30 to $40 thousand dollars . . . please have them contact me.' It was a long way from the £225 Albert had splashed out to buy the watch in the first place, particularly when its authenticity had been so widely dismissed. Were the Johnsons so confident that the watch would eventually be proved authentic and leapfrog in value or were they just taking a calculated risk that they would get a better price before it was exposed as a fake?

Even the slightest possibility of losing the watch to Texas was troubling Robert Smith. Smith, who had tried unsuccessfully to buy a quarter share of the watch back in July 1993, wrote to Doreen Montgomery on 20 January 1994, suggesting that a consortium consisting of Smith Gryphon, Shirley Harrison and the Johnsons should agree to keep the watch unsold until all agreed it should be. 'Pecuniary benefit doesn't come into it. Far from it. It may cost a lot to keep the watch accessible. I believe the watch is very important to "our mutual property", and we should think of ways to encourage the Johnsons not to sell it at too early a stage.' Having explained this idea to the Johnsons themselves, he believed they were very sympathetic to the idea and suggested a round-table discussion on the future of the watch as soon as possible. 'The watch', Smith concluded, 'is vital in establishing the authenticity of the Diary.'

Both Diary teams were now preparing books. Shirley Harrison and her team were updating their research for the paperback version, due out in October. Paul Feldman and his team, now the video was released, had their own plans for a book and, indeed, a second video. Like a gathering storm, the two teams of researchers descended on Liverpool, seeking to prise out any hitherto undiscovered morsels about James and Florence Maybrick and anyone else mentioned in the Diary. In the case of Paul Feldman, his curiosity would not end with the cast list of the Diary. Over the next few months Michael and Anne Barrett, the Johnsons and many others connected with them would find their lives, past and present, subjected to the most extraordinary inquisition. It was hard to imagine anything escaping Feldman's trawl. He revealed to Shirley Harrison, for instance, that he had obtained print-outs of the Barrett's telephone calls for 1993 and noticed a large number of calls to Billy Graham, mostly at a time when Anne would have been at work.

Commissioning tests on the Diary had been a major problem for Shirley Harrison. Once Robert Smith had reduced the advance for the book from £50,000 to £15,000 (which had to be shared between Shirley Harrison and Michael Barrett) as a result of Dr Baxendale's negative report, she had been left with perilously little money with which to try to establish the document's authenticity. Consequently, a number of experts had been invited to indulge their curiosity in the document for fees that were considerably less than normal. Should the book prove highly successful, their generosity would not be forgotten. Unfortunately, estimates of the book's success and how great that generosity should be varied sharply.

The first hint of trouble had arrived back in November 1993, when Harrison contested an invoice from handwriting expert Lawrence Warner for £500 for a trip to London. This was, she told him, 'out of all proportion with the rest of the team who in various ways have from fascination with the diary donated a phenomenal amount of time to helping us'. Warner's invoice would indeed be out of all proportion with two other members of the team, but not in the way Harrison meant.

On 23 February 1994 Harrison received a letter from Sue Iremonger, who told her she was delighted at the success of the Diary and was pleased to hear it was selling just as well in the US. She was enclosing invoices from herself and Nicholas Eastaugh, further to their interim invoices. Harrison was shocked. Iremonger, who had already been paid £500, was now claiming a sum of £11,062 including VAT. Eastaugh, who had received £2,000, was claiming a further £17,103.30 including VAT. A fortnight later Iremonger wrote to Sally Evemy to explain the situation. While there was no contract in place for fees to be charged, both she and Eastaugh had been led to understand that they would be paid upon conclusion of the project. Her interim invoice, she believed, pointed out the approximate number of hours spent on this case and intimated the level of remuneration expected. Having spent so much time on the Diary both experts had forfeited a great deal of paying business and the fees they were submitting now took this into account. 'Nick and I,' she wrote, 'feel that it is not unreasonable to expect payment as Robert and Shirley are continuing to benefit from the work we have put into this case.'

Shirley Harrison was having none of it. Though the two experts had written jointly, she replied individually as there were 'separate issues' involved. 'Your swingeing invoices,' she wrote to Eastaugh, 'amount to considerably more than I have earned for three years' work. The sums mentioned are out of all proportion to money expected or received by anyone involved in the project.' There was an added sting in the tail. Harrison had been personally hurt, she told Eastaugh, as she had been fighting his corner since his 'unguarded statement to the *Washington Post*' contributed to Warner's ultimate withdrawal from the project, which in turn led on to the alarm expressed by publishers of her book worldwide. To Iremonger, she wrote of the complete misinterpretation of what she had believed to be the friendly, informal spirit in which they had agreed to work. 'I suspect,' she wrote, 'that you now have the mistaken impression that megabucks are pouring in.' She had written to Eastaugh at the outset that she would not forget her friends. She would not: 'I am proposing shortly to send a "thank you" cheque to you and some of the others who have shared a project which took us all by surprise and to whom we are so grateful.'

Dr Eastaugh was not happy. Shirley Harrison had not appreciated his considerable contribution to the success of her book, nor the extra stress and unsociable hours the work demanded. Lest she forget, he outlined a number of key benefits she had received from him. He had delayed invoicing, knowing that money was not going to flow until the book was on sale. He had established early on that he could not work on the project 'gratis' to any substantial degree, yet Harrison, Doreen Montgomery and Robert Smith had always been prepared to 'quite freely ask of my time'. Most of all, it was his contributions to the 'scientific side' that added immeasurably to the credibility of their claims for the authenticity of the Diary. As a result of the lack of positive appreciation for his work, Eastaugh was now 'therefore going to withdraw my permission to use any of my material . . .'.

Dismayed that the two experts were taking 'advantage of a wrongly imagined commercial bonanza', Harrison wrote back that there could be no question of a compromise on additional invoices of £28,000 following payment of earlier invoices of £2,500. Though letters would follow from Sue Iremonger's lawyers, the claims would not be pursued further.

In March 1994 Shirley Harrison and Sally Evemy journeyed to Liverpool in pursuit of information. Perhaps most significantly, they spoke to one of the electricians who had worked in Battlecrease House during the renovation work. Vinny Dring had a clear recollection of finding two books in what had been James Maybrick's dressing room, both about 10 by 8 inches with stiff ribboned spines, which he threw into a skip. Unfortunately, Harrison, who felt that Dring's account was honest, found that the skip owners had not kept records. There could be no proof of Dring's story but Harrison believed it at least offered one plausible explanation for why the Diary had emerged when it did.

Meanwhile, Paul Feldman and his team, now comprising Melvyn Fairclough, working full-time on the project in London, and Carol Emmas in Liverpool, were feverishly tearing into the records of virtually everyone connected with the Diary, from James and Florence Maybrick to Michael Barrett and Tony Devereux. To make matters worse, owing largely to legal reasons communication between the two teams was now virtually nil. Often, Harrison claimed, she would arrive for an interview, only to find Feldman's team had already been there.

Feldman was developing a number of theories to explain the Diary's journey from Battlecrease House to Michael Barrett. Briefly Feldman countenanced the possibility that the Diary had indeed been found during renovations at Battlecrease House. In his book *The Final Chapter*, published in 1997, Feldman describes receiving an astonishing call from an employee of the electrical contractors involved, who told him that two colleagues had mentioned something to do with Battlecrease House and taking the Diary, wrapped in brown paper, to Liverpool University to have it authenticated. Liverpool University, Feldman says, confirmed the visit of the two men but could add no further detail. Feldman's contact promised to verify his account on camera. On 8 March 1994 Feldman wrote to electrician Jed Owens, claiming he had evidence that Owens was directly linked to the discovery of the Diary: 'If our lines of enquiry become known to the Press, it is likely to result in a continual line of questioning to you direct from many sources, increasing the possibility of Scotland Yard reopening their investigation. You will have nothing to lose by discussing the information we have.' Speaking to the authors of this book in November 2002, Feldman says it became clear within a matter of days that this potential theory for the Diary's provenance was going nowhere.

So the Battlecrease House theory of the Diary's provenance was discarded. But Feldman's growing conviction that Barrett was lying about where he obtained the Diary would create increasing havoc on the lives of the Barretts and many connected with them. Somebody, possibly everybody, connected with the Diary and even with the watch, Feldman decided, must be withholding information. Even Billy Graham, Anne's elderly and now ailing father, was brought into the picture, with Feldman suspecting that he might be descended from James Maybrick and was possibly connected to a recently discovered group of Maybrick descendants in Peterborough.

Now out of contact with both Diary teams, and trying to restart her life as a single mother, Anne Barrett, in January 1994, made her first visit to a solicitor to get advice about divorcing her husband. Largely for financial reasons she decided to go for the two-year separation period. Within the next three months, however, events outside her control would make her reconsider her options. Thus far, she had remained an off-stage character in the Diary story. This too would change as the year unwound. Unknown to her, one cause of the new pressures that lay ahead came with the latest development on the film front. All had gone quiet on Paul Feldman's deal with MGM and he realised their interest was on the wane. Now he turned to New Line Cinema. MGM had wanted to be sure the Diary was genuine but New Line had a different demand.

Feldman was developing his latest theory that Billy Graham might be descended from an illegitimate line of James Maybrick's. 'Might be' was not a term that fitted naturally into the Feldman lexicon. Pretty soon it became 'was'. Unfortunately for Feldman, this new certainty appears to have been conveyed to New Line, to whom he had claimed that Anne Barrett was the sole surviving heir of James Maybrick, the author of the Diary. Now the company wanted a signed release and consent form from her. Their satisfaction on Anne Barrett's status as sole heir would remain a condition of the agreement. Furthermore the Barretts were requested to supply a warranty that, to the best of their knowledge, the Diary was authentic. On 26 April 1994 Feldman received a 'Grants of Rights and Assignment' letter for Anne to sign. Unknown to New Line, signing at this stage presented two problems. First, Feldman had no proof for his claim that Anne was the sole surviving heir. Secondly, he had no idea where she was.

If things were looking bad for Anne, for her husband they were hitting rock bottom. His current depressed state of mind and his growing sense of isolation and confusion, not to mention his hostility towards Paul Feldman, can be gauged in a taped interview he conducted with Keith Skinner on 14 April 1994 in Liverpool Central Library. Skinner by this date was working part-time for Feldman on a consultative basis. It is clear from the conversation that Barrett, who is sober throughout the interview, is highly resistant to Feldman's line of inquiry and the way he is going about it. After initially refusing to tell Skinner the date of Anne's birthday (Feldman wrongly believed it to be 21 October, the same day that Florence Maybrick died), Barrett gives him both Anne's real birthday, 23 October and Caroline's, the previous day. 'Why,' he demands angrily, 'is Anne brought into this? I sincerely object to Anne being brought in. My marriage is on the rocks because of this book so I sincerely object to her being brought into this.'

After Keith Skinner confesses his own doubts as to the wisdom of the line of investigation Paul Feldman is following, and describes the confusion and damage it is causing, Barrett reveals his own theory for Feldman's insistence that he is lying. Convinced that Feldman's doubts about his story are connected to the 'multi-million dollar' film deal he is trying to sign, and to Feldman's need to have a good provenance in order to complete the deal, he advises Feldman to listen to the Diary. 'There's a very apt line in the Diary and I know the Diary inside out and back to front. "Chickens running around with their heads cut off." That's exactly what you've [Feldman] been doing, running around with your head cut off because you can't see the truth plain in front of you, because the truth is very simple – Tony Devereux gave me the Diary.'

Skinner also asks about Barrett's word processor. Barrett tells him that the Diary notes were scribbled in his own (very bad) handwriting 'all over the place'. He claims to have bought the word processor second-hand to input the notes, Anne showing him how to use the keyboard and correcting his spelling. He didn't, he says, keep the hand written notes. He also claims that he used the word processor to type the transcript of the Diary which was kept on disc. He also makes clear that his first knowledge of the book *Murder, Mayhem and Mystery* was after he claims to have been given the Diary by Devereux, which he now dates to late May 1991, having bought it in the history section of WH Smith's.

Barrett also claims that he would have spoken about the Diary to a number of people at the British Legion club he frequented, even before Tony Devereux died, though he is sure Devereux himself did not tell anyone. He would have told some friends that his mate Tony had given it to him. 'Everyone,' he concludes, 'knew I had something.'

Skinner, observing at close quarters the turmoil created by Paul Feldman's increasingly frenzied search for the truth, noted the effect of all of this on the man at the centre of the maelstrom. 'Considerable pressure', he says, 'was put on anyone in Liverpool, by Paul Feldman, who might be able to answer questions about the Graham family background. Mike Barrett resolutely stuck to his story that Tony Devereux had given him the journal, but became increasingly more and more bewildered, angry and frustrated by Paul Feldman's insistence that he was lying and concealing knowledge of the true provenance. Barrett's world, emotionally and financially, slowly collapsed around him and he sunk deeper into alcoholic confusion.'

As Feldman's pursuit continued, Barrett alternated between blunt confusion and, as if turning the tables, offering a series of clues himself, for instance ringing Feldman out of the blue and offering the information that Anne was a Maybrick. It became a game, albeit a one-sided one, as Barrett's drinking became more and more desperate. According to Skinner, who describes the period January to July 1994 as 'a time of total madness', 'Barrett's life was falling apart and he was trying to find out what Feldy [Feldman] thought he knew by playing a cat and mouse game with Feldy and pretending he not only knew what Feldy knew about the origins of the Diary, but that he knew more than Feldy knew about the origins of the Diary – and this just confirmed to Feldy that all his hunches and beliefs were correct.'

If Feldman, or Shirley Harrison for that matter, were able to prove the Diary was genuine, it would not just be the value of the book and the film rights that would be affected. If that really was the signature of Jack the Ripper at the close of the journal, its value would potentially rocket. But who exactly did own the Diary? On 23 March 1993 Michael and Anne Barrett had sold ownership of the Diary to the publishers, Smith Gryphon Ltd, for a nominal fee of £1. On 23 May 1994 the same parties agreed to a transference of ownership, again for £1, from Smith Gryphon Ltd to Keychoice Ltd (the Barretts had signed to confirm their agreement to this on 21 April). Both companies were wholly owned by Robert Smith. The final transfer of ownership would take place on 8 December 1999, when Smith transferred ownership from Keychoice to himself personally and wound up the company. His reasoning for this, he told the authors of this book in January 2003, was that this would dispense with the costly annual auditing of Keychoice; as he solely owned the company anyway, he considered it purely a technical change of ownership. The objective of setting up Keychoice, according to Smith, was to ring-fence the Diary's ownership should Smith Gryphon cease to exist. (In 1997 the publisher did, indeed, go into administrative receivership, Smith says, and without the transference to Keychoice the receivers would have been obliged to sell the Diary to the highest bidder.)

Ownership of the watch, however, appeared to be a more fluid matter. Texan collector Robert E. Davis, already rebuffed once, was still interested in adding the watch to his growing collection of historic artefacts (which now included a watercolour by Adolf Hitler). After reading Harrison's book he wrote to her on 21 April 1994, saying that he was 'convinced beyond any doubt' that the case was solved. As the value of the watch was predicated on whether James Maybrick was Jack the Ripper, Davis wanted Harrison's opinions concerning its authenticity. With so much money involved, Davis, still in contact with Albert Johnson, was moving slowly.

For Michael Barrett, whose world was disintegrating around him, there could be little escape from the Diary. Not only was he still being hounded by Paul Feldman but he was the subject of other investigations too. Nick Warren, editor of *Ripperana*, was deeply unconvinced by the Tony Devereux provenance and had interviewed the three Devereux sisters for their views. Now he wanted Barrett's response. Initially, Barrett, who Warren now believed had begun to look like James Maybrick, had refused. However, on 6 May 1994 he was able to furnish some answers, via Doreen Montgomery, which she believed had been typed by his sister at his dictation. In answer to the vital questions concerning the *Murder, Mayhem and Mystery* book, he claimed not to know where the Devereux sisters came up with the idea that he had lent it to Tony Devereux, though he did admit to understanding why they were upset about the Diary. 'I would also like to point out a sworn affadavit [*sic*] has been made in connection with the Diary. This has been lodged with my solicitor for quite a considerable time. The contents . . . are obviously confidential . . .'

Two days later Warren sent Montgomery a copy of the draft article he proposed publishing. 'Don't worry,' he wrote in a covering letter, 'we shall not ask what Scotland Yard discovered on your client's W.P. (since we already know).' Montgomery responded quickly. 'Of course we know what the SFS [Serious Fraud Squad] found – a transcript of the Diary! There's nothing sinister in that.

Right from the word go, everyone knew that Mike had bought a WP precisely to transcribe the Diary, in order to study its contents more easily.' The flurry of letters between Warren and Montgomery concluded some weeks later, after Warren accused Montgomery of having an insulting attitude to the bereaved family of Tony Devereux. He would not be communicating further with her on this matter, but she should be assured 'that you will find I am not a good man to cross'.

Warren had also sent the forthcoming article to Michael Barrett. It was not well received. The article, entitled 'The Diary of Jack the Ripper – A question of Provenance' – (By the Editor, in cooperation with the family of the late Mr Tony Devereux), appeared in the July 1994 issue of *Ripperana* and repeated a number of the points made to Martin Howells in the interview that failed to make the final cut of Paul Feldman's video, but there were some additional pieces of information. Describing their father as a compositor on the *Liverpool Echo*, Anne (Nancy) Steele maintained his spelling would have been too good for him to have forged the 'semi-literate' Diary and that he thought of Barrett as a journalist who had contributed features to a magazine, so the sisters were consequently surprised to see him described as an ordinary 'Liverpool bloke'. The article confirmed, for the first time, that the copy of *Murder, Mayhem and Mystery*, which the Devereux sisters had said was borrowed from their father, but which they believed belonged to Michael Barrett, had been taken by the two Scotland Yard detectives.

The article also revealed that Gerard Kane, who was suspected by some to have penned the Diary, owing to a perceived similarity between his signature and the handwriting in the Diary, had been interviewed by Scotland Yard and duly eliminated from the investigation.

Describing Michael Barrett as 'almost unspeakably sad', the article suggested he had never intended to make substantial royalties from 'this project', but only really wanted enough for a small greenhouse. The article concludes with a question: 'Mr Barrett has written of a secret affidavit, which he has lodged with his solicitor. What does it say?'

The Diary of Jack the Ripper, purported to have been written by James Maybrick. (*Robert Smith*)

Battlecrease House, where James and Florence Maybrick lived during the period of the Ripper murders and where James's death led to his wife's trial and conviction for his murder. (*Evans/Skinner Crime Archive*)

Michael Barrett, pictured nursing an injured hand, during an interview with Shirley Harrison and Keith Skinner on 18 January 1995. (*Evans/Skinner Crime Archive*)

Paul Feldman (right) and Ripper author and editor of *Ripperologist* Paul Begg (centre) inspect the grave of James Maybrick in February 1993, accompanied by Michael Barrett. (*Paul Feldman*)

Anne Graham outside the Public Record Office in Kew, London, in April 1995. (*Evans/Skinner Crime Archive*)

Anne Graham (far left), pictured with fellow nurses at Canberra Hospital in 1972, during her five-year stay in Australia. (*Anne Graham*)

Here, in the middle bedroom at 12 Goldie Street, in the alcove between the chimney breast and the window, Anne Graham claimed to have hidden the Diary behind a sideboard. (*Evans/Skinner Crime Archive*)

12 Goldie Street, the Barretts' home, pictured in 1993, the year in which the Diary was published. (*Robert Smith*)

Billy Graham, Anne's father, who claimed to have first seen the Diary in 1943, pictured at his then home in Dorrington Street, Liverpool, at Christmas, 1973. (*Anne Graham*)

Outhwaite & Litherland, the Liverpool auctioneers where, in his affidavit of 5 January 1995, Michael Barrett claimed to have bought the Victorian scrapbook in which the Diary is written. (*Evans/Skinner Crime Archive*)

The Bluecoat Art Shop in central Liverpool, where Michael Barrett claimed to have bought the ink used to forge the Diary, pictured in 1994. (*Evans/Skinner Crime Archive*)

Shirley Harrison, author of The Diary of Jack the Ripper, at the entrance to the Saddle Inn, where Michael Barrett and Tony Devereux used to drink. (*Evans/Skinner Crime Archive*)

Rigby's pub in Dale Street, Liverpool, across the road from Barrett's solicitors, Morecrofts. Here, on 24 March 1993, Michael Barrett and Anne Graham signed over ownership of the Diary to publisher Robert Smith for £1. (*Evans/Skinner Crime Archive*)

Smith Gryphon's original publicity for the launch of Shirley Harrison's book on the Diary. As a result of media criticism, the subtitle, *The Discovery, The Investigation, The Authentication*, would be covered with a sticker that read: *Is It Genuine? Read the evidence, then judge for yourself.* (*Evans/Skinner Crime Archive*)

Fleet Street quickly picks up the Liverpool Post's breaking of the Maybrick/Ripper connection. This is from the *Evening Standard* of the same day, 22 April 1993. (*Evening Standard*)

Is this the face of Jack the Ripper?

by Colin Adamson

Florence Maybrick: Murdered her husband, now thought to have been the Ripper

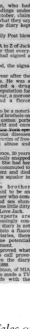

James Maybrick: Accused of the murders

THE final piece of a jigsaw which has baffled criminologists for 105 years was slotted into place today when Victorian cotton broker James Maybrick was named as Jack the Ripper.

Maybrick, a bizarre character who took arsenic to boost his sex life and was later murdered by his wife with a dose of the same poison, is accused of the notorious Whitechapel murders in a forthcoming book.

Publishers Smyth Gryphon, who had hoped to keep their new findings under wraps until publication in October, claim their case is solidly based on what they say is a fully authenticated 62-page diary kept by the Liverpool businessman.

But today, the Liverpool Daily Post blew the closely-guarded secret.

Paul Begg, co-author of The A to Z of Jack the Ripper, told the newspaper that everyone who had seen the diary had signed a confidentiality agreement.

He says: "The diary is signed, the signature is Jack the Ripper."

Maybrick died in 1889, the year after the Ripper killings. He was a womaniser and a drug addict with a reputation for violent behaviour, a morose disposition and a fierce temper.

He was said to be a notorious frequenter of brothels on his travels to cotton ports around the world and once admitted to a New York specialist in nervous diseases that he was a "victim of freeliving, alcohol abuse and other excesses".

His wife Florence, 20 years his younger, finally snapped and killed him. She had her death sentence commuted to life imprisonment and died penniless and in squalor in America in 1941.

Maybrick's brother Michael was said to be an amateur composer who composed songs and sea shanties, including one little ditty called They All Love Jack.

Although experts are becoming increasingly convinced that the diary is not going to turn into a fiasco like Hitler's Diaries, there was always one potential hole in the argument.

No one had proved what antique dealers call provenance — where the diary had been since 1888.

But Paul Feldman, of MIA Production, who made a TV film to coincide with the book, revealed in Monday's Evening Standard that he had final proof.

"It was hidden in the man's home and came to light when something was touched that had not been touched for 105 years," he said.

If the new book does, in fact, point the finger directly at Maybrick, it will be the first time he has been linked with the Ripper murders.

So far, the vast army of Ripperologists has thrown up no fewer than 72 suspects, from Lord Randolph Churchill and the Duke of Clarence to Queen Victoria's doctor, Sir William Gull.

The diary is said to have been written by "a husband and father from north of Watford."

Among the more comprehensible passages is: "I will take the first whore I encounter and show what hell is really like.

"All the bitches will pay for the pain. Before I am finished, all England will know the name I have given myself."

Did *Tales of Liverpool – Murder, Mayhem and Mystery* alert Michael Barrett to the Maybrick connection in the Diary or did it provide material for a forgery? (*Evans/Skinner Crime Archive*)

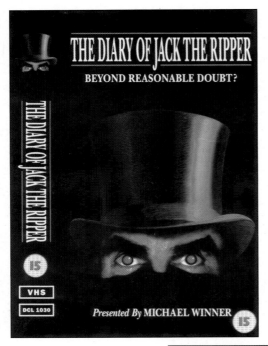

Beyond Reasonable Doubt?, Paul Feldman's video about the Diary. (*Evans/Skinner Crime Archive*)

The original artwork for *Exorcist* director William Friedkin's proposed film on The Diary of Jack the Ripper. (*Evans/Skinner Crime Archive*)

Michael Barrett's reply to the draft copy Warren had sent him was dated 13 May 1994 and appeared underneath the article. His state of mind is not difficult to fathom. The text is reproduced as it was printed in the issue:

What you have written is defamatory. It is now 17 minuts [*sic*] past 7 Friday morning. At 9 o'clock I will be seeing my Q.C. in order to take action against you. Carry on which is ridiculous accusations and we are all going to end up in court, which is no fault of my own. I have a Q.C. who has been with me from the beginning. P.S. Sorry that you should feel so strongly about this. It dose [*sic*] not happen to be my fault. Look forward to hearing from you. And I particularly look forward to seeing you in court. Michael Barrett.

Warren replied that he would be most pleased to publish Barrett's message in the next edition of *Ripperana*, as 'it confirms existing opinions of you'. 'You are exceedingly unwise to threaten me,' he continued, 'since I now hold all the cards.'

Meanwhile, the relentless pursuit of birth certificates continued, with Paul Feldman seemingly determined to prove that none of the major protagonists were who they said they were. Michael and Anne Barrett would each, in turn, face their own identity crisis. But first it was Anne's father, Billy Graham. On 10 May 1994 Keith Skinner, unaware of Feldman's desire to speak to Anne, rang Barrett from Paul Feldman's office to ask if he knew Billy Graham's birthday. Skinner told Barrett that he was exasperated by Feldman's insistence that Billy Graham was not Billy Graham and just wanted assurance that they had the correct birth certificate for him. The answer came from an unexpected source. Anne Barrett was in the house but was abrasive and challenging when she came to the telephone, though she did confirm that Skinner did indeed have the right birth certificate.

The next day Skinner wrote to Barrett, enclosing a letter to Anne and a copy for Barrett, explaining the need to research her family tree through the last four generations, as Skinner understood had already been done with Michael Barrett and Tony Devereux. The reason he needed to do this was due to Paul Feldman's latest theory, one that Skinner hoped and expected to disprove, that Anne Barrett was a descendant of James or Florence Maybrick!

Paul Feldman's belief that the Diary had emerged via either Michael or Anne Barrett's ancestors was about to be given considerable impetus. On 17 May 1994 he received a fax from Keith Skinner to say he had discovered that Florence Maybrick had used the surname Graham after leaving prison in 1904. It was around this time that Anne Barrett, née Graham, received Keith Skinner's letter via Michael Barrett. The suggestion that research into her family tree was necessary to disprove any ancestral link to James or Florence could not have made happy reading. Anne recalls her reaction on reading the letter: 'Had an argument with Michael and said something about being sick and tired of people invading my privacy and I threw the letter at him and left.'

Anne might have been fed up with people invading her privacy, but given half a chance they would be doing it a great deal more. Paul Feldman in particular was anxious to investigate his growing conviction that she was a Maybrick and also to persuade her to sign the 'Grants of Rights and Assignment' form needed to conclude the film deal with New Line. Now living in semi-anonymity with Caroline in a friend's flat, Anne received a note from Feldman via Carol Emmas. Her friends Audrey and Eric had been receiving calls from Feldman. Anne was becoming angry. Her father, she later told Keith Skinner, told her to contact Paul Feldman after seeing the note. She refused, being 'sick to death of the Diary and the constant harassment and intimidation from Michael which was happening day and night'.

Doreen Montgomery was greatly concerned for Anne, who remained her client. Offering her help and support during this 'traumatic' time, she felt that a recent development in her husband's life might offer some hope. 'I have learned of the emergence of Jenny,' she wrote on 17 June 1994, 'who appears to be providing a shoulder to lean upon and, it would also seem, some strong words of advice to Mike. It would be good to feel that at least she is keeping him off the drink. He assures me that their relationship is not a physical one and, indeed, couldn't be. But you doubtless already know this.' Was it possible that Montgomery's well-meant communication triggered a disastrous chain of events for the Diary?

In early June 1994 Robert Smith and Richard Nicholas, solicitor to the Johnson brothers, concluded an extension to the agreement allowing Smith Gryphon permission to reprint the pictures of the watch and Dr Turgoose's report and also to use the equally positive report by Dr Wild in Shirley Harrison's forthcoming paperback edition of the book. The money offered reflected the problems the Diary had encountered. At this stage Smith Gryphon's UK edition was the only one planned. 'I am afraid,' Smith says in the covering letter, 'there will be no paperback bonanza.'

The investigation into Anne Barrett was intensifying. So determined was Paul Feldman to uncover the truth that he employed the services of a private detective agency, initially to investigate Albert Johnson and wife Valerie as well, though this was abandoned as Feldman homed in on Anne. The initial report (an extra £600 was requested for further work) included a surprising discovery:

We are also able to confirm that all medical records relating to the above subject [Anne Barrett] were officially destroyed in 1976. On enquiring into the reason, we discovered that this was 'due to the security risk associated' with the subject. We can confirm that only government officers would have the authority to destroy such records. Our informant has confirmed that the subject left the UK for Australia some time in the past due to an investigation being carried out. All other records relating to the maiden name of this subject have been deleted from all public records. We have discovered that records do exist appertaining to her maiden identity and although difficult to obtain we are now concentrating our efforts on this objective.

Even for the mildest of conspiracy theorists, this was an incitement to speculate. Why did no public records exist for Anne Barrett? Why had her medical records been destroyed and who had the 'records appertaining to her maiden identity'? For Paul Feldman, this could only add to his conviction that somehow key players in the Diary story were withholding vital information from him. Whatever reasons there might be for the absence of her records, Anne Barrett's privacy was clearly due a further invasion. But even as the spotlight was beginning to focus on Anne, her estranged husband was about to swing it back to himself, in the most dramatic manner.

The first to hear the news that would create such havoc and dismay in the Diary camp was Shirley Harrison. During a trip to Liverpool with Sally Evemy on 22 June 1994, they paid Michael Barrett a visit at the house of Jenny Morrison, the woman alluded to by Doreen Montgomery, and with whom he had recently been staying. In the 1998 edition of *The Diary of Jack the Ripper* Harrison describes what came next. 'He led me into the garden and with much emotion poured out the story of how he had forged the Diary. He was bitter and angry that he had not seen his daughter and threatened to tell everything to the national Press. His reasons for such actions were also confused. He kept repeating that all he wanted was to see Caroline, but he then pursued a course of action that made this less and less likely.'

For more than two years since that first call to Doreen Montgomery, in the face of what at times had been almost unbearable pressure, Barrett had resolutely stood his ground. His testimony as to how he obtained the Diary might have been questioned, but his stubbornness in defending his story had been a factor in keeping the Diary afloat in difficult waters. All along the question had been, if it was a modern forgery then who was responsible? Now, it seems, there was an answer. One that very soon would find a much wider audience.

Anne Barrett first heard of her husband's bombshell two days after he had confessed to Shirley Harrison, when, she recalled later, a 'shame-faced Harold Brough [the *Liverpool Daily Post* journalist who had first broken the Diary story] turned up on my door-step and told me about Michael's revelations to the *Daily Post*. He added that he had left him dead drunk covered by a blanket in the middle of the living room floor. He asked me for a comment which he obviously intended to print so I said the first thing that came into my head which was something like, "I will fight like a tiger to protect my family" – I can remember walking up the stairs thinking "What the hell did I say that for?"'

The next day, Saturday 25 June 1994, Anne, along with the rest of the population of Liverpool, was able to read in full her husband's confession. Under the headline 'Fresh Mystery in Jack the Ripper Diary Saga', Brough revealed Barrett's dramatic recanting of his original story and confirmed that he had signed a statement for the paper claiming he had compiled the material himself. 'It was so easy it is untrue,' Barrett is quoted as saying. 'I fooled the world. I would like to get recognised, even in my grave.' This was categorically denied by Anne. 'The whole idea is total rubbish,' she said. It was all, Barrett told the paper, down to money. 'I did it because I could not pay the mortgage. So I thought, "what can I do?" and the only thing I am good at – apart from being a scrap metal merchant – is writing. So I thought I would write the biggest story in history.'

At the end of the article, Brough strikes a warning note. 'But he [Barrett] was unable to explain how he managed to write a book which fooled experts or answer basic questions about how he found the old paper of the Diary or old ink.' In truth, it didn't seem to matter to Barrett, who was exultant in his achievement. 'But I pulled it . . . I bloody well pulled it.'

The man who had brought the Diary into the public arena had now confessed to forging it. As the news quickly spread, the Ripperologist grapevine was humming. For many there was little surprise that Barrett had finally cracked under the pressure and revealed the truth. They had been right all along and here was their vindication. Surely this was the end of the road for all who once believed that James Maybrick really was Jack the Ripper.

FOUR

'This crazy year'

'Yes, I am a forger. The greatest in history.' Two days after his stunning confession, Michael Barrett was back on the front page of the *Liverpool Daily Post*. This time his story was even more dramatic. Indeed, it appeared to be something of a deathbed confession, motivated by an urgent need to unburden a guilty conscience. 'Now Mr Barrett, who is seriously ill,' wrote *Post* journalist Harold Brough, 'says he has decided to confess to his actions, after being told by his doctor that he has only days to live. "I now feel at peace with myself," he said last night.' Pictured somewhat theatrically leaning on a walking stick next to James Maybrick's grave in Anfield cemetery, Barrett was also now able to give a brief account of how he went about the forgery he had denied for so long. The journal itself, he claimed, was an old photographic album, obtained from Liverpool auctioneers Outhwaite & Litherland, from which he had ripped out the used pages. The much-disputed ink, it now emerged, came from a shop at the Bluecoat Chambers in Liverpool. He had typed the diary on his word processor at home, although he did not say whether the handwriting in the diary was also his. As for his original story: 'Tony Devereux had sod-all to do with it. I wrote it. I fooled the world.'

He had certainly fooled a number of people, including, apparently, his estranged wife. 'He told me he got the diary from Tony Devereux,' said Anne, 'and that is all I know. He is now trying to get back at me because I have left him. The whole thing is an absolute nightmare.' It was a furious response, though some in the Diary camp and outside were at a loss to understand how Barrett's confession could be construed as a form of revenge on his wife.

Nor was Robert Smith, who described the claim as a 'sudden and surprising development', any more convinced. 'I find it remarkable in view of the thorough investigation by Scotland Yard in Liverpool last year, and the many expert opinions indicating it is genuine.' In fact, while not being able to find the evidence to make a conviction stick, the Scotland Yard officers had been reported as saying that the diary was a post-1987 hoax, with Barrett, by implication, as the prime suspect. Had their clear suspicion now been proved right? Barrett himself was under no illusions about the scale of his achievement. 'I decided to write the story of the century. I bloody well did it.'

Had he? As both Diary research teams began an immediate fightback against this latest and potentially most damaging setback, Shirley Harrison asked Sally Evemy to compile a list of points which 'Mike would have had extreme difficulty in collating'. Evemy identified six. How had Barrett discovered the little-known fact that cold hands, not merely numbness, are a symptom of using arsenic? How had he found the information for the line in the diary 'Dearest Gladys is unwell again', when the only passing reference to Maybrick's daughter being constantly ill is in a letter in the Kew Public Record Office (to which, Evemy says, Barrett did not have access)? Where did he find the reference to the hitherto unknown character of Mrs Hammersmith mentioned in the journal? How did he know the importance of Middlesex Street in the East End of London (where, the journal says, Maybrick took rooms), which is not referred to in previous Ripper books? How did he know Maybrick was sometimes called Sir James, or about his great friend George Davidson, both obscure references that it had taken diligence and luck, Harrison believed, for professional researchers to dig up? Shirley Harrison also requested that Barrett write a page of the Diary to demonstrate his ability as a forger and produce his notes.

Paul Feldman, who was bravely telling his team that Barrett's confession was a positive development for the Diary in that it both brought the forgery question into the open and was easily disproved, had a similar set of questions, which Harold Brough printed in the next day's *Post*. In the article Feldman challenged Barrett to say where he had found a number of references that had taken professional researchers months to uncover. These included the little-known facts that James Maybrick was indeed away from home at Christmas 1888, that he struck his wife Florence after the Grand National in 1889 and that there were two, not three, brass rings missing from the body of Ripper victim Annie Chapman. Barrett's confession, said Feldman, was 'total rubbish. The man is a liar.' The owner of the Bluecoat Chambers art shop, where Barrett had claimed to have bought the Victorian ink, suggested it would probably have been manuscript ink, supplied by Diamine, a Liverpool firm. Diamine's chemist Alec Voller was not convinced this would have worked: 'Up to about two years ago we did make a manuscript ink almost identical to that used in Victorian times. However, under analysis, an expert would know the ink is modern.'

The confession would not just have implications for the Diary camp. Since the beginning of what Shirley Harrison described as 'this crazy year', the story of the Diary had become irretrievably entangled with an unfolding domestic tragedy. Writing a year after the event, Anne recalled the personal impact of the article: 'Michael's family were very distressed and most of all Caroline was in a terrible state and I think I had to keep her from school. That very day [27 June 1994] I went to the solicitor's office with the newspaper article tucked under my arm and asked him to start divorce proceedings.' After leaving Barrett in January, Anne had decided to wait for a two-year separation period before divorcing him, which was a simpler and cheaper option. The article changed that. 'This was,' she wrote, 'the last straw in a long line of humiliations and my father was so furious he advised me to start divorce proceedings immediately and promised to pick up the bill.'

If he were to be believed, Michael Barrett was just days from death. Those in Harrison's and Feldman's teams who had come to know Barrett had become aware of his taste for the dramatic and his tendency, when in drink, to make wild claims. But equally there was no doubt that he had been under terrible stress, was drinking very heavily and suffered from a long-standing kidney complaint. Since the separation from Anne, there had been an increase in his drinking and a corresponding deterioration in his psychological state. Just how serious was his condition and how had it impacted on his statement to Harold Brough? Brough himself had told Anne Barrett (who from August 1994 would revert to her maiden name, Graham) that he had left Barrett lying 'dead drunk' in the living room that fateful evening and had pointedly mentioned Barrett 'pouring a whisky' while making his confession in the article.

In fact, it soon appeared that Barrett's ill health and drinking were interlinked. On 30 June 1994, three days after Barrett had given his account of the forgery in the *Daily Post*, the paper carried a much shorter but equally dramatic story. The *Post* announced that Michael Barrett had retracted his confession. A closer reading of the statement from his solicitor Richard Bark-Jones gives a slightly different impression: 'With regard to the statement [confession] made by Michael Barrett that he himself had written the diary of Jack the Ripper, I am in a position to say that my client was not in full control of his faculties when he made that statement which was totally incorrect and without foundation.' There was a sad postscript. 'Michael Barrett is now in the Windsor Unit [alcohol treatment unit] of Fazakerley Hospital [in Liverpool].'

Unlike his confession, Barrett's retraction made little impression. Those who had long ago decided that the Diary was a modern fake finally had their belief confirmed, and from the horse's mouth too. The retraction, which was not even in Barrett's words, came too late. The damage was done. Three days after Bark-Jones's statement, and with understandable relish, the *Sunday Times*, which had denounced the Diary as a fake even before publication, now trumpeted the news to a wider public.

Under the heading 'Scrap Dealer confesses he faked Jack the Ripper diary', Maurice Chittenden, the journalist who had originally investigated the Diary, was clearly taking Barrett's claim at face value: 'The man who fooled the book world – but not the *Sunday Times* – by "discovering" the diary of Jack the Ripper has admitted he wrote it himself.' Noting that the book had sold 50,000 hardback copies in Britain and another 50,000 overseas (as well as being translated into eleven languages), Chittenden described how 'Jack the Ripoff', as he termed Michael Barrett, had admitted spending 'ten days tapping out the 9,000-word confession on a word processor in his Victorian terraced house in Liverpool'.

Restating the evidence that had originally convinced the paper the Diary was a fake, the article also claimed that Barrett's confession had thrown 'a giant shadow over a projected multi-million pound feature film based on the Diary to be made by Ted Turner, founder of CNN, the American television company'. It could also, Chittenden suggested, lead to a reopening of the Scotland Yard investigation. Despite her belief that Barrett was incapable of the forgery, the article quoted Shirley Harrison as though she believed him: 'He said he wanted to confess because he is an ill man and believes he is going to die.' Harrison and Feldman were equally angered by the omission of Barrett's retraction, the only part of Bark-Jones's statement reproduced in the article being the sentence that Barrett was 'not in full control of his faculties'.

After several days in the alcohol treatment unit at Fazakerley Hospital, Barrett returned home to Goldie Street, still in a vulnerable condition both physically and psychologically. Why, after not being in contact for nearly three months, he now decided to call Paul Feldman, on 4 July 1994, is not clear but it would be hard to imagine a more damaging conversation for his fragile mental state than the one that would ensue.

Impervious to the confession, Feldman had convinced himself that the Diary had definitely come down through Anne Graham's family and that Barrett had married a descendant of James Maybrick, but had been given a new identity by the Government along with other members of the Barrett family. His team of researchers had been sent to various public record offices to trace Barretts, Grahams, Johnsons (the watch had not been forgotten) and indeed a host of interlinked families. Birth, marriage and death records for great swathes of the Liverpool public were being scrupulously searched for clues. In the case of Michael Barrett what they found did not appear to add up. It was a recipe for chaos.

In his extensive investigations into Barrett's background, Feldman had found a marriage certificate for a Michael John Barrett and a Susan Claire Jones. The signature, Feldman was convinced, was Barrett's. Furthermore, he recalled that Anne had once told him that her maiden name was Jones, rather than Graham. (In fact, Feldman had got the connection wrong, Anne would reveal later. Jones was the maiden name of her grandfather's first wife.) Keith Skinner had also found an article from the *Liverpool Echo* of July 1974 about a Michael Barrett who had been jailed for twelve months for stealing a handbag from an elderly woman. By the time Michael Barrett made his call, Feldman had put everything together and concluded that, whoever Michael Barrett was, he was not Michael Barrett. The anguish this causes an inebriated but still coherent Barrett is starkly evident in the taped conversation.

'I'm going to tell you something which I don't even think you know,' Paul Feldman begins. He informs him that a Michael Barrett of 12 Goldie Street (actually it was Buckland Street, Aigburth) went to prison in 1974 for twelve months for mugging an old woman. 'Jesus Christ Almighty, may God forgive me,' a shocked Barrett exclaims, before denying that he had ever been to prison. The Michael Barrett who married Anne Elizabeth Graham in December 1975 went to prison in 1974, Feldman persists. He then reads aloud the initial report by the private investigative firm who had discovered that Anne's medical files had been destroyed. An evidently startled Barrett is then informed that his signature is on the wedding certificate of Susan Claire Jones and Michael John Barrett. He, Feldman, can prove that Michael Barrett and Anne Barrett are not who they say they are. 'You're not Michael Barrett!' he announces. 'Who am I then?' a bewildered Barrett asks plaintively. '. . . Because you didn't go to prison and you didn't knock a lady over the head with a handbag.' 'But I am Michael Barrett.' 'Mike, I can prove you're not,' Feldman insists.

Barrett is told his signature is also on the wedding certificate of Anne Elizabeth Graham who married Michael John Barrett; that his daughter Caroline's birthday is not October, as Barrett insists three times, but is either on or around Christmas Day and that the

Michael Barrett who went to prison has the same national insurance number as him. Barrett denies again he went to prison. Feldman believes him. He is not the Michael Barrett who went to prison. He is not capable of mugging an old lady. No, the truth is that he is not Michael Barrett at all. Even to a detached spectator, the conversation is confusing. In Michael Barrett's already precarious mental state, the traumatic impact of this sabotaging of the known facts of his life is clearly evident in the tape-recorded conversation.

Even the names and whereabouts of Barrett's sisters are questioned, with Feldman expressing doubts that Barrett has a sister called Elaine. If Barrett claims that Caroline's middle name is Emma, why is it down on the electoral forms for 1988 and 1989 as Elizabeth? Barrett ponders his reply for a moment. 'You want an honest answer? One – kidney failure; two – cancer; three – I was probably bloody pissed at the time.' By now, obviously anxious to bring this terrifying conversation to an end, Barrett agrees to see Feldman in person the next day. Feldman will drive up to Liverpool from London with the documents to back up his arguments.

True to his word, and accompanied by locally based researcher Carol Emmas and co-owner of the watch Robbie Johnson, who by now had become friendly with Feldman and often acted as his chauffeur/guide on his trips to Liverpool, Feldman arrived on the doorstep of 12 Goldie Street at 11am on 5 July 1994. The scene that met their eyes, when Barrett was finally roused from sleep, was not a pleasant one. 'The room,' Feldman wrote in his book *The Final Chapter*, 'was no longer like the one I recalled on my first visit to the Barretts. The furniture had gone, the warmth had gone, it was no longer a home.' By the chair where Barrett had been sleeping was an empty whisky bottle and an overflowing ashtray. He couldn't remember when he had last eaten. While Robbie Johnson heated up some soup he found in the kitchen, Barrett now faced up to the man whose huge investment in the Diary he had so recently and emphatically sabotaged.

One of Feldman's first requests was to ask Barrett to roll up his trouser leg. Slowly Barrett did as he was bid. The Michael Barrett jailed for mugging an old woman, Feldman had learned, had a scar on his leg. Challenged on the phone, Barrett had denied having such a scar. Yet as he rolled up his trouser leg, a scar was revealed. For a moment, Feldman, whose bombastic nature had already unnerved and infuriated Barrett on a number of occasions, was wrong-footed. He *is* the Michael Barrett who mugged the old woman. Having denied the accusation, Barrett, whose voice is slurred throughout the tape, falls back on diversionary measures, trying to interest Feldman in card tricks. It was, perhaps, with some understatement that Martin Fido would later describe this whole episode as 'the most insane piece of Ripper research ever with Feldman lifting Mike and Anne straight out of a Len Deighton novel'.

Presented with the signature on the marriage certificate of Michael Barrett and Susan Claire Jones, Barrett can only say, 'I don't mind admitting that's my signature; the whole point is, who's Susan Claire Jones?' At first Barrett sticks to his story that he wrote the diary. 'I'm one of the world's greatest writers and nobody happens to believe it.' 'Did you forge the watch, too?' Feldman asks. There is a silence. No, Barrett did not forge the watch, nor does he know who did.

Later on, Feldman angrily tells Barrett about the financial repercussions of his confession on him. 'The diary's genuine,' Barrett replies. 'Not the point, you've said you forged it. You fucked up everything I worked for for up to two years . . .' 'I never wrote the diary in the first place,' Barrett mumbles. 'I never wrote the diary.' 'All those so-called historians,' Feldman continues, 'which you can't stand the sight of any more than I can, because you know they're arseholes, they're all saying, "Ah ha, we told you so."' 'I never wrote the diary in the first place,' Barrett repeats.

Towards the end of Feldman's visit there is a telephone call that will have dramatic consequences for the course of the Diary story. Lynn, Michael Barrett's sister, rings to check how he is. Feldman answers and, towards the end of the conversation, gives Lynn his contact numbers, in case she should need to call him.

Not long afterwards Melvyn Fairclough made another discovery. Michael John Barrett had been born in the same road in which Michael Barrett (the Diary owner) had been brought up. Anne Graham, whose new telephone number Feldman did not have, had not yet responded to a letter asking her to contact him. Impatient to solve this seeming mass of contradictions, Feldman decided to ring Lynn Barrett.

It was not a well-received call. Though polite, Lynn was upset and not pleased that Feldman had obtained her phone number. 'How did you get my number?' she demands at the outset. 'You gave it me,' Feldman claims. 'No, I didn't,' she insists. Clearly, she was infuriated at the digging around he was doing and the kind of questions he was asking about her family. Feldman then attempts to explain why he is trying to sort out the apparent discrepancies in the records of Michael and Anne, which also include Lynn's sister and parents too. He knows the Diary is not a forgery, as her brother claims, but he needs to know how it came from James Maybrick into the hands of Mike Barrett. An exasperated Lynn finally almost pleads: 'I'm telling you, Paul, you will never find anything out about this family connected with the book because we didn't know anything about the Diary until Mike told us it was coming out.'

Feldman then insists she is involved, because Anne and Mike are involved and have received money from him and so anyone connected with them has to be involved as well. Lynn, who remarks that none of her family have received so much as a bar of chocolate from Anne and Barrett, disagrees. The conversation ends.

The evident distress shown by Lynn Barrett would have dramatic consequences for the Diary. If her brother's confession had thrown a new perspective on the Diary, the information Feldman would soon receive as a direct result of Lynn's anger with him would propel the story to another level again. Meanwhile, within a few days of Feldman's call to his sister, Michael Barrett received a letter from Shirley Harrison on the subject of his confession. Roger Wilkes, a BBC scriptwriter, Barrett was told, would soon be in touch to 'try to repair some of the damage you have done recently'. Wilkes would not be doing a programme for the moment but would like a short statement from Barrett for the record. 'Hopefully, you will be able to tell him the truth about the origins of the Diary – and not what you said to Harold Brough. We would all like you to see him – it is vitally important.'

As the Diary team worked hard to undo the terrible damage inflicted by Michael Barrett, the investigation into his family was still causing chaos. Like a man possessed, Paul Feldman had latched on to the notion that the secret of the Diary's provenance lay in the Barrett family and he would not let go. Keith Skinner, who by now had detached himself from the mass of contradictory evidence Feldman and Melvyn Fairclough were building up, attempted to make sense of Feldman's current reasoning. Skinner's notes, dated 14 July 1994, offer a revealing snapshot of Feldman's thinking, as well as shedding some light on why Feldman was pursuing everyone connected with the Barretts with such zeal and suspicion:

> Paul F. believes the Diary to be real and written by James Maybrick. Believes it to be inherited by Mike Barrett who is not the Mike Barrett in the picture. Believes his identity has been changed – and he has been given either an invented background or someone else's background – and the records have been so altered to make it impossible/extremely difficult to trace his true identity. Barrett's true identity probably descends from one of the illegitimate children of James and Sarah (Maybrick's mistress). This 'deception' must involve other people, who know what is going on, but every record cannot be doctored to accommodate all of these people. Therefore they have to be on their guard at all times – or when people start asking questions – and consequently may betray themselves because what they disclose does not match what is written in the existing (and probably) forged records.
>
> The 'cover up' of authorised documents is only at superficial level, and has probably been done with government cooperation, because nobody suspected anyone would dig as deep as PF. Thus it is the discovery of MB's prison record which has alerted those in the know – and generated panic – as witness Doreen Montgomery's letter to PF.
>
> Anne becomes a security risk the day she marries Mike Barrett.

But what of the couple at the epicentre of this gigantic conspiracy theory? The alleged security risk, Anne Graham (Barrett), had been

103

trying to keep out of the spotlight as much as possible. She had ignored repeated requests from Paul Feldman and his team to contact them and was becoming increasingly upset about the problems he was causing her own and Barrett's family and friends. Meanwhile, she was pressing ahead with divorce proceedings, as she made clear in a letter to Barrett, dated 18 July 1994:

> As you know I started the divorce proceedings the day the *Daily Post* printed the story [Barrett's confession]. I did not go for marital breakdown as that is only possible after a two-year separation. I know you will be getting the divorce papers shortly and they will no doubt upset you. I am sorry for that Mike, I don't want to add to your burden, but I am afraid that you left me with no choice after speaking to the newspapers.
>
> I am warning you now about the divorce papers because if you manage to stop drinking again, I don't want you to use it as an excuse to start drinking again.

Critics of the Diary, including Melvin Harris, suspected that this letter, which later came into his possession, was actually a clear threat that Anne would pursue divorce proceedings if Barrett persisted with his forgery claim. Furious at this intrusion into her privacy, Anne insisted, in part of an extensive rebuttal of Melvin Harris's criticisms that she wrote to Paul Feldman in July 1995, that she had told her husband within weeks of leaving him (on 2 January 1994) that she had every intention of applying for divorce. To her friends and family, she blamed the rift on the physical and mental abuse she had endured, largely as a result of Barrett's alcoholism. This, she said, had been going on for the last few years of her married life and was nothing to do with the Diary.

As well as the divorce proceedings, Anne had other worries to contend with. As she told Keith Skinner some two years afterwards, the damage being done by Feldman's persistence was rebounding on her. One evening in mid-July 1994 she received a very angry telephone call from Michael Barrett's sister Lynn, complaining about the call Feldman had made to her. 'I felt very guilty that I had brought all this worry on their heads as they had been very good to me and I was obliged to them for helping me get away from Mike. I rang Paul Feldman about 11 p.m. that evening, a few minutes after Lynn had rung. I was furiously angry with him for pestering Michael's family and worrying my friends Audrey and Eric [witnesses to the Barretts' wedding] with his questions.'

Feldman, according to the account he gives in *The Final Chapter*, told Anne that he had bought the film rights and spent almost two years of his life and a great deal of money trying to establish the truth of the matter. He wasn't going to let go now. The conversation rapidly descended into what Anne described as a 'huge shouting match'. Now Anne heard the theories which Feldman had been formulating over the last few weeks. Her reaction? 'I thought he was mad,' she told Keith Skinner. 'I also realised that he was not going to let go and my first thought was that if I could sit down with him and sort through the Barrett family background he would realise they were perfectly normal with nothing to hide. My ultimate aim was to stop him contacting the Barretts who did not want to be involved in the Diary and did not see why they and their family should be investigated.'

The conversation, Anne said, went on for about three hours (in his book Feldman estimates it was four hours). Long enough anyway, that halfway through, Anne decided to give him her phone number so he could ring back and save her telephone bill. Confused by Feldman's theories and worried that the press might get hold of them, Anne says she was most worried for Barrett's parents, particularly his father, who was ill. By the end of the call, Anne realised she had no option. 'I was certain that I would be able to convince him that the Barrett family was completely real and that Michael and I were who we said we were if I met him face to face.' 'If I agree to meet you, will you back off from the Barretts?' is the version Feldman remembers in his book.

Two days later, on 23 July 1994, Feldman, chauffeured once more by Robbie Johnson, arrived at Anne's flat, characteristically late for the agreed meeting, having stopped to buy a couple of Walt Disney videos for Caroline and a massive bunch of flowers for Anne. He was in for a surprise. Anne received the presents but made it clear that Feldman was not coming in – her strategy, she told Skinner, being to 'confuse the enemy'. Instead, they agreed to do their talking in the Moat House, a restaurant/bar not far away, where, according to Anne, 'we settled in the back bar which was empty and there we stayed for the next six hours [Feldman says three or four] or so, only stopping to have a quick lunch'.

It was an exhausting ordeal for both parties, but one which would be vital in developing the story of the Diary. For Anne, the objective was to prove to Feldman that his theories were out of line. 'I tried to convince him that his researchers and detectives had given him wrong information; his air of mystery and the ridiculous conclusions he had drawn affected my rather macabre sense of humour and at one time I think I had convinced him I was working for MI5!'

Anne had brought documents and photographs to try to prove to Feldman that she and Barrett were precisely who they said they were. According to Feldman, she was at least partly successful in this. He did eventually accept that the marriage certificate between Susan Claire Jones and Michael John Barrett was 'a red herring', despite the remarkable similarity with Michael Barrett's signature, and felt she had explained away one or two other discrepancies too, enough, at least, for him to write, 'I felt I had been a fool and my only consolation was that my conviction would lead me to the truth anyway.' Whether it *would* lead to the truth remains a matter of heated debate, but what is certain is that the much-doubted provenance for the Diary, already severely damaged by Barrett's confession, was about to change forever.

Anne has a different recollection of what was achieved. 'Towards the end of the meeting I was exhausted,' Anne told Keith Skinner, 'and felt I had come up against a brick wall. He [Feldman] would not be convinced (or pretended not to be convinced) over the Barrett family – so I told him in no uncertain terms that Michael knew nothing about the origins of the Diary and that when my father died the truth would come out.'

Here, finally, was something to entice Feldman to let go of the Barretts. If Anne was telling him the truth, the Diary, it seemed, had not journeyed from the hands of James Maybrick to Michael Barrett. The spotlight, as Anne wished, would turn away from the Barrett family. But, if that was her sole intention, it would be a Pyrrhic victory. Now the focus, inevitably, must shift to her own family, and, in particular, the very last person she wanted to be hauled into Feldman's net. 'My main worry during this time was my father,' she told Keith Skinner. 'I was trying to get us a decent home so he could come and live with us as I did not want him to have to go into a nursing home as he was very close to needing 24-hour care.'

The meeting had been held to try to answer Feldman's doubts about the Barretts. From his point of view, it had achieved a great deal more. Out of the blue he now had a new, or at least drastically revised, provenance for the Diary. 'I assume the Devereux story was rubbish?' he recalls asking Anne. She looked embarrassed. 'No, it was not. I gave it to Tony. I've always wanted to apologise to the Devereux family.' 'Why did you not give it to Mike direct?' Feldman asked. 'Maybe I will tell you that story when I know you a little better,' Anne replied.

The story had moved on. It was now claimed that Tony Devereux *had* given Michael Barrett the Diary but that Devereux had received it from Anne. In truth, this account appeared to make even less sense than the original story. Dramatic new information, however, would soon emerge to clarify this new version. And the most extraordinary claim would not come from Anne at all.

Meanwhile, totally unaware of this latest news, the other Diary team were at loggerheads over the legal fees owing to Mishcon de Reya. Smith Gryphon had been advised by their lawyers that the 'authors' of the Diary book, Shirley Harrison and Michael Barrett, should be liable for their share of the legal fees of £57,205.07, the bulk of which was attributed to the *Sunday Times* action, and the negotiations of film agreements with Duocrave and New Line Cinema. Doreen Montgomery, acting on behalf of both her clients, was outraged. On 22 July 1994 she wrote to Smith, leaving him in no doubt as to her feelings on the matter.

Hoping to avoid another legal spat, Smith wrote a long letter back to her, outlining his position. Smith believed that Montgomery had not understood the extent of Smith Gryphon's financial outlay on the Diary. 'The central issue,' he wrote to her on 25 July, 'is the outlay this company has had to make, to defend the book and "the diary" from commercial annihilation.' It would be wrong, he felt, to lay all the blame at the door of the *Sunday Times* when the 'Exocet' came not from that paper but from the article in the *Washington Post* that had triggered the Rendell report. This was based on a statement by Nicholas Eastaugh, the consultant chosen by Shirley Harrison, whom she had not asked to sign a confidentiality statement. It was this that led to the commercial damage brought about by the cancellation by Warner, following the Rendell report.

The legal and commercial problems arose because 'we believed the Diary is genuine and because the book is based firmly on that premise. When Warner and Rendell cried "fake", we were faced with a spate of legal and commercial threats.' The situation was not made easier by a 'large army of ill-wishers' who were determined to 'smash the diary commercially'. They included Melvin Harris and the editor of the *Sunday Times* who had claimed on television to have 'blown the book out of the water'. The legal argument with the *Sunday Times* was largely concerned with whether it would be in the public interest for their article to be published. The judge decided it was. At least Mishcon de Reya had successfully delayed publication of the article until the end of September 1993, when it caused only minimal commercial damage.

Smith acknowledged that Montgomery had expressed considerable misgivings over doing a deal with the *Sunday Times*. So had he. As a result, he had tightened the wording of the agreement, which had prevented them publishing their article earlier. Other legal advice had been necessary too, to deal with potential or actual copyright or ownership problems and the negotiation of film contracts. As regards Paul Feldman, 'we are in the excellent negotiating position we are today re film contracts because of our lawyers'. As a result of their retaining various rights for the authors, Feldman had been 'restrained from unilaterally entering into an agreement with New Line, which would have warranted authenticity. Just think where that would have landed us all, with

Mike's recent statements being used to substantiate claims running into telephone numbers.'

Montgomery had been puzzled as to why Robert Smith had claimed not yet to have made any profit, given the healthy sales of the book. It was not, he replied, so difficult, pointing to almost £60,000 of legal costs, advertising and promotion costs (London Underground poster campaigns and the like), posters and four-colour presenters for the bookshops, and the high production values of the book itself, all of which had combined to 'virtually eliminate the profits at this stage'.

While not yet aware of the nature of Anne Graham's revelations, Doreen Montgomery knew something was up. Montgomery had remained loyal to Anne through a deeply traumatic period, and she had expected loyalty in return. 'I am not quite sure why Paul Feldman should be the recipient of your confidences,' she wrote to Anne on 25 July 1994. 'Whatever he has promised you, I assure you, can be nothing to the ultimate benefits you could receive from the book and attendant rights.' If, that is, Anne was interested in such benefits. 'You have said, I know, that you are not interested in money,' Montgomery acknowledged, 'but, willy-nilly, there will certainly be some for you and Caroline, as Mike's family, and it would be ludicrous of you not to keep us in the picture and apprised of what is going on.'

For the time being, though, the revelations were restricted only to Paul Feldman's team. On 26 July, three days after the meeting with Anne Graham, Feldman rang Keith Skinner to fill him in on the new developments. Anne, according to Feldman, had rung him the day after their meeting, very upset and frightened, later calling again to say she was coming to London, with Caroline, to see him. She had told Feldman that her first sight of the Diary was in a wardrobe in the family house in Stalisfield Grove, Liverpool, just before they moved (which dates it approximately to 1969/70).

Worryingly for Anne, who would soon become aware of it, Feldman told Keith Skinner that he had a new theory. Anne had said she was not Anne Elizabeth Graham. Paul now believed her real name was Emma Parker, a name he had seen in Michael Barrett's address book with Anne's name marked next to it. Feldman was convinced that the Barretts' wedding certificate was forged.

Anne had worries enough without this new identity scare. There were still problems with her estranged husband: 'I was also being continually hounded by Michael night and day. I couldn't even walk down the street without tripping over him; although the original statement in the newspaper had been retracted, I never knew what he was going to say next.' Most disturbing of all was the report from the private investigation agency, which Feldman had shown her, that her medical records had been destroyed: 'I had an awful niggerly [*sic*] feeling that I knew what it was about. He told me that there was a strong possibility that this information would become public and although this had been the first I knew about it, if it was due to the reason I was beginning to think it was, the implications just didn't bear thinking about.'

It was arranged that Anne and Caroline should spend a couple of days at Feldman's house outside London, where Caroline would have the company of Feldman's own daughter. A few days later they set off, not by train as planned, but taxi (paid for by an impatient Feldman), all the way from Liverpool, because of a rail strike. Having got so close, he was not going to let slip the opportunity to find out all Anne knew. Anne told Keith Skinner that she had her own reasons for wanting the meeting to go ahead as soon as possible. 'I had spoken to someone over my fears about the government report and he had filled in the background for me and by now I was convinced I knew why the government had been involved and destroyed the records.' The implications, should this be leaked to the press, Anne said, would 'cause some pretty heavy problems for a third party and possibly Paul Feldman himself'. Unwilling to release the man's name, she told Skinner, she decided to make up a story and hope that Feldman fell for it.

After a dinner in which everything but the Diary was talked about, Feldman recalls, he suggested that he and Anne talk in his office. Suspicious that their conversation might be bugged, Anne insisted they talk in the garden. 'So Paul and I went to sit on the steps that led into the rose garden . . . I told Paul that after I married

Michael I had an affair with an SAS officer who was posted to Ireland and went deep undercover, that he was shot and badly injured but brought out of Ireland back to England. I suggested that because of our close relationship this was why the government had put a protection order on me. He thought it over for a minute and told me plainly I was lying. I burst out laughing and said something like, "it was worth a try".'

In fact, Anne told Feldman, the story *was* substantially true. The man, however, was not a lover but someone closely connected with her and she was worried about these details being disclosed as the IRA were still active (IRA activity had increased in the months leading up to their August 1994 ceasefire). Though Feldman believed her account, he remained, she says, convinced that there was another motive for the government's action. However, the exchange had lessened the tension between the two and Anne now agreed to continue the conversation in Feldman's office. Indeed, Anne recalls 'spending most of the day and the night [she would spend two days in all at Feldman's] in Paul's office being bombarded with questions'.

According to Anne, communication improved as the two got to know each other and she gave him crucial information about the Diary, but the massive conspiracy theory that Feldman had conjured had still to be fully punctured before any other issues could be addressed. This would not be easy. At the outset, she recalled, 'he was still working around all the information he had uncovered over the last few years and I was being bombarded with theories and information'. The first item on the agenda, Anne insisted, was to make him believe fully that 'I was who I said I was and Michael was indeed Michael Barrett'. Otherwise, there could be no discussion of the Diary.

It was now Feldman's contention that there had been a swapping of identities with people close to the Diary and that somehow Anne had taken on the persona of an Emma Parker, the name he had seen in Michael Barrett's address book with the name Anne alongside. Barrett couldn't recall who Emma Parker was. Neither could Anne when Feldman mentioned it to her. There was only one solution.

Feldman rang the number. It took two fairly confused telephone calls to establish that Emma Parker was a schoolfriend of the Barretts' daughter Caroline. Another theory had bitten the dust. Progress was being made.

Michael Barrett and his family were now out of the equation, Feldman had decided. Now he needed to investigate the possibility that the Diary had come down through Anne's family, the Grahams. Feldman's research team had uncovered in Peterborough what he believed was a line of illegitimate descendants of James Maybrick, from his relationship with his mistress Sarah Robertson. For a while Anne and Feldman discussed the possibility that her father Billy Graham was connected to them.

The discussion led to Feldman suggesting that one member of this line, Sheppard Shalgrave Maybrick, who had disappeared from the records after his first birthday, could actually be Anne's father, as their ages would have been similar. 'Anne listened to me without comment,' he wrote in *The Final Chapter*. 'Then, quite unexpectedly, she said, "You might just have something here, Paul. Believe it or not, I know very little about the Diary. I first saw it in 1968 or 1969, when Dad was about to move house. I was packing up a lot of things and saw it in a black trunk with white writing on it [she told Keith Skinner later that Paul Feldman then said that Florence Maybrick had owned a tin trunk with white writing on it]. In the trunk was some tropical gear and a crucifix. All I have ever really known is that Dad was given it on Christmas Day 1950 by his stepmother Edith. She told him that his granny had left it to him."'

After more than two years in which Michael Barrett had stuck unflinchingly to his story that Tony Devereux had given him the Diary, we had, in the space of one month, seen Barrett claim he had forged it himself, and now Anne Graham, his estranged wife, was claiming that it was in her father's possession over forty years previously. Which, if any, of these stories could be believed?

Now, Feldman says, Anne's attitude to him began to change. Her suspicion and hostility had disappeared. He believed she finally understood just why he needed to pursue his investigation in the manner in which he did. He too, he says, began to understand that her caution, even deceit, was not due to financial reasons or other selfish motives, but to her overriding need to protect her family, both daughter Caroline and the man whom she dreaded being dragged into Feldman's line of fire, her father Billy Graham.

Anne had her own theory of how the Diary had made its way into the family, suspecting, she told Feldman, that it had emerged via a servant in the Maybrick household. She had learnt that her father's step-grandmother, Elizabeth Formby, had been friendly with Alice Yapp, a senior servant/nurse in James Maybrick's household, who detested Florence. Anne believed Yapp had stolen the diary and given it to Elizabeth. Because Granny Formby 'could not read or write and the servant had seen no monetary value in it, it had just been left and ended up with my dad'.

Feldman, who had wrapped his life around the journal for nearly two years, wondered what Anne had thought when she first saw it. Her answer must have seemed a strange one. 'Not a lot really, Paul,' he says she answered. 'Jack the Ripper was to me a bogeyman of my youth. I'm not sure that I even knew he was real. I briefly looked at it, but left it to read at another time. I was busy at the time packing. When I eventually did ask my dad about it he was doing his [football] pools and just ushered me away. You didn't ask twice.' Years later, Anne claimed, after her father's second wife died in 1989, he moved into sheltered accommodation and gave her some of his possessions to store, as his own space was limited. Anne says he handed the Diary over to her with the words, 'You may as well have this'.

Though no longer a teenager, as she was when she claims she first saw the Diary, Anne said that even then she had no interest in it. Having been given a diary allegedly written by Jack the Ripper and then, to all intents and purposes, ignoring it, was just one element of Anne's story that sceptics find puzzling. The other was her claim that she gave it to Tony Devereux to give to her husband. Why? She told Feldman:

Mike had lost his self-esteem. He was drinking a lot and I blamed myself for the problems we were having. He wasn't working: I was, and I enjoyed it. Mike was keen on writing, so, one day, on the spur of the moment, I decided to give him the diary. I thought he would try to write a novel around it. I never thought he would try to get it published. I gave it to Tony for two reasons, though. I didn't want Mike to know I was helping him. If he was going to be successful, I thought it best to distance myself. I suppose the most important reason, though, was that I didn't want Mike to know it had come from my family. Mike would have pestered my father to the extreme.

Anne claims she chose Devereux as the instrument of her plan as he was 'close to Mike at the time and I happened to know where he lived'. Devereux lived about a six- or seven-minute walk from the Barretts. Another two hundred yards further on was the Saddle pub and opposite it was Caroline's school. Anne says she wrapped the Diary in brown paper and tied it up with string before taking it to Devereux. It was a short conversation: 'I just told him to give it to Mike and to tell him to do something with it.' It certainly coincided with the story that Barrett had first given to the world, the story that so many had disbelieved. But was this new, amplified account any more likely to convince the sceptics, especially as many had now written off the Diary completely following Barrett's confession of forgery?

Would-be believers have to discount the convenience of Anne's story coming to the fore at this crucial time, not just in terms of the prospective film deal (which Paul Feldman continues to insist did not hinge on the provenance), but seemingly as part of a rescue package launched by the Diary camp to undo the damage Barrett had caused. What better way, the sceptics might argue, than to effectively take Barrett out of the picture, while still retaining the integrity of his original story? And, even if one accepts that someone could be so lacking in curiosity about a diary allegedly signed by the world's most notorious serial killer, the idea of giving the document indirectly to one's husband as an inspiration for a novel seems almost less credible than Barrett's original story.

However, unlike Barrett, it should be said that Anne Graham has never deviated from this story. Even at this time, she told Keith

Skinner, the Diary was not a subject of any interest to her. 'My priority at that moment was to my father – I just wanted him to be happy for his remaining months of life.' But now, given the nature of the story she told Feldman, it would no longer be possible to keep Billy Graham out of the picture. The story had not yet been completed. That task would fall to Billy Graham himself. And his contribution would top anything that had come before.

A significant turning-point in Anne's decision to open up, she told Keith Skinner, came when Paul Feldman promised to protect her from the media, Ripperologists and 'all other interested parties'. With this anxiety removed and having already revealed so much information, she felt there was little point in holding back any more. It was inevitable, she now realised, that her father would become involved. Feldman was determined to interview him and asked Anne to get his permission. It was granted.

Anne's visit to Feldman had not gone unnoticed. It should not be forgotten that there was at least one party who would be extremely interested in knowing what Anne had told Feldman. Shirley Harrison had been busy updating the story for the paperback edition of *The Diary of Jack the Ripper*, due for publication in October 1994. Due to the virtual communication breakdown between herself and publisher Robert Smith with Paul Feldman, she had no way of knowing about the extraordinary developments taking place at Feldman's house. But Michael Barrett had discovered that Anne had been to London, via Caroline's piano teacher. It was, he told Harrison, her first trip since they were married. 'There must be a reason,' Shirley Harrison noted in a memo to Doreen Montgomery dated 28 July 1994.

Michael Barrett was in Robert Smith's thoughts that day too – and not, perhaps, the kindest of thoughts. Richard Bark-Jones, Barrett's solicitor, had faxed a demand for outstanding royalties to Smith on his client's behalf. Furious, Smith faxed back an immediate reply. He pointed out that the *Sunday Times* article based on Barrett's confession had been repeated extensively in many of the book's major markets, including Australia, America and Germany, while Bark-Jones's retraction statement had barely featured in the

115

press coverage at all. Smith had already encountered a number of booksellers, he told Bark-Jones, whose universal reaction had been, 'Well, it was a fake after all.' He was also worried that Smith Gryphon would now have to face legal claims from trade customers who had bought the book as well as overseas customers who had acquired rights. Smith also expected that sales of the forthcoming paperback in the US and UK would be 'severely reduced'. 'There is the additional worry,' he added, 'that Mike might make some other public indiscretion, or that he and/or his wife Anne may commit a further breach of their agreement with us, given the current very strange behaviour of the both of them.' He went on:

> Rather than threaten us with steps to be taken for recovery of royalties, you should consider how unprecedented it is for an author to make public statements to the press on a controversial book which completely undermines the validity of the book he has been contracted to write. The commercial damage cannot yet be calculated but I am already in receipt of a letter on the subject by one of our major customers.

Intriguingly, Smith told Bark-Jones that Michael Barrett had given him an explanation for his confession – 'that he wanted to get back at Anne', claiming that she had written to him on sexual matters a day or two before his first statements to the press. 'A marital problem,' Smith wrote, 'does not provide cause to risk wrecking a commercial venture which has taken me, Shirley Harrison and Doreen Montgomery to the limits of our physical and mental endurance.'

Meanwhile, unknown to Smith, Montgomery and Harrison, Paul Feldman was travelling to Liverpool for his eagerly awaited meeting with Billy Graham on 30 July 1994. Staying overnight with Robbie Johnson, according to an account he gave to Keith Skinner, he woke up at the time he was due at Anne's flat, and, as had become customary, was late for the meeting. Robbie Johnson dropped Feldman off and was told to come back at noon. Feldman came armed with presents, flowers for Anne, another Disney video for

Caroline and a bottle of Scotch for Billy. He also brought a leather case filled with photograph albums and research material. Feldman was ushered upstairs. There, waiting in an armchair in the living room, was Anne's eighty-year-old father, Billy Graham.

The interview began with Feldman's belief that Billy's brother Harry, who had died as a child, might in reality have been Jack Maybrick, who also died young, and was one of the illegitimate descendants of James Maybrick that Feldman's researchers had discovered. Jack Maybrick was the brother of Sheppard Shalgrave Maybrick, who had disappeared from the public records at the age of one in 1914 and who, Feldman suspected, might be Billy Graham himself. Graham now looked at some of the photographs of this Maybrick line that Feldman had brought. Nothing rang a bell. Nor, it emerged, was it conceivable that Graham could have been one of them. The conversation moved on to James Maybrick's wife, Florence.

Feldman produced Nigel Morland's book *The Friendless Lady* about Florence Maybrick and read out what he believed could be a vital paragraph from the book, concerning Florence's movements after being released from prison in 1904:

Feldman: 'In January of that year she was moved from Aylesbury Prison to the House of Epiphany . . .'
Graham: 'Yes.'
Feldman: 'On the banks of the Fal, in Cornwall, where . . .' [At this point Feldman handed the book over to Graham and pointed to the reference].
Graham: (Reading from book) 'As "Mrs Graham" . . . If my dad could see my old girl down there. (Continues reading) 'she was to try . . .'
Feldman: 'When Florence came out of prison, Billy, she called herself Mrs Graham.'
Graham: 'Did she? She must have had a crush on the old fellow, eh? (Laughs) I don't mind you saying that it is . . . about him you know, eh?'
Feldman: 'She called herself Mrs Graham . . .'
Graham: 'Yes. Dirty old get . . .'

It is an extraordinary exchange. Billy Graham appears to be trying to make some link between his own family and Florence Maybrick. Feldman, despite his obsessive attempts to link the Diary with Barrett or Anne, appears to miss the inference altogether. In his book *The Final Chapter*, he offers his inexperience as an interviewer as the reason he now left this subject for the time being and led Graham into a different area of discussion. But even as this developed, Graham's mind was still switched on to the earlier conversation. Initially Feldman seems slow to pick up what he is saying, apparently still trying to make a connection between Anne's family and James Maybrick. Billy Graham, however, was making a very different connection.

> Graham: 'Well, I was working out with my father – being her son.'
> Feldman: 'Say that again!'
> Graham: 'It's possible – being her son – my father – being Maybrick's son. Because at the time he'd be – I can't work it out – you could. He'd be er – she was fifteen when she had him. Well that's possible . . .'

Neither Anne nor Feldman appears to understand the connection that Billy Graham is making. Feldman confirms that Graham's father was born in 1879 and Graham does some working out, 'and how old would she have been then? – fifteen'.

> Feldman: 'Sorry, I will just recap on this. You are saying there was talk that Billy, your dad, may have been Maybrick's son?'
> Graham: 'No. It's only what I'm finding out now like.'

The confusion continues with Graham unable to make the other two understand who he is talking about. Finally, Graham mentions America.

> Feldman: 'Oh, you're talking about Florence?'
> Graham: 'Yes. Yes. She was in America when she was only

fifteen.'

Feldman: 'Yes.'

Graham: 'Right. Well she could have – she had a child didn't she – before?'

Feldman: 'Before she married James?'

Graham: 'Be—no. You know – she had – the Maybrick one, had a child before she married him.'

Feldman: 'Did she?'

Anne: 'Who told you that?'

Anne's surprised intervention seems to momentarily set her father back.

Graham: 'Eh?'

Anne: 'Who told you that?'

Graham: 'Somebody told me that, didn't they?'

Anne: 'I don't think anybody's ever told you that, Dad.'

Graham: 'I'm sure they have.'

Anne: 'When?'

Feldman: 'Hold it – we might have good news here. Go on, tell me more, Billy.'

Graham: 'Oh well – Somebody told me that.'

Feldman: 'That she had a child . . .'

Graham: 'While she was in America, before she got married to, er, the other fellow.'

Feldman: 'And what . . .'

Graham: 'She had an illegitimate child. Where did she get Graham from?'

Feldman: 'Billy, you might just have cracked the whole case.'

After the months of pursuing a Maybrick/Barrett connection, even a Maybrick/Johnson connection, Feldman had now been steered towards a remarkable new possibility. The true provenance of the Diary may have come from a quite different and totally unexpected source. Towards the end of the interview Anne's daughter, twelve-year-old Caroline, entered and, being informed of what her grandfather had revealed, asked, 'We're not related to him [the Ripper], are we?' 'No, my darling,' Feldman answers, 'you are related to her [Florence].'

Whether that was true or not, Anne's attempt to take the pressure off the Barretts had certainly worked a treat. Paul Feldman now had more than enough to be getting his teeth into with her own family to give the Barretts a second thought. And, as far as he was concerned, he now had a provenance for the Diary that went back to 1950. Many Ripperologists believed that there were items of information in the Diary that could only have been accessed after 1987. If Anne and Billy were to be believed, that could only mean one thing. The author of the journal was not just James Maybrick, he was also Jack the Ripper.

FIVE

'I just wanted to burn the Diary'

However vague his recollection, Billy Graham had provided a startling new prospect for Feldman to investigate: the possibility that his father, William Graham, was the illegitimate son of Florence Maybrick. If this were Graham's attempt to provide a plausible background for his daughter's story, it would not have been difficult to create. All he needed to do was work out Florence's age at the time of his father's birth and then introduce a family legend that she had an illegitimate child at fifteen. But there was a danger in such a story. All information found thus far suggested Florence had not travelled to England until after this date. Would Billy Graham risk leaving Anne with a story that could be so easily disproved?

Billy Graham told Feldman that his grandfather, Adam Graham, had been a blacksmith from Hartlepool. Even if Florence had been in England at the time, it seemed an unlikely liaison. Feldman, however, was sure that he had made the breakthrough. Anxious to uncover as much information as he could, he took Graham back to the moment it was claimed he had been given the Diary by his stepmother Edith on Christmas Day 1950, along with a letter from his step-grandmother Elizabeth.

Feldman: 'Okay, so Edith never told you where this came from when she gave it to you?'
Graham: 'No, no, no.'
Feldman: 'There was no letter or anything like that?'
Graham: 'No. Oh, she mentioned something about me Ganny. I remember she said, er – "Ganny said, 'here y'are – that's yours'".'
Feldman: 'That's yours.'

121

Graham: 'Yes, and I didn't take no notice of it, because she was good to me, my Ganny, she was all right.'

Feldman worked out that if Florence had an illegitimate child when she was fifteen, it would have been born in 1878/9. William Graham was born in 1879.

Before the interview Anne had made it clear to Feldman that she did not want her elderly father, whose illness (already suffering with a heart condition, he had been diagnosed with a tumour) was causing him increasing pain, to be questioned for more than an hour. Graham, a Second World War veteran and long-standing member of the British Legion, was also anxious to meet some old friends at the local branch. With a growing sense of urgency, Feldman now returned to Graham's vague memory of being told that Florence had a baby at fifteen. 'Try to remember a bit more,' he exhorted. Frustratingly Graham was finding recall difficult.

Graham: 'Oh, I am trying to think, somebody mentioned it, that she had a child before.'
Anne: 'Possibly a conversation you overheard with your Granny or something?'
Graham: 'Yes, yes. They used to talk, they used to talk a lot about that case, you know – years after, they used to speak about it.'

Clearly Feldman would not get his answer this time. But there were other areas, too, that needed looking at, if this story were to be believed. The provenance of the Diary had been doubted from the outset, and Barrett's forgery claim had nearly finished it as a subject for serious analysis. Yet the man who said he had seen the Diary as early as 1950, and who even believed he may have had a clear link to Florence Maybrick, had kept quiet throughout. Why, Feldman asked, did he not tell the whole story in the beginning?

Graham: 'It's only – when, when she told me you were having trouble trying to get this film to come off.'

Feldman: 'Well, there is a lot of things we've had trouble with.'

Graham: 'Yes.'

Feldman: 'So at the beginning, you just didn't want to be bothered.'

Graham: 'I wasn't bothered – no, I wasn't interested.'

Feldman: 'Okay, I understand.'

Graham: 'Tell you what – I've never read the book [*The Diary of Jack the Ripper*]. Have I, Anne? I won't read the book and I won't read the papers if it's getting pulled to pieces.'

One of the reasons the Diary had been 'pulled to pieces' was the unlikely provenance Michael Barrett had supplied for it. Now, to Feldman's delight, he was being presented with the suggestion that it had emerged into the Graham household, indirectly, from Florence herself. Feldman appeared not to be interested in another possibility that Billy Graham offered, that Granny Formby was linked with Battlecrease House and was a friend of a nurse or 'skivvy' who gave evidence at the trial. Though unable to recall the woman's name, Graham had been told as a child that his step-grandmother had tried to help her get a job with a local ship-owning family, the Holts. Graham, however, never saw the woman herself. 'I didn't see half that came to the house – had to get out, you know – and then the old girl used to get the cards out.'

Remarkably, Graham appeared never to have had the slightest curiosity as to the Diary's origins. Had he, Feldman persisted, not asked his stepmother why he had been given the book? 'No,' Graham responded. 'I never bothered. I never looked at it any more – I didn't want to know it. I'd been away for ten years, you know, without a leave and then when I come back, I'm stuck over in Germany and France and everywhere. I was never home – but I never seen them [his parents] for just on thirteen years – when I came back I was only with them a couple of months and then I got married, couple of weeks more or less.'

By now Anne, Graham and Feldman had been joined by Anne's daughter Caroline and Robbie Johnson, whom Caroline had found sunbathing on top of his car outside. It was, perhaps, a sign of Feldman's inexperience in research methods that he was happy to allow this contamination of the watch and Diary sources, not least as there would be accusations of collusion between both camps. Johnson's arrival also introduced a slight tension into the atmosphere. When, some weeks earlier, Feldman had wanted to renew contact with Anne, he had asked Robbie to pass on a message to her to get in touch with him. She had told Johnson in no uncertain terms to leave her alone. A certain frostiness was now evident between the two.

Johnson was also clearly staggered by the developments, which Feldman had updated him on, and shocked that Anne had not shared this information earlier. 'Anne, you need throwing out the window. Jesus, I can't believe all this. You mean that we're going to get a few bob after all this. So, he was Jack the Ripper?' 'Obviously,' Feldman replied, 'he was Jack the Ripper.' As the conversation progressed, it became evident that Anne was upset by Johnson's rebuke. 'I had my reasons,' she told him. 'He [she indicated her father] is one of them. Caroline also, she is the reason for not answering questions.'

With Graham becoming tired, the meeting drew to a close. Feldman did not yet have the detailed information he needed, but the interview had proved a turning-point in his investigation into the Diary. He asked Graham if he would be happy to tell his story on camera. 'It's so important,' he tells him. 'You are such an important part of history and I think it is, you know, what that would do, don't you?'

Graham: 'Yes.'
Feldman: 'What that would do for your daughter and your granddaughter. Would be a big difference for the rest of their lives.'
Graham: 'That's why I'm doing this now, not for me, I don't need any money.'
Feldman: 'I know you are . . .'
Anne: 'Don't push him into this if he doesn't want to do it.'

There was one more exchange of interest before the interview ended. 'The rumour is in the family,' Feldman clarifies one last time, 'that your dad was the son of Florence?' 'You can say that. It's no skin off my nose', is Graham's curious reply. Was he giving Feldman the go-ahead to reveal the family secret, or giving him *carte blanche* to say what he needed? Whatever, the day, even in the extraordinary saga of the Diary, had been a memorable one.

In *The Final Chapter* Paul Feldman recounts driving back to London and turning over the events of the day in his mind. Anticipating the reaction of the Diary's critics, he was sure Billy Graham was not lying to protect himself or his daughter from prosecution for forgery and fraud. Florence Chandler was thought to have come to England in 1880 on the sea voyage during which she had met James Maybrick but, if Billy Graham was right, she must also have been in England in 1879 or probably earlier. This, surely, could be proved. Feldman couldn't believe that Graham would have lied, thus 'hurting the people he loved most – and I could not accept that he would do that. I had not just witnessed some kind of performance staged for my benefit: I had seen real people, and real emotions.'

Feldman rang Anne from the car. She was, he heard, 'still in a state of shock' from this new possibility for the Diary's provenance. 'I always thought,' she told Feldman, 'the thing [the Diary] had been nicked from the Maybrick house, although when I had heard about the Maybrick illegitimate children I had wondered. I certainly didn't expect this.'

Feldman was clearly thrilled with the new Graham family connection to the Diary. But Anne knew that there were others who, when they heard, would be angry that it had not been shared with them from the outset. If her story, rather than Barrett's forgery claim, were true, their lives would have been a great deal easier if the details had been revealed earlier. According to the account she gave Keith Skinner, Feldman told Anne that he was arranging a meeting with Shirley Harrison, Robert Smith and Doreen Montgomery to let them hear the taped interview with Billy Graham. 'I came to the conclusion,' Anne told Skinner, 'knowing the other people as I did, and all the problems they had faced in the past, that they deserved some sort of explanation from me and that if Paul walked into that meeting without my support and just the recording of my father, that this would end up causing me and probably my father a continuous stream of phone calls, explanations and probably visits.'

Anne told Feldman she was going to make a recorded statement, 'with a few apologies thrown in', for the benefit of Smith, Harrison and Montgomery. Written on the weekend of the interview with her father, she read it out to Feldman over the telephone on Sunday night, 31 July 1994. Feldman recorded it and offered no suggestions for changes before it was played over the phone to Harrison, Smith and Montgomery (it is also addressed to Paul Feldman). This is the most detailed account of her story that Anne Graham has given.

I suppose I knew it was inevitable that one day the truth about the Ripper Diary would be revealed. I apologise most sincerely that it has taken so long, but I felt I had justifiable reasons.

I realised some time ago that the snowball effect had intruded so deeply into your lives and this has been a heavy burden for me to carry. The Diary was never meant for publication, not by me.

First, I would like to confirm that I have not taken any money from Paul Feldman, nor has my father, nor has Paul offered me anything more than his protection. The following part of this letter is the story in its entirety, I leave you all to work out the best way to present it to the Press, with as little harm to us all as possible. That also includes Mike, I do not want him hurt any more than he has been already.

I think it was in 1968/9 I seen the Diary for the first time. I was living with my father and maternal grandmother and we were leaving the house as my father was about to remarry after being widowed some years previously. My grandmother was going to live with her son. In my bedroom was a fitted cupboard. I discovered the Diary in a large metal trunk at the back of the cupboard. I read the first page and put it away to read when I was not so busy.

Sometime later, after reading most of the Diary, I took it to my father and asked him what he knew about it, if anything. He was doing his pools at the time and wasn't very interested. He said his Granny's friend had given it to her and his mother had given it to him. I asked him if he had read it and he said he had started to, but the writing was too small – I left it at that.

For the sake of clarity I will tell you the story I eventually pieced together from different things he told me. My father's step-grandmother, whose name was Formby, was a great friend of the nurse who worked at Battlecrease. Granny Formby accompanied the nurse when she gave evidence at the trial.

On Christmas 1950, just after I was born, my father's stepmother Edith come for Christmas dinner, she brought a suitcase with various books and documents my father had entrusted to her care during the war, and in it was the Diary. She told my father his grandmother had left it to him. After my stepmother's death we bought the house in Goldie Street to be near my father. It must have been around that time he gave me the Diary among lots of other things he no longer wanted. I never showed it to Mike – Why? – I honestly don't know. I didn't like having the Diary in my house and jammed it behind the cupboard in the spare room.

Sometime later, I can't remember how long, Mike started drinking, he was desperately trying to write, but didn't seem to be getting anywhere. It was all very frustrating and was making things difficult between us.

I thought of giving him the Diary then so that he could use it as the basis of a book. I was hoping he would be able to write a fictional story about the Diary. I knew if I gave it to him and told him its history he would be badgering my dad for details and by this time he and my father were beginning to irritate each other.

So I came up with the plan of giving Mike the Diary via someone else, that way he could not connect it with me or my family. My only motive was to give Mike something of interest to do without it coming from me. I found some brown paper which had been lining the drawer and wrapped the Diary with it and tied it with string.

I took the parcel to Tony Devereux and asked him to give it to Mike and tell him to 'do something with it'. This he faithfully did. What he thought about it all I have no idea. Whether he eventually told Mike where he got it from, I've no idea. I never seen Tony again. I apologise to the Devereux family for being brought into this, but then I never realised what would happen.

I suppose I was very naive because far from using it as a basis for a story Mike started to investigate it. When he said he wanted to get the Diary published I panicked and we had a big argument and I tried to destroy the Diary. I don't mean I destroyed any of the pages, I just wanted to burn the Diary in its entirety. Anyway he contacted Doreen just the way he said he did, and I just hoped the Diary would live or die on its own merits – so I just let everyone get on with it. I never realised the problems it would cause.

The reason I am making this statement to Paul is so that I don't have to repeat it again and again to twenty different people. I also have no intention of allowing my father to be hounded to death; he has an inoperable tumour and a heart problem and is eighty years old. I seen Paul the other day simply to clear up the problems caused by his investigating the Barrett family and my friends. I realised then how out of hand everything had gone and reluctantly came to the decision that things had to be sorted out one way or another.

I hope you can understand why I did not in the end come to you, Doreen. If I had, the whole machinery would have gone round and round [and] I could not cope with it. I have a great respect for you and everything you have tried to do in the past. As far as breaking contracts are concerned I suppose you will have to do whatever you think is right. I know nothing about the contracts, I just signed what Michael told me.

In conclusion can I just say that I have never been interested or cared who Jack the Ripper was, neither has my father. All these people who are obsessed by a hundred-year sex murderer seem to me to be most pitiful. Since 1889 there have been two world wars, the threat of nuclear annihilation, the breakdown of the ozone layer and the scourge of Aids. I am afraid the identity of a man who wouldn't even be thought of today if his *nom-de-plume* had not captured the public's imagination comes very low on my list of priorities.

Anyway this is my story, do with it what you will. I hope it makes up in some ways for the secrecy I took on to protect my father and his family.

Robert, I give you your paperback; Shirley, I give you your story; Paul, I give you your film; Doreen, I hope I give you back the occasional night's sleep.

It had not been an enjoyable experience, Anne acknowledged later. 'It's not an easy thing to do – confess to the whole world you have been an idiot – and prepare for the consequences.'

On the Saturday that Paul Feldman interviewed Billy Graham, he had also seen Michael Barrett, who claimed he had something for him. Threatening to go to the press with his story of forgery, he presented Feldman with a sample of his handwriting, using the last few lines of the Diary to prove how easy it had been. Unfortunately he had not managed to reproduce the words correctly. The handwriting was even less convincing than the text, and was obviously different from that of the Diary. Was Barrett playing a game of double-bluff, taking an unusual route to disprove the allegation of forgery by his inept attempt at copying the Diary's handwriting?

That afternoon, Saturday 30 July 1994, Paul Feldman, returning to London, rang Keith Skinner from his car phone to keep him abreast of recent developments. By the time the events were relayed to Skinner, Feldman's excitement had stripped some of the ambiguity from Billy Graham's words. According to Feldman's interpretation, Graham's father *was* the illegitimate son of Florence and it was all documented. All they had to do was find the birth certificate of William Graham, which Feldman confidently expected to show Florence Chandler (later Maybrick) as the mother. Previously they had been looking for a Liverpool birthplace, now they must try Hartlepool. As the conversation developed, Skinner questioned

Feldman's belief that Billy Graham's father was the product of a liaison between Florence and Adam – and was assured that it was beyond doubt.

The next day, Sunday 31 July, unknown to Anne, Paul Feldman, still bubbling with excitement, rang Billy Graham to try to expand on the key elements of his story. Like a hypnotist regressing a patient, he took Graham back to the day he was given the Diary by his stepmother, Edith Formby. It was, Graham recalled, Christmas 1950, when Anne would have been just a few weeks old and his father William had not long been buried. Feldman asked what she said when she gave the Diary to Billy. This time Billy's account was different. 'Well she never said anything,' he told Feldman, 'she just passed the books over to me and I just glanced at it and seen it was small print and threw it in the box and the box has been there ever since. It's been in the box since I left Sleepers Hill and Anne took it. She's seen it, I haven't. I didn't even know it existed. But I heard something about my granny was going to leave me the book.'

Graham had no idea why he was the recipient of the Diary, save for the fact that his step-grandmother was very fond of him. In the light of a line of forthcoming research Paul Feldman would undertake, Graham revealed an interesting aside about Granny Formby's antecedents who, he believes, were descended from the Flynn family, then one of the biggest shipping owners in Liverpool. Questioned again about the rumour concerning Florence Maybrick when she was a teenager, Graham replied: 'Yes, well there was some talk about you know, I wasn't supposed to listen, but no one would be there only my mother, grandmother and father and there used to be an old lady who used to come and see the old granny, every night, they would be talking about the murder, you know.'

Crucially Feldman pressed Graham on the baby Florence was alleged to have had before meeting Maybrick. 'Yes, so I heard,' Graham said. 'I heard that bit of the conversation, but I wasn't supposed to be listening, you know, I was in the back kitchen.' Pressed further by Feldman, Billy said that someone mentioned that she had the baby 'early, around about fifteen or something'.

Feldman: 'And who was that baby, Billy?'
Graham: 'Oh I don't know, I haven't got a bloody clue [Laughing] about that! No.'
Feldman: 'Billy, when we spoke yesterday, you thought that your . . .'
Graham: 'Father was . . . yes.'
Feldman: 'That your father was?'
Graham: 'Yes, well it fitted in, didn't it, with his age? That's the way I thought it.'

This was some way from Feldman's statement to Keith Skinner that William Graham *was* Florence's illegitimate son. While Graham is fairly emphatic that there was a rumour regarding Florence having had an illegitimate child at fifteen, he appears to be merely suggesting that it was possible that the child was his father, as he would have been born around that time and it would have explained Florence's decision to call herself Mrs Graham when she left prison. This, it seemed, was not a family legend but something that Graham had conjectured himself during or just before the first interview. It is also clear that while Graham does recall a nurse from Battlecrease House being friendly with his step-grandmother (and his stepmother too), it is not necessarily Alice Yapp, the senior servant whose evidence was pivotal in convicting Florence.

Was the Graham link nothing more than the musings of an ill, elderly man trying to please his questioner? There was some circumstantial evidence to support the idea. After her release from prison in 1904, Florence had eventually travelled back to the US, where she lived until her death in 1941. Not only had she used the name Graham on her release from prison (her original family name, it should be noted, was Ingraham), but Paul Feldman's researchers had dug up an intriguing newspaper article from the *Sunday News* of 1 May 1927. It is an exclusive interview with the 'sad-faced, gentle-voiced' Florence, now with 'hair turned to silver', on her second and final trip to England since leaving in 1904. In the article Florence, who feels 'death's shadow hanging over me', states she has only one objective to her visit, 'to effect a reconciliation with members of my family, if that be possible. To that end I am trying to clear myself of the charge of murder of which I was convicted and sentenced to death.' The journalist had met Florence some time after the first interview and found her desolate after being rebuffed by the family. 'It is bitterness worse than death. . . . All the years that have passed since that terrible day when I heard the verdict of guilty I have longed for my children, who were but babes at the time, and the mother hunger in my heart was so strong that I felt I must make this journey now in the hope of seeing them.'

Florence had not seen her children from the moment of her arrest, nor had Gladys or James (Bobo) ever been in contact. Raised under the influence of their paternal uncles, their alienation from their mother would have sprung from the conviction that she was indeed guilty of murdering their father. Sadly, in the case of James, who died in April 1911 (after accidentally swallowing cyanide in mistake for water while working in Canada), no reconciliation would have been possible anyway. A few weeks after his death, Florence had told the *Chicago Daily Tribune*, 'This boy has been dead to me for more than twenty years.' Why, then, did Florence talk of making this journey in 1927 in the hope of seeing 'them'? Was she referring to another child? Remote or not, the possibility that William Graham was her son could not yet be eliminated.

On 1 August 1994 Melvyn Fairclough, now looking for a birth registered in Hartlepool rather than Liverpool, unearthed William Graham's birth certificate. He had been born on 9 January 1879, when Florence was fifteen. Florence, however, was not registered as the mother, whose name was given as Alice Graham, formerly Spence. If Florence were the mother and Adam Graham the father, Feldman reasoned that she would need to have been in England in early 1878.

No one had seemed more surprised than Anne at her father's suggestion. Even so, she was beginning, for the first time, to become intrigued in the Diary story. She had long denied any interest in Jack the Ripper, but the possibility of a family connection had begun to fuel her interest in Florence Maybrick and from this period Feldman would increasingly call on her to help with his Liverpool-based research. Her first task, on 1 August 1994, the day after Feldman's telephone interview with her father, was to visit Liverpool cemetery to establish a date of death for her father's younger brother, Harry (Henry) Graham, who had died as a child.

Shirley Harrison and her team now knew all about Anne's story. Soon they would try to investigate it for themselves. But though Anne now held the key to the future of the Diary, Michael Barrett had not been forgotten. Shirley Harrison, Doreen Montgomery and Robert Smith were still receiving regular late-night calls from him. On 2 August 1994, just three days after presenting Paul Feldman with his 'evidence' of forgery, Barrett wrote a letter to Harrison, giving a very different account of the Diary. The letter reveals the extent of his alcoholism during this period and the emotional impact of the family separation, particularly from Caroline. Written in a shaky hand (Barrett says that without the help of a bottle of Sicilian wine, it would be totally unreadable), and with appallingly bad spelling, he expresses contrition over the damage he has done: 'I never ment to hurt you, Anne, Caroline, my familly and Doreen and all. I owe every one a big appoje (God my spelling is terrible). Funny thing I always whonted to be a writer, but I never had it in me. It was allways Anne who ended up writing articals, that had my name on (and there were very few). Anne was the one who allways had the idears (she did not however write the Diary). Tony relly give me it.'

Facing the possibility of death – the doctor at the Windsor Unit had apparently told Barrett that he would not make Christmas if he carried on – he tells Harrison that he has only ever been in love with one woman in his life and that will never change. His feelings for Caroline were never in doubt. 'They were my world. But my world fell apart. I miss them both so much.' He will apologise to them all in person. 'I am sorry I let everyone down.'

He had also let himself down. While his confession must undoubtedly have impacted on sales of the Diary, his total income from it to date was significant. Sadly, little appeared to have been retained. On the same day that Barrett wrote to Harrison, his agent Doreen Montgomery was writing to give him a breakdown of the cheques that had been sent either to his bank account or to him and

Anne personally (the latter amounting to £2,000). By 2 August 1994 the sum was over £47,000. It was, Montgomery felt, 'quite alarming' if Barrett had nothing to show for it now.

Shirley Harrison was now urgently trying to research the latest twists in the story before the deadline for her paperback. It was proving a nightmare. With just weeks to go, she had first to react to the terrible damage that Barrett had done and now had to speedily evaluate and research the astonishing news from Anne and her father. Indeed, at this point Feldman was not even allowing her access to Billy Graham. Her frustration is recorded in a memo to Robert Smith, dated 8 August 1994, written after speaking to Keith Skinner.

Skinner, she informed Smith, had echoed her own sentiments: 'I am very, very sad because I think Paul is committing suicide with his refusal to allow anyone else access to Billy or Anne,' she quoted him as saying. Harrison was concerned that, as it stood, 'any outsider could blow Anne's story to pieces'. She would not waste time researching the story without first speaking to Anne and her father: 'If her story is true she has nothing to fear from me at all. If her story is not true then she is in trouble. But in this case truth will out.'

'I also said [to Skinner] that we all desperately want this story to be true – and that we are all, in our ways, wanting to protect Paul's investment by making sure his revelations are supported.' Harrison's concerns about Feldman acting as researcher himself were also made clear. 'I will not conduct interviews via Paul because his technique is utterly amateur and taints his material. Nor will I support the story in public even though I think it may be true. But Paul's behaviour makes me less and less sure.'

The same day Harrison's irritation with Feldman was again aired in a memo to Keith Skinner. Two or three weeks previously, when Feldman still believed that Anne Graham was descended from James Maybrick's illegitimate line, a contact Harrison had 'nursed' at the British Legion in Liverpool had received a telephone call from 'some bloke' in London, saying he wanted to get in touch with Anne and that he had found a link between the Diary and

Anne and Billy. He also said he could make Anne a millionaire. Harrison was 'less than happy about this conversation, and the way the waters around my contacts have been muddied'. More importantly, 'this kind of talk in a community like Liverpool is appalling . . . besides which it shows the way that Paul has been talking to Anne and contaminates the Diary'.

In discussion with Keith Skinner, Harrison and Sally Evemy were formulating a plan of research to help them deal with the latest developments concerning the Diary, even as the first proofs for the paperback were being prepared. But, as Harrison wrote to Robert Smith, 'this is utterly useless until Sally and I have met Anne. We must speak not only to her but various members of the family. Paul surely must realise that whereas we will treat her gently, the Press will not. She'll be torn to shreds and I am not prepared to defend her story unless I have heard it from her own lips and made up my own mind.'

Having made himself a vital witness in the Diary story, Billy Graham knew he would have to face further questioning. Now he agreed to another face-to-face interview with Paul Feldman, this time with Keith Skinner in attendance, to be held on Saturday 13 August 1994. Feldman had told Anne he needed Skinner present 'as an objective witness'. This time Anne decided it would be easier for her father if the interview took place at his sheltered accommodation. Skinner, who arrived at Anne's flat before Feldman, soon became aware of the pressure she was under. 'During the time before Paul arrived,' Anne recalled, 'Michael rang the doorbell and as I thought it was Paul I answered the intercom without checking out the window as was usual. Michael became abusive over the intercom and I had to take the fuse out.'

Anne, Feldman and Skinner then drove to Graham's sheltered accommodation for the interview. Again, Anne recalls, she instructed Feldman that her father could not be questioned for more than an hour. While Anne cleaned up in the kitchen, Skinner was finally able to press her father on a number of points he had picked up from the transcript of the first interview. This transcript itself was to create serious problems as it had been rapidly prepared by Paul

Feldman's secretary from a tape that was difficult to comprehend and was then circulated by Feldman as evidential support of his breakthrough. Few people, if any, could understand or follow what they were reading (the tapes were later painstakingly transcribed in February 1996 by Keith Skinner and Anne Graham).

Skinner was particularly interested in the identity of the nurse or 'skivvy' from Battlecrease House who was a friend of Elizabeth Formby, Graham's step-grandmother. Billy revealed that she would have been 'fifty-odd' at the time of these visits (Alice Yapp, whom Feldman believed it was, would have been in her late fifties at this point). Skinner elicited more information on the Diary itself. It emerged that when Graham came home from leave in 1943 (he had joined the army in 1933), he recalled seeing a tin box in his room upstairs that he had never seen before. Inside was the Diary. 'But I seen this book and I just seen very small print and I just put it down – didn't want to know.' Then, on Christmas Day 1950, his stepmother brought the book plus Graham's and his father's birth certificates and gave it all to him. Skinner picked up the discrepancy. Had he first seen the Diary in 1943, not 1950? Graham assented. In 1943 his father and Uncle Billy were also living at the house. When Graham returned after the war, they had moved on but still had the tin box.

Graham also expanded on the rumour that Florence had an illegitimate child. 'Yes, well, they used to talk about her in the shops and all that: she had a kid before she was married and all this. It was a terrible thing in them days – you had to turn your face to the wall if that happened to you. You were condemned right away – you were an outcast after that.' Questioned by Feldman, Graham appeared convinced they would discover that Florence Maybrick was in Hartlepool in 1879. Feldman and Skinner then concluded the interview and said their goodbyes. There were still areas that needed expanding, still questions to answer, but that would have to wait until next time.

Not everyone was delighted by the new provenance. With the paperback version of Shirley Harrison's book due in October, Doreen Montgomery, as she wrote to Paul Feldman on 17 August

1994, was anxious that he wasn't presenting the media with another opportunity to ravage the Diary. 'The fact that Billy – and Anne – have made these revelations, does NOT make them kosher! You have to take on board the extreme scepticism of the Press – and public – and my acute anxiety is that they will not accept the statements at face value. Indeed, why should they?'

For Shirley Harrison, time had run out. On 9 September 1994 the paperback edition of *The Diary of Jack the Ripper* went to the printers without her being able to question Billy Graham. It was a serious omission but one that she could do nothing about. 'Shirley wanted to meet my father,' Anne wrote later, 'and interview him with Sally and Keith, and I did try to arrange a visit, but he was getting weaker and was suffering a great deal of pain and was also undergoing long visits at the hospital and in the end it was just not possible.'

Harrison had, anyway, formed an opinion of Anne's story. 'I am very much inclined to believe her,' she wrote to Doreen Montgomery on 30 August 1994, 'largely because she says she thinks Paul's linking her family to the Maybricks is "bullshit" and she is much more inclined to think it was passed by the servants to her great great [*sic*] granny Formby. If Anne were on the make – or spellbound by Paul – I think she would be supporting the other story.' Anne was not, Harrison told Montgomery, impressed by Feldman and had told him so. 'She says he makes her head spin and she doesn't understand what the hell he's talking about.' Anne, she said, had also discovered that Barrett had put a detective on to her (Harrison had not believed Barrett when he told her this information). 'He's probably promised a share of the megamillions,' she believed.

Despite Harrison's initial scepticism, Barrett had indeed employed a private detective, former Liverpool policeman Alan Gray of Proctor & Collins Investigations. The original commission, according to Gray, came on 14 August 1994 and was to search for Anne. This particular job would, Gray says now, last for two weeks, though soon afterwards Barrett would employ him on another matter altogether. This timing, however, is curious. Barrett knew precisely where Anne was on 13 August, as Keith Skinner had been told about him shouting through Anne's intercom on that date and Gray's commission seemed to end at just about the time that Anne, at least temporarily, moved out of Barrett's range. Towards the end of August she was found a house to rent by a locally based housing trust, a consequence, she says, of her estranged husband's 'constant harassment', and she was able to move her father in to live with herself and Caroline. It was at this point, too, that she decided to revert to her maiden name.

For a couple of months, at least, Anne had gained a precious respite for her father and daughter. Back in London, researchers might be feverishly trying to put flesh to the bones of the Graham family's revelations, but Anne was determined to keep the Diary at bay: '. . . I wanted Caroline to have a happy environment and not to have to dodge newspaper reporters, which had happened in the past. I was sick of the pressure Michael was putting on us with his nocturnal visits and drunken aggression and the reports he had initiated in the newspapers.' For protection, she says, she turned to Paul Feldman. 'Paul was very good and managed to fend people off as I was not prepared to answer questions and give explanations while I was trying to nurse my father.'

Genuine or not, Graham's provenance had been more than timely for Paul Feldman. While the New Line film deal did not demand a warranty that the Diary was authentic, Anne had had to sign a 'Grant of Rights and Assignment', saying she was the sole surviving descendant of James Maybrick. Paul Feldman maintains to this day that New Line were solely concerned with protecting rights and not interested as to whether the Diary was written by James Maybrick. Doreen Montgomery, as she wrote to Shirley Harrison, was not impressed. She understood that Anne was to sign an affidavit to confirm that the Diary was by James Maybrick. And while Paul Feldman had told Robert Smith that the rights clause should never have gone in, who, Montgomery wondered, had put the thought in New Line's head in the first place?

Anne's story would unquestionably give the Diary a new lease of life after her husband's damaging confession of forgery. But neither had helped the financial well-being of those involved with the Diary. If Anne had been forthcoming at the outset with her current declaration, Doreen Montgomery wrote to Michael Barrett on 31 August 1994, none of the *Sunday Times* affray would have occurred and Robert Smith would not have been given such a 'whacking great legal bill'. Barrett did not escape either, Montgomery telling him that he had to accept responsibility for his statements to the *Liverpool Post*. It was a serious matter.

Two days later a royalty statement was drawn up for Barrett that perfectly summed up the current situation. Of total royalties due of £53,218.82, Barrett's 50 per cent share of £26,609.41 had been reduced by legal expenses of £24,223.27; by his share of the Word Team's (Shirley Harrison and Sally Evemy) expenses to 10 July 1993 of £2,105.77; and by Doreen Montgomery's commission of 10 per cent – £238.61 and VAT of £41.76, to the grand sum of precisely nothing.

The statement, with an accompanying letter of explanation from Doreen Montgomery, was sent to Michael Barrett on 13 September 1994. She was anxious that he understood that Shirley Harrison had received equal billing for expenses; indeed, she had borne the expenses up to the publication of the hardback, some £9,864.18, entirely on her own. Should the film deal go through there would be money enough to settle outstanding bills and start afresh but in Barrett's own interests, she advised, he should allow Rupert Crew to pay certain amounts into his account each month. 'I don't want to keep on harping on the amount of money you have got through,' she told him, 'but I do have to say that £40,000-odd is a considerable sum and I just can't bear to think of it having been wasted.' After asking him not to speak to the press, as they wanted release of the new story to coincide with publication of the paperback, Montgomery added her pleasure that Barrett was now on board again. 'I am so glad, incidentally, that you now feel that the picture told by Billy and Anne is a true one. Thank God for that.'

Surprisingly, the new account of the Diary's provenance would stay secret until fairly near the publication of the paperback. In an article in the *Sunday Telegraph* on 25 September 1994, under the heading 'Could This Crucifix Finally Solve the Ripper Mystery?', the recent developments were brought into the public arena, but with an added twist. Not only did the article cover Billy Graham's story, but it also quoted Paul Feldman's latest belief – that a crucifix given to Anne by her father could once have belonged to Mary Kelly, the last and youngest of the Ripper victims.

The article looked in some detail at Feldman's claims for the Graham link with Florence Maybrick, including information that had recently come to light from two different sources that Florence had indeed been in England in 1878 and 1879. Another recently uncovered nugget was also included. After Florence's death, her address book was found with all the entries beginning with G ripped out. But what of the crucifix?

At the same time as Billy Graham claims to have given Anne the Diary, in 1989, he also gave her a crucifix, left to him, like the Diary, by his stepmother Edith in 1950. Nothing had been thought of the crucifix until Feldman discovered that it could quite possibly be the same as those worn by the Sisters of Mercy nuns at the Providence Row convent, Spitalfields, where Mary Kelly had once lived. Today nuns at the same convent, the paper reported, still wore a slightly smaller version of the highly distinctive 4-inch silver and black cross, which featured a skull and crossbones. Feldman claimed the coincidence was another sign that Maybrick was the Ripper, who liked to bring back mementoes from his victims: 'The crucifix tells us that there's a clear link between the Diary and Whitechapel.'

Robert Smith was still dealing with the fall-out from the last bout of bad publicity. Those in both Diary camps had been furious at what they saw as the irresponsible attitude of the press when it came to reporting Michael Barrett's alleged confession. In a letter to a *Sunday Times* reader, on 3 October 1994, Smith aimed his venom at the *Sunday Times*, for the hugely damaging article written by Maurice Chittenden. 'They know the true circumstances of the confession – I spent an hour on the phone with Chittenden beforehand, and so did several other people. I told him about the watch, but he didn't want to know. He also ignored a medical report from Fazakerley Hospital, Liverpool, on Mike's state of mind.'

It wasn't the best of environments in which to launch the paperback version of Shirley Harrison's *The Diary of Jack the Ripper*. Michael Barrett's 'confession' had seen the Diary nose-dive in the credibility stakes, and Harrison had not had time to mount a proper investigation into that or even to deal with Anne and Billy Graham's new story. A vital opportunity had been missed. Nevertheless, when the book was released in paperback on 6 October 1994, it soon became clear that the level of public interest in the Diary, in the UK and US at least, had not diminished in the period since the hardback first brought the Diary to world attention. Some 13,000 copies were to go on sale nationwide, 'a very high number these days', Robert Smith informed Doreen Montgomery. Jack the Ripper was still news. The Diary was still alive. Just.

SIX

'Oh costly intercourse'

In normal circumstances a book about the possible identity of Jack the Ripper would result in a flurry of publicity, a healthy dollop of sales and, occasionally, the odd howl of derision, before its author shuffled off centre-stage to make way for the next interloper. These were not normal circumstances. By rights, Michael Barrett's confession should have been the final nail in the coffin, but the Diary was not like other Ripper theories. It soon became clear that the publication of the paperback edition of Shirley Harrison's book was not going to be the end of the story. Somehow, despite the scepticism and, occasionally, outright hostility from certain quarters of the media and many Ripperologists, the public were not so dismissive. Within a few weeks the paperback had sold 10,000 copies and gravitated to the best-sellers list. Without the various contributions of Barrett, the *Sunday Times* and its more vociferous critics, the Diary, proven or not, would surely have topped the list, and not just in the UK. Include the vast potential of the US market and the overall loss of revenue becomes enormous. Add to that the increasing tension between Paul Feldman and Melvin Harris, accentuated by the film deal with New Line, and it was no wonder that feelings were running so high. The pressure to prove or disprove the Diary had never been so intense.

A few days before the paperback edition hit the shops, Michael Barrett had thrown another considerable spanner into the works. Towards the end of the journal, after the murders of the five generally acknowledged Ripper victims had taken place, the author had slipped what appeared to be a direct quotation into his work:

Sir Jim will cut them all
Oh costly intercourse
of death

The first line, not untypically for the Diary, had been crossed out. But where did the second and third lines come from? They seemed to be lines of poetry and not, judging by the quality of the doggerel otherwise offered, of the author's creation. Harrison and her team had trawled through several anthologies of poetry but failed to find an answer. On 30 September 1994 Martine Rooney, Paul Feldman's assistant at Duocrave, took a telephone call from Michael Barrett. He had discovered the source of the quotation.

Keith Skinner, a few weeks later, would interview Martine Rooney to clarify what had been said. According to Rooney, Barrett told her that he was sitting with the book in front of him. She later realised that he must have seen the real version because he knew that the Diary was wrong: 'Oh costly', he told her, correctly as it transpired, should have been written, 'O costly'. The significance of the telephone call, however, went far beyond the fact that Barrett had been the first to reveal the source of the quotation. As far as Rooney could recall, Barrett was claiming that his awareness of the source was proof he had forged the Diary. How else, he asked her, could he have known it? On hearing of Barrett's find, Feldman's reaction was to dispatch Carol Emmas and Anne Graham to Liverpool Central Library to see if they could find the author of the quotation, whom Barrett had still not identified. It would prove a fruitless search.

On 3 October 1994 Keith Skinner learnt for the first time of Barrett's discovery when he received an answerphone message from Shirley Harrison. 'Mike seems to have found "Oh costly intercourse of death" – quite by chance. Is in the *Sphere Companion to English Literature* Vol 6, MB thinks – did not even make a note of it!' Three days later, on 6 October, came confirmation of the quotation, when the library faxed Harrison the relevant pages from the anthology. Interestingly the author of the Diary had made another mistake:

143

> O costly intercourse
> Of death(s) and worse,
> Divided loves . . .

The poem from which these lines were taken is called 'Sancta Maria Dolorum' and it was written by Richard Crashaw, a seventeenth-century English poet. Ironically, if the Diary really were the work of James Maybrick and he was an admirer of Crashaw's, the two would prove to have something in common. Crashaw also died an early death and, like Maybrick, it was suspected that he was poisoned.

Intriguingly, Paul Begg would later discover a more tangible link. Crashaw's father William had been appointed to St Mary Matfellon (the white chapel from which Whitechapel takes its name) in 1618 and Crashaw appears to have lived in the area from the age of five until at least thirteen. Though ranked with other religious poets of the calibre of John Donne, Crashaw was not exactly a household name. How had Michael Barrett managed to track down a line from a poem by such an obscure poet, little known outside academic circles? Not surprisingly, there would be several different explanations.

Initially, according to Harrison, Barrett said that he had found the quotation by chance, which would have been an extraordinary piece of luck. Paul Feldman, however, claimed Barrett told him that he had asked 'everybody at Liverpool Library whether they knew the source' (indeed, Feldman suspected that Barrett had written to several university English departments for the answer). Skinner received a fuller version of events in a conversation with Shirley Harrison on 11 October. Barrett, she said, had been upset by remarks in the paperback, an early copy of which he had read in late September, which had described him as an alcoholic. Determined to show that this was an unfair description, and to prove how resourceful he could be, he then spent a week in Liverpool Library trying to find the source of the quotation.

A day later Shirley Harrison left another message on Keith Skinner's answerphone. The story had just become more complicated. To

Harrison's dismay, Barrett was now claiming that a copy of the Sphere volume containing the relevant quotation had actually been in his possession long before the Diary had been brought to public attention. Not only that, she told Keith Skinner, but Barrett was using this fact as proof that he had forged the Diary.

Harrison phoned Barrett's friend Jenny Morrison, who corroborated his story. It seemed that after the Hillsborough Disaster of April 1989, when ninety-six Liverpool football supporters were crushed to death at an FA Cup semi-final, Barrett had decided to help raise money towards the appeal. Among a number of publishers he contacted to donate books for selling were Sphere Books, who sent several volumes from their literary criticism series, including a volume containing an essay on Crashaw. Deciding that these books were too academic for sale, Barrett put them in the attic and forgot about them. During the summer of 1994 Barrett had taken them around to Morrison's house in case her teenage son found them useful for his studies (though in the end they proved unsuitable). Barrett, Harrison claims, had told her that he only recalled possessing these books after finding the quotation. Barrett also told Harrison, on 12 October 1994, that he was seeing his solicitor that very afternoon, and was taking the Sphere volume containing the quotation with him.

For those who believe that Michael Barrett was involved in forging the Diary, the Crashaw quote is a key piece of evidence – the kind of evidence that Alan Gray, the private investigator that Barrett had employed back in August, was actively seeking in order to help him sell his forgery account to the newspapers. On 7 November 1994 Gray recorded a meeting with Barrett in which the subject of the quotation is raised. By this stage Gray, who clearly believed Barrett's forgery claim, was becoming frustrated at the lack of solid evidence he was able to find to back the claim. The two men were at Barrett's home at 12 Goldie Street and were soon to set off to visit the auctioneers where Barrett said the blank journal in which the Diary was written was obtained. Barrett claims that he created the Diary on his word processor from Tony Devereux's original research, but that the handwriting was Anne's.

Anne might be denying this but there was, he told Gray, a vital piece of evidence to prove the forgery. 'And another thing Anne forgot,' he claims, 'is, "O sweet intercourse of death".' 'What does that mean?' Gray asked. 'Did you write it?' Barrett told Gray he was missing the point. Gray did not appear at this stage to realise the significance of the quotation. 'Show me something on paper with the proof,' he told Barrett. Barrett then showed him something, which Gray reads.

Gray: 'I found it in the lodge – [Amends to] in the library?'
Barrett: 'Do you know where I found it?'
Gray: 'That's what you said on this paper you've given me. Is that your handwriting? You were drunk when you wrote this?'
Barrett: 'Go to my solicitor and my solicitor will find it – he will give you – and you're dealing with my solicitor – he will give you a document copy.'
Gray: 'A document copy of what?'
Barrett: 'Page 130, nobody could find "O sweet intercourse of death". "Chickens running around with their heads cut off. Chickens running around with their heads cut off", which I wrote. Nobody, nobody could find, "O sweet intercourse of death". And the only person who could find "O sweet intercourse of death" was myself.'

Barrett then insisted that he told Paul Feldman 'months ago, I mean months, that "O sweet intercourse of death" was a fucking phoney'. He went on to emphasise that the book containing the source of the quotation was lodged with his solicitor, but Gray was focused on visiting the auctioneers.

Barrett had other things on his mind at this stage, too. Alan Gray reported him as being infuriated by Anne Graham's divorce action. This was to have other repercussions too. Anne's solicitors, Deacon Goldrein & Green were now investigating Anne's rights regarding the Diary. Anne, Doreen Montgomery explained to them on 10 October 1994, was not a party to the publishing agreement between her husband and Shirley Harrison, though she was to the collaboration agreement. Furthermore, had Anne volunteered her recent statement regarding the provenance of the Diary at the outset, as the provisions of the collaboration agreement demanded, it might have prevented the hugely expensive legal battle with the *Sunday Times*, two-thirds of the costs of which were borne by Harrison and Barrett. In the light of this, and of Barrett's 'confession', Montgomery believed that Shirley Harrison's costs and lost agency commission should be underwritten by the Barretts, 'before any sums are payable to Mr Barrett or Mr and Mrs Barrett'. At the moment, in any case, 'there are no sums to their credit'.

The next day it was the turn of Barrett's solicitor, Richard Bark-Jones. 'Barrett', Montgomery wrote to him, 'continues on a destructive course. I have no idea how we can stop him, or prevent him damaging his own cause, as well as ours. And, at the same time he continues his quest for money, acting as if it were his due, despite the fact he has caused such chaos for his publishing partners.'

That was not the way Michael Barrett saw it. Listening to a tape of him and Alan Gray, made on 24 October 1994, it is clear that Barrett believes he is the victim of exploitation. The tape begins with Alan Gray waiting for Barrett to emerge from the offices of his solicitors, Morecrofts, where he has been discussing the royalties he believes he has been denied. When Barrett does come out, the two wait in Gray's car for a journalist from the *Independent* to turn up for an interview which Barrett says has been pre-arranged. Barrett is hoping the journalist will pay him for his story so he, in turn, can pay Gray. The *News of the World* has already withdrawn an offer to buy Barrett's story, he tells Gray, who is clearly worried that Barrett is saying too much to these papers.

Gray then drives Barrett back to 12 Goldie Street, after it became clear that the man from the *Independent* was not going to appear. Barrett promises to show Gray how he forged the Diary. 'Have you perpetrated a fraud?' Gray asks. 'Yes, no question of that. I've proved that beyond doubt,' Barrett replies. Leaving Barrett's house, Gray, who is off to 'make further enquiries', records that, 'he's pouring his heart out now. They're all having a go at him. He's fed up with it and he's making a clean breast of this terrible, wicked forgery and it is wicked to involve the Maybrick family. . . .'

Whatever money he had or had not received, Michael Barrett was clearly broke. Worse, he now stood to lose 12 Goldie Street. On 31 October 1994 the matter reached court. A letter sent to the court by Barrett's solicitors, Morecroft, Dawson & Garnett, on his behalf, claimed that Smith Gryphon were withholding royalties from their client that presumably might make up the deficit in his mortgage payments. Robert Smith was having none of it. In a letter faxed to the Bristol & West, Barrett's building society, to be read out in court, he denied holding back any royalties to Barrett. 'I confirm that we gave a full account of all the royalties due to the authors of *The Diary of Jack the Ripper*, Michael Barrett and Shirley Harrison, together with a cheque in settlement of £9,428.93 including VAT on 5th September. I understand that after deduction of monies owed by Mr Barrett to his co-author, there were no monies available to Mr Barrett.' Smith did have some good news on the financial front. Smith Gryphon had received the sum of £70,000 for the purchase of the film rights to the Diary. The bad news was that Barrett might not receive his share before the end of June 1995.

Morecroft, Dawson & Garnett were still not convinced their client was getting his due. The same day they dispatched a letter to Doreen Montgomery. Michael Barrett had informed them that £12,000 had been received by Smith Gryphon for the video rights of the Diary. Could Montgomery confirm receipt of this sum and let them know when Michael Barrett would get his share?

As far as Barrett himself was concerned, he told Alan Gray on returning from court, there was no doubt about the matter. 'They're taking me to the cleaners.' His solicitor, he said, would be entering litigation to reclaim the money owed to him. Meanwhile Barrett had twenty-eight days to come to some arrangement over the house. Back at 12 Goldie Street, Gray's attempts to extract some solid evidence for Barrett's forgery continued. He had been talking to some contacts in the newspaper world but now he and Barrett had to find ways to prove the forgery. He quizzed Barrett on a couple of promising points. Where, for instance, did he find out about the initials on the wall behind the body of Mary Kelly? From *The Jack the Ripper A to Z*, Barrett replies. As for the name Mrs Hammersmith and the idea of the two murders in Manchester, they were purely 'my imagination', Barrett claimed.

To the evident disappointment of Alan Gray, who had been pursuing openings, Barrett was now anxious to avoid talking to the newspapers while litigation was being pursued. He was also increasingly fearful of Paul Feldman, telling Gray that he had been threatening him, actually telling Barrett that it was not beyond his capability 'to get a couple of scousers to fill me in'. Gray was concerned that Barrett had told him the ink used in the forgery was Quink, not Diamine as he said now. 'You got it wrong, did you?'

A few days later Barrett's finances were on the mind of Doreen Montgomery, who wrote to Morecrofts to explain the current financial situation regarding the Diary. Barrett had gone through 'as much as £40,000 during the year in question, apparently with nothing at all to show for it. In fact, the imminent loss of his home tells its own sorry tale. And, of course, it is a tangible fact that Mr Barrett has undermined the whole sales potential of this book, world-wide, by his press comments, albeit hastily retracted.'

At last came good news for the Diary. At the recent Frankfurt Book Fair a press release from Smith Gryphon announced that the Diary's publishers, in association with MIA Productions (Paul Feldman), had concluded a deal with New Line Cinema for the film rights to the controversial *Diary of Jack the Ripper*. The director would be William Friedkin (best known for *The Exorcist* and *The French Connection*, for which he won an Oscar) and one of the illustrious names being mooted for the lead role of James Maybrick was Jack Nicholson. The release could be as early as the end of 1995. According to Robert Smith, negotiations had been prolonged owing to the controversy over the authenticity of the Diary. 'However, after investigating all the evidence including the latest revelations published in the paperback of the Diary, New Line were convinced and rapidly concluded the outright purchase of rights in the title for a high figure.'

Meanwhile, despite the recent publication of the paperback, Harrison was still actively researching the Diary. In November 1994 she received from magazine publishers D.C. Thomson copies of three articles that Michael Barrett had written for their *Celebrity* magazine in 1988. If Barrett had written the Diary, he would have needed more literary ability than his correspondence had hitherto shown. Could these articles cast any light on his potential in this area? Barrett's editor at D.C. Thomson, David Burness, confirmed that Barrett was a valued contributor: 'As I told you, Mike was always very reliable in the time he worked for me. I'm so sorry that his life seems to have gone so desperately wrong.'

Having implicated himself, Barrett was obviously suspect number one for the alleged forgery. But there were some who considered that his estranged wife was better qualified for the job. By agreeing to undertake some research for Harrison, Anne Graham did herself few favours in this regard. On 2 November 1994 she sent Harrison a one-page report on the history of the Hillside Laundry Company in Peel Street, Liverpool, where Elizabeth Formby (Billy Graham's step-grandmother) had once worked. Harrison was exploring the possibility that it was here that a member of the Maybrick household had handed over the Diary. Anne's efficiency alerted suspicion. Writing to Keith Skinner after reading the report, Ripper expert Martin Fido declared himself 'flabbergasted' that it was not the work of a professional researcher. A consistent sceptic towards the Diary, he was now surprised that she would ever have 'let such a badly researched and misspelled document [as the Diary] go out!' Worse, from Anne's point of view, he now believed she could have concocted the basic story of Maybrick as the Ripper 'with one hand tied behind her back'.

Shirley Harrison was too concerned with the erratic behaviour of Michael Barrett, however, to worry over any possible encouragement she might have given to those who believed Anne Graham was the forger. She was one of a number of those in the Diary camp who would regularly receive long, rambling and sometimes abusive telephone calls from Barrett, often clogging up their answerphone tapes, and 3 November, it seems, was a particularly bad day. Barrett began, Harrison later wrote to Doreen Montgomery and Robert Smith, at about 7 a.m., telling her that he had reported Anne as a missing person to the police and that they were coming to see him. Harrison rang the local police to tell them Anne was not missing but suggested a visit to Barrett would be helpful. Soon after, Barrett was on the telephone again to say he was meeting the *Sunday Mirror* outside his solicitor's office that very day with 'all the evidence'.

At 10 a.m. Barrett was on the telephone again, sobbing uncontrollably with the news that his father had just died and he was organising the funeral. Harrison rang his priest, who was unable to shed any light: 'He was utterly fed up with Mike and could do nothing.' During the night 'it all started again, from four onwards. He was aggressive and unpleasant. I said, "You should be thinking of your mum" and he said "Don't worry about that". He was off to the newspapers . . . etc., etc.' So disturbed was Harrison that she rang the police and reported 'harassing phone calls'. At 9.45 a.m. Harrison rang Paul Feldman who, she discovered, had been receiving similar calls: 'Mike had been alternating between us.' When Harrison rang Barrett's sister Lynn a few minutes later, she learnt that Barrett's story about their father dying had been 'confabulation'.

Harrison and Feldman were not the only ones getting alarming calls from Barrett. On the morning of Sunday 6 November 1994, as he recorded on tape that day, Alan Gray received a very worrying message from Barrett claiming that his door had been kicked in during the night. Terrified, he arranged to meet Gray some distance from his house, near the Everton football ground. It is clear from Barrett's taped voice that he was genuinely alarmed. He told Gray that he was asleep in his bedroom at the back of the house when, around 3 a.m., he was woken by a banging on the door and windows. He was convinced that Paul Feldman had 'promised to blow me away'. Gray tried to reassure him, promising to investigate before both men made a full report to Walton Lane police station. He was, however, annoyed to learn that Barrett had already rung Shirley Harrison, who he believed was 'in cahoots' with Paul Feldman. Now Feldman would be alerted.

According to Harrison, in a memo written the next day to Robert Smith and Doreen Montgomery, Barrett told her he was living in a state of fear as a result of several death threats from Feldman, who, he alleged, had threatened to 'break his head' and get a Liverpool gang on to him. However, having reached 12 Goldie Street, Alan Gray could see no new damage to the front door, though he confirms that Barrett had showed him some slight damage to the paint. The two men duly reported the matter to Walton Lane police station, where a police constable promised to convey the message to a Detective Abrahams. Barrett told Gray that he heard the threat (he believed there was just one man involved), 'I am fucking well going to fucking kick you, Barrett.' Gray believed they were putting the frighteners on him. 'They are doing a good job,' said the clearly terrified Barrett.

At Barrett's house Gray continued his quest for solid evidence after being given the 'worst cup of tea' he had ever had in his life. He had tried several times to take possession of a compass that Barrett claimed was part of a job lot with the Victorian journal he had bought at the Liverpool auctioneers. When he asked again, Barrett was evasive. 'Don't start grinning at me,' Gray cautioned him, 'you're either with me or not.' Later, Gray was to be told that the compass was given to Barrett's sister Lynn, who threw it away to protect him. However, if pressed by Gray, she was likely to deny doing this, as she would wish to protect their mother.

The day was not wasted, though. Gray saw the name 'Dorothy Wright', which Barrett had written on the tape of an interview he conducted with the clairvoyant for *Celebrity* magazine. Suddenly there was an excited edge to his voice: 'By Christ, I've seen that Y somewhere else,' he told Barrett. 'I haven't seen that in the Ripper Diary manuscript, have I? By Christ I've tumbled you at last. You wrote the manuscript.' Now, surely, it will be easy to prove. 'Doesn't anybody understand?' complained Barrett.

Unfortunately, having accepted that it was his handwriting, there was still a problem for Barrett. 'You said Anne did it,' Gray said, 'you're still saying it's all her handwriting.' Barrett now said that it was fifty-fifty. 'And we can prove that?' Gray asked.

The first page of
James Maybrick's
will, dated 25 April
1889, and
described in 1891
as 'written in a
large shaky hand',
which proved so
controversial in the
Diary debate.
(*Evans/Skinner
Crime Archive*)

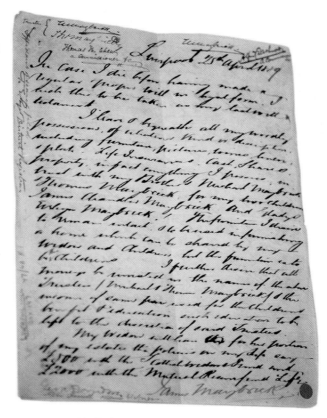

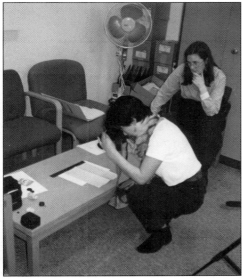

Liverpool-based researcher Carol
Emmas, of Paul Feldman's team,
photographing Maybrick's original
will at Somerset House, London,
on 23 October 1995, watched by
Tess Tippling, record keeper at
Somerset House. (*Evans/Skinner
Crime Archive*)

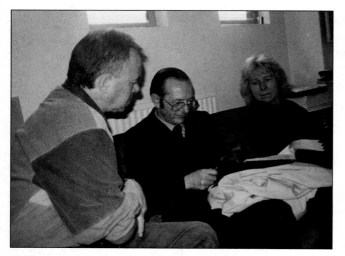

Alec Voller (centre), head chemist at Diamine Ink, examines the Diary at the London offices of Smith Gryphon Publishers on 20 October 1995, as Martin Howells, who wrote and co-directed Paul Feldman's video on the Diary, and Shirley Harrison look on. Voller stated that the ink used was not Diamine, as some critics had claimed. (*Evans/Skinner Crime Archive*)

Document examiner, Maureen Casey Owens, of the Rendell team, studies the Diary in Chicago in August 1993. Kenneth Rendell, whose report would brand the Diary as a fake, looks on. (*Robert Smith*)

The Diary awaits testing at the Department of Colour Chemistry at Leeds University in November 1994. (*Evans/Skinner Crime Archive*)

Ripper author and historian Donald
Rumbelow (left) and *Ripperana* editor
Nick Warren, at the Grey House book
launch. (*Ed W.G. Chick*)

Below: Leading Diary sceptic, Melvin
Harris (left) and TV presenter and true
crime aficionado Jeremy Beadle, in the
kitchen at Camille Wolff's house during
the launch of Grey House Books' *Who
Was Jack the Ripper?* on 25 January
1995. (*Ed W.G. Chick*)

'Bluff and Bluster?' Paul Feldman points
the finger at Melvin Harris during their
legendary confrontation over the
authenticity of Maybrick's will at
Camille Wolff's house. (*Ed W.G. Chick*)

Two copies of the *Sphere History of Literature, Volume 2* (near centre of picture), photographed in situ at Liverpool Central Library, in which Michael Barrett claimed to have discovered the source of the controversial 'O costly intercourse of death' quote used in the Diary. (*Evans/Skinner Crime Archive*)

Mike Barrett has, on occasion, claimed that he ordered this red diary with forgery in mind, but, more recently, because he wanted to compare the appearance of a standard Victorian diary with the Maybrick Diary given to him by Tony Devereux. (*Evans/Skinner Crime Archive*)

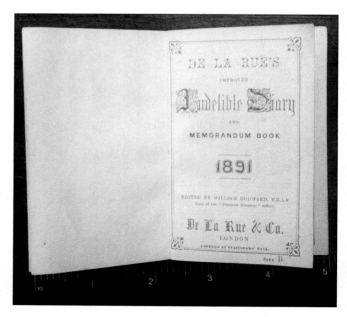

‘I am Jack’, ‘J Maybrick’ and the initials of the Ripper victims, scratched inside the Maybrick watch. (*Albert Johnson*)

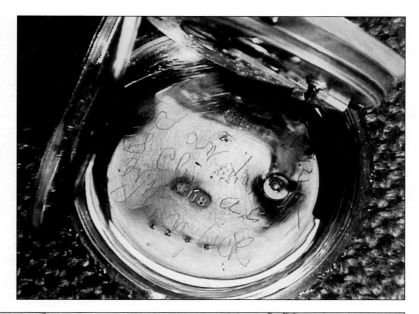

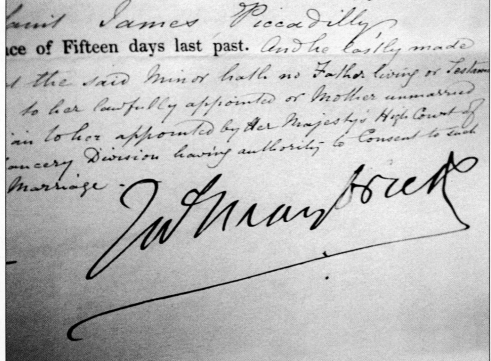

James Maybrick's signature on his marriage licence. (*Evans/Skinner Crime Archive*)

Shirley Harrison questions Mrs Murphy of Stewarts the Jewellers in Wallasey, Merseyside, where Albert Johnson bought the Maybrick watch. (*Evans/Skinner Crime Archive*)

From left to right, Albert Johnson, owner of the Maybrick watch; Robert Smith, original publisher of the Diary; Shirley Harrison, author of *The Diary of Jack the Ripper* and Ripper author and researcher Melvyn Fairclough, being questioned at the 2001 Jack the Ripper Conference in Bournemouth. (*Manon Rosat*)

Private detective Alan Gray (left) with his employer, horologist and Diary sceptic Stanley Dangar at the latter's house in Spain in 1998. (*Janet Dangar*)

Albert Johnson and his wife Valerie at the Bournemouth Ripper Conference. (*Robert Smith*)

Albert Johnson's younger brother Robbie, whose tragic death in Spain in 1995 would spark rumours of murder. (*Peter Cavanagh*)

From left to right, Peter Jepson, Anne Graham, Annie Jepson, Paul Feldman, Shirley Harrison and Brian Maybrick at a gathering of the descendants of the 'Peterborough Maybricks' held in that town in November 1994. (*Paul Feldman*)

Barrett now provided Gray with a more detailed background to his forgery claim. The initial cause, he said, was the death of Billy Graham's second wife Maggie on New Year's Eve 1987. After Maggie's death, Anne wanted to move near her father, who would now be alone. Consequently, they moved across the city and bought 12 Goldie Street, exchanging a low housing association rent for a large mortgage (and a deposit of £600). Not only was there now a 'crippling' financial pressure but Barrett was not happy in the new neighbourhood. He was therefore incensed when, no sooner had they moved across the city, 'disrupting our lives', than Billy moved into sheltered accommodation. In order to address their financial problems, Barrett formulated a plan, to which Anne assented: they would forge the diary of Jack the Ripper. Now they had done it, she didn't want to know him. He had sacrificed everything and had been 'left in the shit to defend myself'.

The first challenge was to find a new candidate for Jack the Ripper. Maybrick, a wifebeater and 'bastard', was a perfect candidate. Barrett offers the fact that his grave was desecrated in 1962, apparently as proof of his low standing. 'Who did that?' Gray asks. 'You told me Devereux did that.' Barrett confirms that. Devereux, he says, was obsessed with the Ripper. They both decided that Maybrick was the ideal candidate. Then Devereux died in June 1990 (actually August 1991) when they were 'all getting into it'. Devereux had given Barrett his research, which Barrett then checked for himself. Barrett created the Diary on his word processor and Anne then wrote it into the journal. He promises to specify which sections he wrote himself (ones she had been having trouble with) later. The money needed to buy the journal – £50 – was donated by Billy Graham. When the forgery was completed, they sought a literary agent and made the phone call to Doreen Montgomery.

Alan Gray was still anxious to seek out actual proof of this story. The next day (this being a Sunday) they would get samples of the Diamine ink used, the pen and nibs, which Barrett said would cost no more than 50p. Barrett also observed that the kidney-shaped stain on the cover was his work, to signify his own kidney problems.

The following day, 7 November, Gray arrived at 12 Goldie Street to take Barrett to the auctioneers Outhwaite & Litherland to confirm how the journal was bought. He was not pleased to discover that Barrett had reverted to the claim that Anne wrote all the diary. 'You've not got to be seen as telling any more lies. You got to be seen as telling the truth,' Gray cautioned him. Outside Outhwaite & Litherland Fine Arts Auctioneers and Valuers, in Fontenoy Street, central Liverpool, Barrett confirmed to Gray that this was where the journal was bought, in the name of Williams. There was a problem with the timing, though. Barrett initially claimed this was in 1987. 'Now, we've had another date. We had 1990 the other day,' Gray reminded him. However, while Barrett tried to work out the correct date, the conversation moved on. It now transpired that Anne alone, not Barrett, bought the job lot which included the journal and compass. How, Gray wondered, did Barrett discover that a Victorian journal was for sale?

Barrett: 'Sheer bloody luck.'
Gray: 'You walked in here . . .'
Barrett: 'No, no, no, we can trace it in actual fact. . . . em, how did I find out? . . . when it really comes down to it, it was sheer bloody luck.'

Barrett, apparently forgetting his explanation of the previous day, then informed Gray that the kidney shape on the cover of the Diary is actually a stain from a real kidney dropped on it by Anne. Barrett was intent on going into the offices to check the auctioneers' records but Gray felt it was not the time, especially given Barrett's current state. 'To get them to look into records,' he said, 'we will need some pretty heavy guns. It has to be done professionally with a phone call and follow-up.' Barrett eventually agreed, though he told Gray that he had been three times before to check and on the second occasion the girl in the office confirmed the name Williams and their address were on record. Having established the auctioneers, Gray felt it was time to leave it for the day; they would make an official approach to confirm Barrett's account later.

Alone, drinking heavily and facing the imminent repossession of his house, Barrett was hardly enjoying the fruits of his alleged forgery. He also claimed to believe that his life was under threat from Paul Feldman. His wife Anne, despite their early differences, saw Feldman in a very different light. In fact, she did not believe she would have survived the trauma of the last few months without him. 'He has been continually criticised for keeping me under wraps,' she wrote later, 'but very few people knew what was happening. I heard rumours that he had paid huge amounts of money for my story, and that my father was in a private nursing home – paid for by Paul of course and that Caroline and I were living in London. Rubbish! The truth was that my father was dying of cancer of the oesophagus and getting worse every day. With the help of my stepbrother's wife and the support of district nurses we nursed him around the clock. It was a heart-breaking process to watch and wasn't helped by the pressure put on me by Michael, who although he had not found our new address was not above going to the hospital when my father was admitted and harassing him there, and continually telephoning my friends and writing to my father's old flat.' It appears from the taped conversation between Alan Gray and Barrett on 7 November 1994 that Barrett had still not traced Anne's new address on that date. He was getting closer, though, having discovered (correctly) that it was a housing association house and the name of the road it was off. Sometime in the next few days, Anne now said, Barrett would finally track her down.

In early November Paul Feldman decided to host a 'conference' of the Peterborough Maybricks (allegedly descendants of James Maybrick through an illegitimate line) and also invited Anne, Shirley Harrison and Albert Johnson. During this weekend Anne received a call from Liverpool to say her father was dying. By the time she reached the hospital, on 12 November 1994, Billy Graham had died of a massive heart attack. 'Paul, Shirley and Keith came to the funeral,' Anne wrote, 'where the vicar had arranged a police presence as Michael had telephoned some of my friends and told them he intended to disrupt the service.'

From the separation from Barrett in early January 1994, through the personal repercussions of his confession, going public with her own account of the Diary's background and now the death of her much-loved father, it had been a traumatic eleven months for Anne. The death of Billy Graham also meant that there was now no other corroboration for Anne's account of how she obtained the Diary. This would become an increasingly important matter, with financial and even legal ramifications. Although Paul Feldman insisted that he had not needed a new provenance for the Diary to complete the film deal with New Line, it clearly remained an important factor, as revealed by Robert Smith's letter to Doreen Montgomery on 28 November 1994. Warning Montgomery that the first batch of royalties on the recently released paperback would not be high, Smith had decided to hold back the money due to Harrison, Barrett and Anne Graham on the sale of film rights (the agreement with New Line had finally been signed on 19 September). Due to an ongoing campaign conducted by the Committee for Integrity, a group set up by Melvin Harris to expose the truth about the Diary, it was not impossible that New Line's money could be retracted.

Robert Smith was particularly worried about the two men at the heart of the conflict: 'The situation between Feldman and Harris worsens and Harris has made it clear to me that his major campaign is to persuade Richard Saperstein at New Line that Feldman has duped him. With both Feldman and Harris threatening to sue the other for libel, there is a nasty situation.' However, there was hope, Smith maintained, of Harrison's various scientific investigations proving Harris wrong and he had a *Sunday Telegraph* journalist standing by to publish should that be the case. Should such scientific proof materialise, he was happy to release the money. However, 'if it ever turns out, as Harris claims, that Feldman paid Anne money to make her story up for the benefit of persuading New Line to sign the Agreement, then we will be needing the best legal advice available. I'm not sure that our innocence would be enough to protect us.'

Doreen Montgomery was still doing battle with Barrett's solicitors, Morecrofts, who were anxious to reclaim what they believed was his rightful share of royalties from the video and the expenses which they claimed were wrongfully deducted from the book royalties. Replying to Morecrofts on 30 November, she pointed out that Shirley Harrison had only recently asked Michael Barrett to settle his 50 per cent of all her research and writing expenses. But he 'apparently has not a single penny to show for all the money which has been paid over to him'. As a result, it was decided that deductions would have to be made at source. Barrett was 'certainly not a victim at our hands'. She also pointed out that the money Morecrofts referred to was not for the video rights (already paid) but for the sale of film rights (which Robert Smith would that same day confirm to Morecrofts as being for £70,000), and it had not been received by Smith Gryphon in time to be included on their end-of-year statement.

During all of this the Sphere book had not been forgotten. According to an account given by Alan Gray to the authors in December 2002, the *Sunday Times* had shown some interest in Barrett's story but wanted to see some solid proofs:

Mr Harris then contacted me for the *Sunday Times* and asked for the book [the Sphere volume] to be produced. It was some time before Barrett got around to this mainly because he was in debt to the solicitors and was keeping out of sight. The other thing was that I was working on several other cases and could not give any priority to Barrett. So it was not until Tuesday December 6th [1994] that I met him outside his solicitors in Dale Street and he went in and brought out the Sphere book and handed it over to me. I do not know just how long it had been there since it is not proper to ask solicitors such a question without their client being present to give permission and Barrett was out of favour at that time.

Melvin Harris's alleged campaign to encourage New Line to terminate the film rights purchase agreement was given its first public airing in the 'Londoner's Diary' section of the London *Evening Standard* of 8 December 1994. Allowing that few documents had stirred the public imagination like the Diary, the article announced (wrongly) that CNN, 'the excitable American television station', had paid in the region of £1 million for the film rights. 'This', it continued, 'could prove to be a costly mistake for New Line Films, the CNN subsidary. For I hear that Harrison and her publisher Robert Smith (of Smith Gryphon) have decided to conduct tests to determine the age of the ink used in the Diary – a decision reached after hearing allegations that the ink contains a preservative first marketed in 1974.' Melvin Harris, whom the article named as the man responsible for instigating the ink tests, was absolutely sure of his ground. 'There is now no doubt whatsoever that they [*sic*] are a recent fake,' he claimed. 'The identities of the three people involved in the forgery will soon be made known.'

The *Evening Standard* returned to the subject of the Diary in a full-page article written by journalist Mark Honigsbaum on 13 December 1994. 'The chilling signature of a mass killer, or a brilliant forgery? The battle of words over the latest Ripper "disclosures" is getting more brutal by the hour' ran the introduction. Harris's promise to disclose the identity of the forgers was again mentioned (a claim Harris later said should have been preceded by the words 'it is hoped that'), as was Harrison's renewed attempt to authenticate the Diary scientifically. The article also had a stab at identifying the rather grandly named Committee for Integrity, which, it revealed, comprised various Ripperologists, some of whom had once been part of the Diary team, plus handwriting experts and scientists. The nature and extent of the committee's membership would itself become a matter of controversy in succeeding months. That Melvin Harris was at the helm, however, seemed indisputable.

'Hardly a month passes,' reported Honigsbaum, 'without a new revelation from Harris, purportedly proving that the journal is a fake. His latest is that ink in the Diary contains chloroacetamide, a modern preservative agent first marketed in 1974. He claims Mike Barrett has admitted faking the Diary with Diamine, an ink he bought in Liverpool containing chloroacetamide. Moreover, when Harris had both the Diary and a sample of Diamine tested by independent analysts in October both tested positive for the preservative. QED, the journal is a modern forgery.'

But the Diary team, Honigsbaum reported, had also subjected the ink in the Diary to further tests, this time at Leeds University's

Department of Dyeing and Colour Chemistry, where they had failed to find any trace of the preservative (though, it should be noted, their first test had found a trace, which was put down to contamination). Furthermore, when the Leeds team compared the journal to two documents from the 1880s they found the inks were identical.

The article ended on a disturbing note, revealing that Michael Barrett was apparently in a critical condition having recently severed an artery while attempting to break into Anne's home in Liverpool. With a macabre sense of humour, it contrasted this with a quote from the Diary: 'I have not allowed for the red stuff, gallons of it in my estimation. Some of it is bound to spill onto me.'

After the outright assault from the *Sunday Times* and the sceptical tone of the earlier 'Londoner's Diary' piece, this article was one of the few to give both sides of the Diary debate a hearing since it was first published. Still it did not go far enough for Shirley Harrison. Not only did the Diary camp have doubts over the extent of the Committee of Integrity, but, as Harrison made clear in a letter to freelance journalist Paula Adamick just after the article appeared, she felt that the Integrity part of the title should also have been questioned. 'Melvin's entire *raison d'être*,' she wrote, 'is de-bunking and destroying. He's become a very vindictive character.' Harrison was also upset at the article's assumption that Robert Smith and not she, was footing the bill for the further scientific testing.

The independent analysis referred to in the article, in which six ink/paper dots were examined, was conducted by Analysis for Industry, whose director is Dr Diana Simpson. On 11 December 1994 Shirley Harrison wrote to her, enclosing the results from the Department of Dyeing and Colour Chemistry at Leeds University, who had 'repeated your tests and performed a number of investigations on my behalf. I enclose a copy of their results for your interest. As you will see these are at variance with your own findings. This is a puzzle. We have no reason to doubt your conclusion, so we think it may be fair to suggest that you have the opportunity to test ink from the diary itself.'

Harrison also wrote to the very first expert she had commissioned, David Baxendale, to offer him an opportunity to look at the Diary again. She informed him that after ten days the Leeds scientists had concluded that 'there was no chloroacetamide but that there was no nigrosine either and that the ink was without doubt an iron-gallotannate ink. They also said the ink was extremely difficult to remove from the paper or to dissolve in solvent.' A few days later Robert Smith wrote to the editor of *Ripperana*, Nick Warren, querying whether another test for chloroacetamide was necessary. 'Alec Voller [then Research Chemist for Diamine Ink] tells me that there needs to be nitrogen present if chloroacetamide is in the ink. Leeds say there was no nitrogen in the Diary's ink. Nick Eastaugh also found no nitrogen.'

So much had happened relating to the Diary in recent months that the watch had, once more, been relegated to a bit part. But not everyone had forgotten it. 'I am still in contact with Mr Johnson about the watch,' wrote Texan collector Robert E. Davis to Shirley Harrison on 13 December 1994, 'and he has promised me first refusal if he decided to sell it. I think his main hesitation lies with the fact that there seems to be considerable question concerning the diary.' Davis was still promoting his interest, directly to the Johnson brothers, a month later, when he faxed them a copy of a letter he had written to the US publishers of Harrison's book, Hyperion, saying he was willing to offer a substantial sum for the watch. 'Please do remember,' he wrote to the brothers, 'I am still interested in buying the watch or being a part owner with you, in order to keep the watch available for future research, and to display it publicly in Liverpool.'

Though it was now well over a year since the failed legal action against the *Sunday Times*, the financial repercussions were still creating discontent. Robert Smith and Doreen Montgomery had long been at loggerheads as to whether the publishers or the authors (Harrison and Barrett) were mainly responsible for the extensive legal costs. On 16 December 1994 Montgomery reluctantly confirmed acceptance of two outstanding legal invoices, providing the lawyers' supporting documentation accorded with Smith's claim that this reflected Harrison's and Barrett's involvement only. However, Montgomery felt that it was totally unrealistic for the whole legal cost to be appropriated to her clients, when viewed in proportion to their revenue. In future, no legal expenditure involving her clients was to go ahead without prior agreement from them and her.

Despite their different standpoints, Melvin Harris and the Diary camp were still in communication, as the current wave of ink testing confirmed. At the beginning of 1995 Harrison sent Harris the reports from Leeds University to examine. It is clear from Harris's characteristically combative reply that he was not impressed. 'Thank you very much for sending me the copy of the reports from Leeds. Unfortunately these reports are fatally flawed, thus your optimism is quite unjustified.' That was just for starters. In a ten-page critique of the Diary, Harris unfavourably contrasted the methods of the Leeds team with his chosen experts, Analysis for Industry. He accused Harrison of misunderstanding the Leeds team when she claimed they saw no difference between the Diary ink and ink contained in two Victorian documents. He also gave several instances of where the Diary 'hoaxers' had blundered, both in terms of known facts about the Ripper and in regard to the life of James Maybrick. He concluded:

Accept this, therefore, as a positive contribution towards reaching the full truth in this matter. Don't let your personal feelings stand in the way of reaching that goal. I, and my colleagues on the committee, are prepared to cooperate fully and freely, without prejudice, in order to make known the real facts in this case.

Melvin Harris now had the Diary firmly in his sights. According to handwriting expert Reed Hayes, who wrote to him on 4 January 1995, he had heard from Sue Iremonger that Harris was now involved in a project to set the record straight on the Ripper case, 'now that new information had come to light'. Hayes too would now describe himself as a disbeliever of the Diary's authenticity, although at one point he had thought it 'quite possibly genuine'.

However, he felt there were two main points against this: the questionable provenance and the lack of similarity between the Diary handwriting and that in letters sent to the police at the time of the murders. Hayes, he told Harris, had been contacted initially by Paul Feldman, who 'attempted, with my assistance, to discredit Maybrick's will'. However, his findings were reported inaccurately in Shirley Harrison's book. Although it was possible that the will and Maybrick's marriage certificate were not signed by the same person, Hayes could not reach a conclusion on the will's authenticity based on signatures written some eight years apart. However, Hayes had stated verbally to Paul Feldman that if Maybrick were dying of arsenic poisoning at the time he signed the will, the signature 'should have shown signs of tremor or weakness, which it does not'.

Melvin Harris, though, was not the most dangerous threat to the Diary. That distinction now belonged to Michael Barrett. If the Diary camp were glad to see the back of the 'crazy year' of 1994, they would not have to wait long to see that 1995 was not going to be an improvement. With the year just a few days old, back leapt Barrett into the fray with his fullest and most damaging version of events yet. In a five-page affidavit, sworn on 5 January 1995 in the Liverpool offices of solicitors D.P. Hardy & Co., he drew a picture not just of a forgery conspiracy which now included his estranged wife and Tony Devereux but of another and much more sinister conspiracy – of which he himself was the victim. It was more or less an amplified account of what he had told Alan Gray back in early November 1994.

Apparently incapacitated after his attempted break-in at Anne Graham's house, which might, he had been informed, result in the amputation of two fingers, Barrett, who gave his occupation as author and former scrap metal dealer, got straight to the point. 'Since December 1993 I have been trying, through the Press, the publishers, the author of the book, Mrs Harrison, and my agent Doreen Montgomery to expose the fraud of the, [sic] *The Diary of Jack the Ripper* ("the Diary"). Nobody will believe me and in fact some very influential people in the publishing and film world have been doing everything to discredit me and in fact they have gone so far as to introduce a new and complete story of the original facts of the Diary and how it came to light.'

Barrett's statement was a complete repudiation of Anne's story; indeed, it wasn't all that dissimilar to the rather sparse initial confession he had made to Harold Brough when the forgery had appeared to be a one-man effort and he was not able to say where he had found the ink and journal. He now revealed that the handwriting in the journal belonged to Anne, either from his typed notes or dictation. The idea, it seemed, had come from discussions between Barrett, Anne and Tony Devereux after Barrett had decided such a hoax would be possible and that James Maybrick would be the ideal candidate. 'He was not "Jack the Ripper" of that I am certain but, times, places, visits to London and all that fitted. It was to easey [sic]. I told my wife Anne Barrett, I said, "Anne I'll write a best-seller here, we can't fail".'

Serious consideration was given by Barrett to the necessary materials, papers, pens and ink. A red leather diary was purchased by Anne for £25 from a firm in the 1986 *Writers Year Book* but when it arrived in the post Barrett decided it was too small to be of use. Anne had since requested and been given the red diary by Barrett. Armed with £50 from Billy Graham, Barrett claimed he had bought the blank journal used for the Diary from the auctioneers Outhwaite & Litherland. Given that this would be the most detailed account of how he claimed to have forged the Diary, and how hotly contested by the Diary camp it would be, it is worth reproducing this section of his statement in full. (We have retained the original spelling throughout.)

It was about 11.30am in the morning when I attended at the Auctioneers. I found a photograph album which contained approximately, approximately 125 pages of photographs. They were old photographs and they were all to do with the 1914/1918 1st World War. This album was part of lot no. 126 which was for auction with a 'brass compass', it looked to me like a 'seaman's compass', it was round faced with a square encasement, all of which was brass, it was marked on the face, North, South, East and West in heavy lettering. I particularly noticed that the compass had no 'fingers'.

When the bidding started I noticed another man who was interested in the itmes he was smartly dressed, I would say in his middle forties, he was interested in the photographs. I noticed that his collar and tie were imaculate and I think he was a Military man.

This man bid up to £45 and then I bid £50 and the other man dropped out. At this stage I was given a ticket on which was marked the item number and the price I had bid. I then had to hand this ticket over to the Office and I paid £50. This ticket was stamped. A woman, slim build, aged about 35/40 years dealt with me and she asked my name, which I gave as P. Williams, Allerton Street, Liverpool 17. I think I gave the number as 47. When I was asked for details about me the name Williams arose because I purchased my house from a Mr P. Williams, the road name I used is in fact the next street to my mum's address, 17 Buckland Street, Liverpool 17.

I then returned to the Auction Room with my stamped ticket and handed it over to the assistant, a young man, who gave me the Lot I had purchased. I was then told to return my ticket to the Office, but I did not do this and left with the Photograph Album and Compass. When I got the Album and Compass home, I examined it closely, inside the front cover I noticed a maker's stamp mark, dated 1908 or 1909, to remove this without trace I soaked the whole of the front cover in linseed oil, once the oil was absorbed by the front cover, which took about 2 days to dry out. I even used the heat from the gas oven to assist in this drying out. I then removed the maker's seal which was ready to fall off. I then took a "stanley knife" and removed all the photographs, and quite a few pages. I then made a mark "kidney" shaped, just below centre inside the cover with the knife.

This left 64 pages inside the Album which Anne and I decided would be the Diary. Anne and I went to town in Liverpool and in Bold Street I bought three pens, that would hold fountain nibs, the little brass nibs. I bought 22 brass nibs at about 7p to 12p, a variety of small brass nibs, all from the 'Medice' art gallery. This all happened late January 1990 and on the same day that Anne and I bought the nibs we decided to purchase the ink elsewhere and we decided to make our way to the Bluecoat Chambers, in fact we had a drink at the Empire Pub in Hanover Street on the way.

Anne and I visited the Bluecoat Chambers art shop and we purchased a small bottle of Diamine Manuscript Ink. I cannot remember the exact price of the Ink. I think it was less than a pound. We were now ready to go and start the Diary.

So much for the preparation. Barrett now went on to describe the forgery itself. Having decided on a trial run using A4 paper, they decided that Anne should write the Diary as Barrett's handwriting was too distinctive. After two days they felt able to 'go for hell or bust'. Barrett had already drafted a rough outline of the Diary, over a few days prior to obtaining the necessary materials for the forgery. Now, over a period of eleven days, Barrett worked on the story and then dictated it to Anne who wrote it into the photograph album. 'Thus,' Barrett stated, 'we produced the Diary of Jack the Ripper. Much to my regret there was a witness to this, my young daughter Caroline.'

According to Barrett's statement, while he and Anne were writing the Diary, Tony Devereux was housebound and very ill: 'In fact after we completed the Diary we left it for a while with Tony Devereux severely ill and in fact he died late May early June 1990.' Barrett said that mistakes had been made during his dictation, giving as examples an ink blot on page 6 which they inserted to cover a mistake Anne had made in putting down 'James' instead of 'Thomas'. Barrett also named the source of the Diary quote, 'TURN ROUND THREE TIMES, AND CATCH WHOM YOU MAY.' This, Barrett stated, 'was from *Punch* Magazine, 3rd week in September 1888. The Journalist was P.W. Wenn.' He blamed Anne for the mistake in writing 'Oh' instead of 'O' in the quote from Crashaw and attributed another ink blot to Anne covering the letter 'A' which she had written down by mistake.

All but one of the original photographs, Barrett claimed, were given to Billy Graham. The one he kept back was 'of a grave, with a donkey standing nearby'. Furthermore, he said, all incriminating material – the one photograph, the compass, all the pens and the remainder of the ink – was taken by his sister Lynn Richardson to her home address, where, after reading her brother's confession in the *Liverpool Daily Post*, she destroyed everything in order to protect him.

The forgery, it appeared, was the easy part for Barrett. It was when Robert Smith took possession of the Diary (from July 1992 onwards) that it 'went right out of my control' and his problems began:

> There is little doubt in my mind that I have been hoodwinked or – if you like – conned myself. My inexperience in the publishing game has been my downfall, whilst all around me are making money, it seems that I am left out of matters, and my solicitors are now engaged in litigation. I have even had bills to cover expenses incurred by the author of the book, Shirley Harrison.
>
> I finally decided in November 1993 that enough was enough and I made it clear from that time that the Diary of Jack the Ripper was a forgery; this brought a storm down on me, abuse and threats followed and attacks on my character as Paul Feldman led this attack, because I suppose he had the most to gain from discrediting me. Mr Feldman became so obsessed with my efforts to bare the truth of the matter, that he started to threaten me, he took control of my wife who left me and my child and he rang me up continuously threatening and bullying me and telling me I would never see my family again. On one occasion people were banging on my windows as Feldman threatened my life over the phone. I became so frightened that I sort the help of a private detective, Alan Gray, and complaints were made to the police which I understand are still being pursued.

Even more controversially, Barrett now accused his estranged wife of working for Feldman against him: 'It was about 1st week in

December 1994 that my wife Anne Barrett visited me, she asked me to keep my mouth shut and that if I did so I could receive a payment of £20,000 before the end of the month . . . She insisted Mr Feldman was a very nice Jewish man who was only trying to help her. My wife was clearly under the influence of this man Feldman who I understand had just become separated from his own wife.'

The affidavit was concluded in the same way, with the exception of the name, as the Diary he claimed to have written: 'I give my name so history do tell what love can do to a gentleman born, Yours Truly . . . Michael Barrett.'

By some way this was the fullest account of his alleged forgery that Barrett would give. On the surface it sounded convincing enough, but was it? By this time Barrett would have had to hand all the information garnered from Harrison's own research, plus the conclusions of various tests on the ink and paper to help him create a convincing account. And, as Shirley Harrison recorded in her book, there were some obvious problems. Tony Devereux had not died in May 1990 but in August 1991. Could the red diary have played a part in the forgery? Anne Graham has a copy of a cheque she wrote to Martin Earl of H.P. Bookfinders in Buckinghamshire for the maroon diary to which Barrett refers. It is dated 18 May 1992, one month after Barrett had taken the Diary to Doreen Montgomery. According to Anne, it was Barrett who ordered it to see what a Victorian diary looked like and to compare it with the journal, and she was furious at the waste of £25. It would certainly have been a poor choice for a forgery. Apart from being far too small for the purpose, it is a diary for the year 1891, three years after the Ripper murders and two after Maybrick died.

What about Barrett's detailed account of buying the journal at the auctioneers? According to Shirley Harrison, Kevin Whay, a director of Outhwaite & Litherland, gave it little credence. Having searched through the company's files and archives on both sides of the alleged sale date, Whay confirmed that 'no such description or lot number corresponding with Barrett's statement exists. Furthermore we do not and have never conducted our sales in the manner in which he describes.' In a telephone conversation with Harrison soon after

Barrett's affidavit was made public, Whay went further. 'Anyone who tells you they have got a lot number or details for such an album from us is talking through their hat.'

There were other mistakes – the *Punch* journalist was Tenniel, not Wenn, for example. The first ink blot Barrett refers to covers the word 'regards', not 'James'. More controversially Alec Voller, who would examine the Diary on 30 October 1995, at a time when he was the research chemist for Diamine ink, gave his considered opinion that the ink used in the Diary was *not* Diamine as Barrett claimed. Nor did the Diary's handwriting look anything like Anne Graham's, though it would obviously have been possible for her to disguise it. Lynn Richardson would later react furiously to her brother's accusation. But if the devil might lie in the details, it was the bigger picture that made the impact. Now the Diary's critics had a full confession to work on. True or false, Barrett's statement would make life much harder for the Diary camp.

This did not appear to deter Paul Feldman. On 7 January 1995, two days after Barrett had signed this damaging affidavit, Feldman was the first ever speaker at the Cloak and Dagger Club, which would become the hub of British Ripperology. Based then in the heart of Ripper territory in London's Whitechapel, at the Alma, a pub decorated with murals and paintings of Ripper scenes and personalities, the club would quickly attract a large membership, all either fascinated by the Ripper or by the East End world in which he wrought his horror. At each bi-monthly meeting an expert in local history, an authority on the Ripper or the author of the latest book on the subject would address the audience. The club magazine, *Ripperologist*, covered the same issues, often in extensively researched and quite remarkable detail. Overall, it is safe to say, the large audience had not been impressed by the Diary. Feldman was stepping into the lion's den. Moreover, he was taking Anne Graham into it with him.

At the outset Feldman asked those who believed the Diary was genuine to hold up their hands, and was not surprised at the miserly response. But he was not a man to be easily intimidated. For the next hour he expounded on the reasons why he believed the Diary

was genuine. If it were a modern forgery, he insisted, the woman he
had brought with him must have helped compose it, possibly in her
living room, with her father Billy Graham, husband Michael Barrett,
Tony Devereux and Albert and Robbie Johnson, for the watch must
be part of the same conspiracy. They would, he said, have had to be
experts on ink, paper, Victorian language and handwriting as well as
on the known facts about the Ripper and the Maybricks. Moreover,
what luck they had enjoyed, when all the subsequent research by
himself and Shirley Harrison, including the discovery of a number of
journeys taken by Maybrick, had failed to find anything to
contradict the possibility that he had been the murderer. How had
the forgers, from a modest two-up, two-down in Liverpool,
discovered what Feldman claimed was Maybrick's habit of calling
himself 'Sir James'? Keith Skinner, Feldman maintained, had
discovered this snippet, from the letters of a young guest at the
Maybrick household, at Wyoming University in the States. No one
before 1970 had had access to this file. 'The person who really owns
this Diary,' Feldman announced dramatically, 'is in this room
tonight and has never had a penny, not one brass farthing from it.
I'd like to introduce you to Anne Graham, please give her a hand.'

A little nervously Anne took the floor to give her story.
Surprisingly, her reception was warm. Nor were the questions at the
end of the meeting particularly hostile, though some listeners might
still have been shell-shocked by the mass of information Paul
Feldman had woven into his talk. Indeed, at the end only one
member of the audience raised a hand to register their belief that the
Diary was a modern forgery. The argument focused not on recent
times but the possibility that the Diary might have been forged at
the time of the trial of Florence Maybrick in order to help win her
release from life imprisonment. Given the mayhem being created by
her former spouse, Anne Graham must have been more than a little
relieved at the way the evening had gone.

Michael Barrett had much to lose financially from his alleged
confessions. Had he kept silent, the sales of the paperback version of
The Diary of Jack the Ripper might have been considerably greater
and, indeed, he had been made aware that his statement was in

breach of the publishing contract he had signed. He knew, too, the potential damage he was doing to the sale of the film rights to New Line. If Barrett hadn't forged the Diary, why on earth would he concoct such a damaging story? One possible answer came within a fortnight of his sworn affidavit when the volatile Barrett himself gave a very different account of events. For those who maintain the Diary is not a modern forgery, this would be the most crucial interview Michael Barrett would give. The meeting, on 18 January 1995, was taped.

Barrett had assented to a meeting at his house with Keith Skinner, Shirley Harrison, Sally Evemy and a mutually agreed 'independent witness' – Kenneth Forshaw, an ex-Liverpool CID man of thirty-two years' experience – to discuss his sworn statement. It was clear from the outset that Barrett had no intention of defending his latest claim. On the contrary, he now announced that the forgery claims were false and that for the first time he would explain why he made them. It was, he repeats throughout the taped interview, a way of getting back at Anne. 'It's all about Anne and it's got to stop. This hatred between Anne and me. It's got to stop today, it's gone beyond a joke,' he tells Keith Skinner, the first to arrive at the house in Goldie Street. When Shirley Harrison follows soon after, with Sally Evemy and Kenneth Forshaw, Barrett is anxious to know if she will be seeing Anne afterwards. He has a private tape and letter he wants taken to her, which, he claims, defends both the Diary and her story. He pursues this request, with increasing vehemence, throughout the interview, until Harrison reluctantly agrees.

Barrett is anxious that the damage to his hand, now in traction, is photographed. It seems to be almost a symbol of the injustice he expresses. As he reveals later, the injury was the result of putting his hand through a glass panel at Anne's house after spending Christmas and New Year alone, not even wanting to be with the rest of his family. Throughout the meeting Barrett, who appears sober (though at one point he vainly tries to bargain for a quarter bottle of Scotch in return for information), returns again and again to his theme of betrayal. He displays great bitterness that Anne has not made contact with him since leaving in January 1994, that she has not tried to help him during his prolonged illness, that she withheld the 'truth' about the Diary from him for so long and, perhaps most painful of all, that she refused him permission to see Caroline. His hurt seems genuine. 'This,' he says, 'is what it's all about . . . the bloody Diary and everything else.'

It was his anger at Anne, he now claims, which caused his initial confession to Harold Brough in June 1994. 'Anne walked out on me on Jan 2. I have been by myself ever since. I've tried to contact her many times but she's refused to have any contact with me. Then, in May [sic], I got so pissed off I came out with this bloody false statement that I wrote the Diary, and it is a bloody false statement, because I wanted to get back at Anne, because after five months I still hadn't seen my daughter.'

Although Harrison and Skinner try to persuade Barrett that his confessions are having the opposite effect to the one he intends, and that the Diary and his relationship with Anne should not be entangled, he will not be diverted from his strategy. He shows little concern for those associated with the Diary team, and no argument can intrude on the personal sense of loss he expresses. Again and again his despair at being prevented from seeing Caroline rises to the surface: 'Now, I haven't seen my daughter for a year and that's a long time and that cut me deep and I mean it cut me deep and I don't give a damn for the Diary, the money or anything else. I just want to see my daughter, that's all I want.'

The revelation that Anne had withheld the truth about the Diary from him stung him almost as much. 'She kept the truth from me for four solid years,' Barrett shouts at one point, 'that was mental cruelty.' In stark contrast to the detailed account of forgery he had recently given, in which the Diary was written by Anne, he now talks of believing her story that the Diary came from her family. 'My argument is not that I don't believe her,' he says, 'I really do believe her story. My argument is this, why didn't she tell me in those four years when I was sitting at that glass table writing away, night in and night out, trying to find the identity of Jack the Ripper . . . I have an absolute right to know.'

171

He reverts to the original account he gave Doreen Montgomery, that the Diary was handed to him by Tony Devereux. He describes a terrible physical fight the couple had when she tried to throw the Diary in the fire to stop him getting it published. 'We had a bloody great blazing argument over that . . . I wanted to do something with it and I couldn't understand why she was having a bloody great blazing argument with me after all the bloody months of effort I had put in, months and months . . . I couldn't understand why all of a sudden she turned around and, "stop Michael" . . .'

He also gives an insight into pre-Diary life for the Barretts, describing the loss of self-esteem he felt at having to become a 'house husband' and how writing seemed to offer him a chance to 'make a contribution to the household'. He confirms Anne's account that she had to tidy up the celebrity interviews he wrote for the children's magazine (for which his interviewees included Bonnie Langford, Kenneth Williams, Stan Boardman and Jimmy Cricket), 'all the interviews, great, but could I get the articles out properly? . . . so, Anne stepped in and I felt she was taking something away from me.'

As to the alleged forgery, he claims that he named the shop where he bought the ink, the Bluecoat Chambers art shop, because it was the easiest to get to, though he didn't go inside. Did he, Harrison asks, have a receipt or lot number for anything he purchased at Outhwaite & Litherland? '126, there is no such lot,' he replies. 'I know there is no such lot', Harrison intercedes. 'I know because I made it up,' Barrett replies. 'Shirley, I was half cut with a bottle of Scotch at the time when I made up the number, it only goes up to 50.' If people believe that he is the forger, Barrett insists, more fool they. 'If it is a modern forgery I must be one of the world's greatest actors and one of the world's greatest experts and I'm not, I assure you, I'm a Liverpool man, a scouser.'

Barrett's abiding resentment and mistrust of Paul Feldman is another theme of the meeting. Feldman is blamed for taking Anne and Caroline from him and for threatening and blackmailing him. Poignantly he talks of the terrible damage the Diary has done to his life. 'Now, I was happy once. Everyone [here] has been in the house when it was a decent house . . . what in the bleeding hell went wrong? I'll tell you what went wrong – the bloody Diary. If Anne had come out with the truth in the beginning maybe none of this would have happened and we would have been ordinary people leading ordinary lives.'

Modern forgery or not, there can be little doubt about the Diary's malign influence on the Barrett household. Despite the money he had earned, Barrett had little to show for it, apart from a drawerful of bills and the imminent threat of eviction from his home. Painting himself as the man who discovered the identity of Jack the Ripper, he has, he says, ended up with, 'no marriage, no daughter, no money, no nothing'. But while he accepts the damage his claims of forgery have done to the status of the Diary, he will not desist until he can see Anne. The forgery claims, he insists, are his only leverage. 'I want to see Anne and if I don't see her I'll still say the bloody Diary is a forgery even if I can't prove it and I'll kick up more shit. I'll kick up all the shit in the world until I can see Anne.' These were not the words the Diary team wanted to hear.

It is hard to believe, listening to the tape of that meeting today, that Barrett's sense of hurt and anger is feigned. But is he telling the truth about the forgery claims? Does he really believe Anne's story that the Diary was in her family and that she gave it to Tony Devereux to give to him? Kenneth Forshaw, the independent witness, was clear on one thing: he did not believe Barrett capable of forging the Diary, he told Keith Skinner after the meeting. But could such a belief survive yet another change to Barrett's story?

Writing to Paul Feldman the next day, 19 January 1995, Keith Skinner described Barrett as

an embittered, broken man. He is genuinely devastated and bewildered regarding Anne's actions over the journal – and all these feelings of betrayal, loss, rejection, anger – when mixed with Scotch – drive him to make damaging statements about 'forging the journal', as a means of 'getting back at Anne'. He has openly, and in front of an independent witness, confessed this is the case – and his belief in the authenticity of the journal remains as intact as it was from the day he identified its author as James Maybrick.

After the meeting with Barrett on 18 January, Shirley Harrison, Sally Evemy and Keith Skinner did visit Anne Graham as promised, and this meeting too was recorded. Though not as dramatic in content as the interview with her estranged husband, it also covers important ground. If Anne's story were true, then she had kept the Diary, unknown to Barrett, in the family house in Goldie Street for some time. How, her interviewers wanted to know, was this possible? The Diary, Anne told them, was kept in their daughter Caroline's room, wedged behind a very heavy old-fashioned sideboard. Behind the sideboard was a ledge, in a small recess, and it was here, she claimed, the Diary sat, with Caroline's games beneath it and other possessions on top. Ushering Caroline in to confirm her description of the room, Anne maintains that, apart from the first few weeks in the house, when Barrett decorated the room, nothing was moved until she retrieved the Diary to give to Tony Devereux.

Given that she had, in the past, claimed to have little affection for the journal, why, Keith Skinner wanted to know, did she keep it? Was it anything to do with its potential monetary value? No, she answers: 'It had a historical value, which I was a bit reluctant to destroy. . . . I didn't like the bloody thing. I couldn't destroy it, but I wanted shot of it. I didn't want it in the house.'

Perhaps the most puzzling aspect of her story, though, was Devereux's apparent willingness to go along with her wishes, despite the fact the two barely knew each other. Anne was asking the world to believe that Devereux took the Diary from her, handed it on to Barrett and then suffered his ceaseless questioning, all without any subsequent recourse to her. What had his reaction been, when allegedly handed the brown paper parcel? 'A bit puzzled. He didn't question me . . . I was very jumpy, "Would you do me a favour?", when I get very nervous I giggle . . . 'would you just give it to Michael and tell him to do something with it.' That was practically it. He said he would do it. If he had said no, I'd have taken it back off him. I hadn't thought the situation out. Only when I was there I felt such a prat because I'd realised I'd done something silly.'

She can't recall if it was during the week or at the weekend, but does remember she had little time to spare with Tony Devereux, having told Barrett she was just slipping out to the corner store to get something. Her main objective was that Barrett would, unlike the celebrity interviews, achieve some kind of creative writing without help from Anne. Her hope was that Barrett 'would have been able to write a book around it or got someone else to write a book around it, a ghostwriter'. Above all, she says, 'I didn't want him to know it was from me.'

While Devereux was an established drinking friend of Barrett's, Anne says she barely knew him. They had met perhaps twice before she allegedly handed him the journal, first when introduced outside the British Legion club, then at the Saddle pub. She confirms that, despite the pressure Barrett claimed to put him under, Devereux never once rang her to complain. She also gives her own account of her attempt to destroy the Diary, which Barrett had brought up earlier in the day:

> I did try to destroy it. I had a big argument about it, a battle royal on the floor. He said he would make millions publishing it. I said, no, he must just do a story on it. He was bewildered at that attitude. It's not very easy when you're telling a load of lies to cover up with an explanation. I'm not that devious. I wanted to be subtle, not suggest things, not lead him, but it didn't work out that way.

Devereux's lack of communication after being given the Diary to hand over to Barrett was just one aspect of Anne's story that some found puzzling. Her indifference to the Diary from her first encounter with it as a teenager also worried people, especially given her stated interest in history. She was, she tells Harrison, Evemy and Skinner, eighteen when she first saw the Diary in 1968 and even then the name Battlecrease House registered. This is probably as a result of conversations she heard in the house as a child, she says, when local history, including the Maybrick case, would have been discussed by her parents and maternal grandparents (who lived with them). It was her sense of history, she says, which would have prevented her throwing it away, even if she didn't like it.

Anne says she has always believed that the Diary was stolen from Battlecrease House by one of the servants and given to Billy Graham's step-granny Elizabeth Formby. She had not discussed the Diary with her father since she first saw it in 1968/9 and did not believe his interest in it was any greater than hers. Though he had a copy of Shirley Harrison's book, it was kept on top of the wardrobe and was never read, though, she is sure, Barrett would have shown him the journal. She recalls a sense of shock during the interview with Paul Feldman when another possibility was mooted by her father:

> I was not aware of any family link. That absolutely took me by surprise . . . he'd worked it out. I didn't think he knew anything about it. I don't know how long he was thinking about, he certainly didn't get it from me . . . even now, I couldn't say when Florence was born. I couldn't have done it like him, off the top of my head. It must have been there and just came out. I was totally flabbergasted.

Asked for a sample of Billy Graham's handwriting, Anne produces a betting slip which was probably written shortly before his death on 12 November 1994 (see illustration). She also creates a sample of her own writing at various speeds: 'I will rhondeveau [*sic*] with you at the Post House.' (There appeared to be no similarity between these two samples and the writing in the Diary.)

While the two people at the centre of the Diary story were giving their accounts, the man leading the campaign to prove the Diary a modern forgery was still not in a position to name the forgers. Melvin Harris had told the *Evening Standard* back in December 1994 that it was hoped that those responsible for forging the Diary would 'soon' be named. In a letter to Shirley Harrison, posted the day of these Liverpool meetings, Harris revealed this would not be possible: 'As for the identity of the forgers, at this point this is simply avoiding the real issue. There are papers dealing with this in the hands of the police, as a consequence I am not entitled to say or write anything more on this matter.' Harris believed that if the Diary

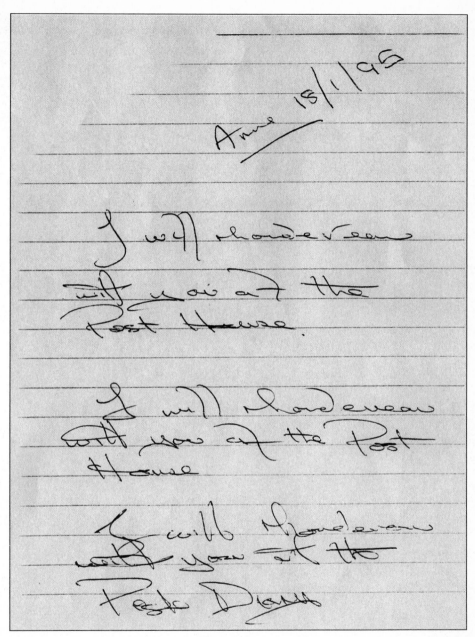

Anne Graham supplied these samples of her handwriting (she wrote the three sentences of varying speeds) in the presence of Keith Skinner, Shirley Harrison and Sally Evemy on 18 January 1995.

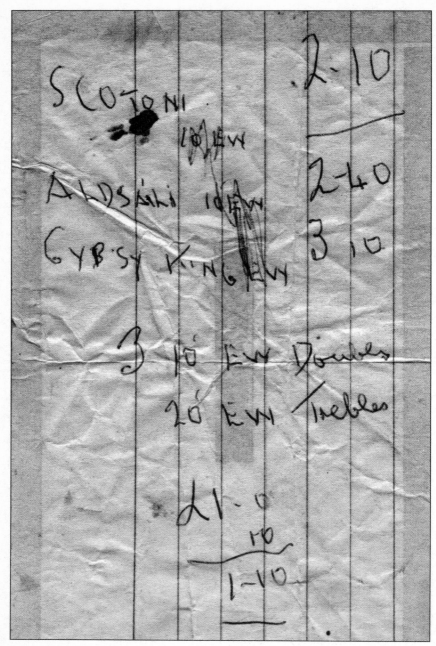

A sample of Billy Graham's handwriting, probably written shortly before his death on 12 November 1994.

could be proved a forgery: there was no need, anyway, to name the forgers. Harris urges Harrison instead to look at aspects that will prove the Diary to be a forgery. 'But the business of the will and the test for the preservative (chloroacetamide) are pressing matters and no one anywhere is restraining us from bringing to light the truth about the handwriting and the ink. Shall we move forward on this?'

The answer to that was no, at least, not together. 'Now that a considerable element of personal abuse has entered your correspondence, and in view of your statement that you cannot name your alleged "forgers" because "there are papers dealing with this in the hands of the police" it seems inappropriate to pursue our dialogue further at this stage,' Shirley Harrison immediately responded.

The meeting between Michael Barrett, Shirley Harrison, Keith Skinner, Sally Evemy and Kenneth Forshaw appeared to have brought Michael Barrett back to his original story. Or so the Diary team thought. But five days afterwards Barrett revealed a dramatically different account of the meeting than the taped conversation appears to show. In a further affidavit, sworn on 23 January 1995, Barrett declared that his four visitors 'tape-recorded everything that was said and the truth is I felt overwhelmed by their presence and I had nobody present to advise or support me'. He went on:

> It was made clear to me that if the Diary was genuine I would be paid all monies due to me by the publisher Mr Smith in June 1995. I was frightened by the situation because I didn't really know which way to go, run or jump, the inducement of money in June 1995 led me to agree with Ann [*sic*] Barrett's story. I backed it 100 per cent. It's still a forgery. The truth of the matter is I have already informed the police it is a forgery, that is the 'Diary of Jack the Ripper', and I have also made a sworn affidavit that the Diary is a forgery.

After describing an alleged physical attack on him by a relative of his estranged wife, Barrett concludes, 'I am not a well man. I am sick, confused at times and under pressure constantly from Ann [*sic*] Barrett, Robert Smith, Shirley Harrison and Feldman, they never let up.'

(Keith Skinner, who was responsible for taping the meeting, strenuously denies there was any talk of financial inducement, insisting that neither he, Robert Smith, who was not even at the meeting, Shirley Harrison or Sally Evemy would have been party to bribery or blackmail. He also points out that the entire proceedings were independently witnessed by a retired senior police officer.)

Within a matter of days, Barrett's affidavit had come into the hands of Melvin Harris. A postscript to a letter written to Shirley Harrison on 4 February 1995 makes his feelings on the matter abundantly clear:

This man should be allowed to state his position freely, without any inducements to please either believers or doubters. Because a large sum of money seems to be on promise, but only IF he goes along with the Anne Barrett line, then any testimony endorsing that line is null and void, as a matter of course. But, in this case, his witnessed repudiation means that you may not make use of anything said on these tapes. They are now meaningless, and I understand that an enlarged statement about this visit has since been made by Barrett, in which the repudiation is repeated and made even stronger by extra details. I have not yet seen this statement. This is an unfortunate turn of events, and since a crime is involved, can we, from now on, have this investigation conducted on a strictly equitable level?

This postscript would enrage the Diary camp. Shirley Harrison faxed Harris's letter on to Paul Feldman and sent a copy to Michael Barrett's solicitor, Richard Bark-Jones, with a covering letter 'detailing the context of that meeting between Keith, Mike and ourselves'. She advised cool heads and for them not to 'rise to this very tempting bait'.

Robert Smith was no happier when Harris sent him a copy of the same letter. There were, he replied on 10 February 1995, 'a number of allegations and legal implications in your letter,' though he felt this was not the place to comment in detail on them.

However, it is an untrue and libellous statement that [referring to Michael Barrett], 'a large sum of money seems to be on promise, but only IF [*sic*] he goes along with the Anne Barrett line' (your words). Michael Barrett's statement is also untrue that: 'It was made clear to me that if the Diary was genuine I would be paid all moneys due to me by the publisher Mr Smith in June 1995.' The tape-recorded meeting requested by Michael Barrett which took place on 18th January 1995; and which was witnessed by a former Detective Superintendent in the Merseyside Police Force, demonstrates clearly that there was no such suggestion made, either explicitly or implicitly. Nor has there been any such suggestion made by me.

In view of this alleged libel, and Harris's own publishing and commercial interests (his book, *The True Face of Jack the Ripper*, had recently been published in 1994), Smith informed Harris that Shirley Harrison and Smith Gryphon could no longer continue their exchange of information and views on the Diary. Nor were Harris, Nick Warren or others permitted to quote in print any words that Smith, Shirley Harrison or any of their colleagues had written or spoken to them, without Smith Gryphon's prior permission. The same restriction applied to their use of any reports commissioned by Shirley Harrison or, indeed, any of the text of Harrison's book.

This 'curious letter', Harris responded on 13 February 1995, confirmed what members of the Rendell team had warned him about Smith – that he 'would prove impossible to work with'. His words reeked of 'dictatorship and thought control'. 'Take them back,' Harris demanded. The letter was concluded: 'For integrity above all things.'

Three days after his 23 January affidavit, Barrett had another to swear, this time written by Alan Gray at his dictation (owing to the injury to his right arm). Having reported Anne's relative to the police, a matter which Barrett notes is now under investigation, he states that he is now staying at an address known only to Gray, 'because this matter is becoming very serious, I have already had threats, my home attacked, and all this is lodged with the police, also my phone wires were cut and now I have been beaten up, perhaps when they find me dead one day they might take me seriously'. He continues:

> On Wednesday 18th January 1995 when they all called at my home I was pressurised by them. Feldman's man Skinner came earlier than the others and started a tape recording off and my very words at the beginning were, 'FELDMAN YOU BASTARD GO AND GET FUCKED, BECAUSE YOU ARE A BLOODY BIG MAN WITH A HELL OF A LOT OF MONEY AND AS FAR AS I AM CONCERNED, I WILL NEVER GIVE IN TO YOU. I REFUSE TO BE BLACKMAILED. [His actual words were 'By the way Feldman, go get fucking screwed, because I'm not scared of you. I've been blackmailed all last year'.)

Again Barrett claims it was made clear to him 'that if the "Diary of Jack the Ripper" is genuine I would get my money in June 1995, however, due to my solicitor advising me some time before this meeting, that I have been granted legal aid to take Shirley Harrison to court, along with Robert Smith, and that if I stay quiet I would get my money, so this being the case I decided to collaborate with these people and Anne's story by supporting the Diary, much to my regret but at the time I did not know what to do. I was also afraid that if Anne and I get arrested for fraud what would happen to my daughter. I did not know who the independent adviser was and I felt a serious threat to me either through the law or if I didn't conform, personal injury maybe. My wife has for the past twelve months kept my daughter away from me and used her to threaten and blackmail me that I will not see her again if I don't cooperate.'

In June 1994, Barrett alleges, Feldman threatened to destroy him and keep his wife and daughter from him (a threat Feldman vehemently denies today). Having credited Tony Devereux as being a 'tremendous help' during the forgery, and reaffirming that he wrote it and Anne transcribed it, Barrett has a warning for the Diary team he has accused of pressurising him to lie. 'I am ready now should it be necessary to speak to the Detective from Scotland Yard who saw me some time ago, Detective Thomas.'

It was back to war.

SEVEN

'Fact not fiction'

Michael Barrett was not the only combatant sharpening his claws for battle. Behind the scenes there had been a growing antagonism between two of the main players in the Diary story, a mutual antipathy that was about to explode. Since buying the video rights to the Diary back in December 1992, Paul Feldman had pursued his belief that James Maybrick was Jack the Ripper with characteristic vigour. In the process he had made significant enemies. One was Michael Barrett, who claimed Feldman had bullied and threatened him with physical violence since his confession and turned his wife Anne against him. Another was Melvin Harris, spokesperson for the Committee for Integrity and the Diary's most vociferous and long-standing critic. Feldman believed that Harris and the committee were attempting to persuade New Line Cinema, which had spent £70,000 on the film rights, that the Diary was a hoax, something that Feldman, who had personally sold those film rights, bitterly resented. Given that neither man could be described as retiring, any meeting between them could be expected to be incendiary.

The venue for their confrontation was Grey House Books, run by octogenarian Camille Wolff and her associate Loretta Lay from Wolff's house in London's Notting Hill area. One of the world's largest true crime dealerships, the house was also a regular venue for literary lunches, attracting guests as diverse as Great Train Robber Bruce Reynolds, Oscar-nominated screenwriter and director Bruce Robinson, and television presenter and true-crime *aficionado* Jeremy Beadle. The occasion was the launch, on 25 January 1995, of Grey House Books' own publication, *Who Was Jack the Ripper? A Collection of Present-Day Theories and Observations*, by leading

Ripperologists and crime historians. Here, amid shelves packed with numerous rare and second-hand editions of books on Jack the Ripper (not to mention books on virtually every famous major crime in the UK and abroad), thronged a collection of Ripper experts, authors and media representatives, including Harris and Feldman.

Aware of the intensity of feeling between the two men, Loretta Lay had forewarned Paul Feldman to avoid a confrontation. She was to be disappointed. As the two came together in the living room, onlookers began to gather from all parts. By the time Loretta Lay arrived, 'everyone was either sitting or standing around the perimeter of the room, it was like an arena, and a hush fell on the audience'. Feldman and Harris 'were starting to circle each other, like gladiators. Paul was stabbing the air with a large cigar, gesticulating, and both voices were beginning to rise.'

The dispute centred around the much-disputed will of James Maybrick. Paul Feldman had suggested that the disparity between the handwriting in the Diary and that in Maybrick's will, written just days before the last Diary entry, might be because the will (which contains Maybrick's signature and two pages of his writing) was a forgery, perhaps created by Maybrick's brothers Michael and Thomas. Feldman had long pointed to a book about the trial of Florence Maybrick, written soon after the event by the lawyer Alexander MacDougall, which disputed the authenticity of this will in Somerset House and argued that there were many discrepancies between it and the will witnessed at the registry. Harris, who insisted MacDougall was using a faulty transcript of a newspaper report in the *Liverpool Mercury* (itself a verbatim report from a clerk at the registry), believed MacDougall's account was fatally flawed.

Speaking to the authors of this book in November 2002, Paul Feldman recalls how the tension built that day. He had brought with him, he says, a Home Office document from Maybrick's trial papers, which confirmed that MacDougall *had* seen the Maybrick will, something which, Feldman believed, dealt a fatal blow to Harris's argument. 'Every time I passed him,' Feldman claims, 'I'd say, "Don't forget, I've got something to show you." I think I showed it to a few other people first and they couldn't wait for me to show him.' According to Feldman, when Harris finally did see the document, 'he went absolutely mad'. (It should be noted, however, that in a letter to Feldman's solicitors, written six months later, Harris claimed that Feldman had *not* brought the evidence with him that day and failed to produce it at a later date as promised.)

The encounter was still on Harris's mind when he wrote to Shirley Harrison a few days afterwards, on 4 February 1995:

> It was fortuitous that you were present when Paul Feldman launched into his diatribe. He had been asked to avoid all confrontation, and for my part, I was there only to please my old friend Camille, but perhaps you will now realise how difficult it has been to discuss the Diary issue on a civilised plane. The evidence I have sent to you was there, with me, but Feldman was not in the least interested in looking at it and judging it coolly and fairly. He seeks to get his way by bombast and dogmatic repetition but I have letters from him which prove that he is not able to read, with understanding, the very documents he insists on 'quoting' from!

In her last letter to Harris, Shirley Harrison had terminated their correspondence because of what she claimed was an increasing level of personal abuse creeping into his letters. Harris did not agree. 'There is not the slightest element of personal abuse in my insistence that you set the record straight,' he wrote, 'but I hold that every writer has the moral duty to correct his or her errors once they have been identified. To refuse to do so is inexcusable.'

Harris had identified a number of contentious points which Paul Feldman had 'thrown' at him some months before the publication of the hardback edition of Harrison's book. Feldman believed these were all supportive of the Diary, Harris that they were all bogus. Harris had also been disappointed to see the same arguments recur in the paperback edition of Harrison's book.

Still angry at the encounter with Feldman, Harris circulated a defence of his position on 15 February 1995. Entitled 'The Bluff

Behind the Bluster', it set out his views on the Maybrick will in no uncertain terms:

> Those of you who were present at the Wednesday signing at Camille Wolff's place may have been a little baffled by Paul Feldman's antics. Briefly he has been angered by the fact that his constant use of a tainted text has been exposed. The text is that found on pages 203 and 204 of A.W. MacDougall's *The Maybrick Case* (1891). This text claims to be a transcript of the will written by James Maybrick and witnessed on 25 April 1889, yet its wording differs in places from the holograph will now at Somerset House. These differences were seized on by Feldman and others as a way of dismissing the evidence provided by the holograph will, whose writing bears no resemblance whatsoever to the handwriting in the fake 'Maybrick Diary'.
>
> The difference in wording is easily accounted for: they are nothing more than the errors of transcription. This can be shown by examining the section quoted by MacDougall that was NOT written by Maybrick, but was added by solicitors on 29 July 1889. In this text also can be found eleven missing words and other errors. This, of course, is never even mentioned by those whose interests are served by ignoring the will.

The various confessions and affidavits of Michael Barrett and his employment of the Liverpool private detective Alan Gray, who had been party to these affidavits, had impacted hugely on the Diary. In his letter to Shirley Harrison of 4 February 1995 Melvin Harris had been anxious to make it clear that neither he nor the Committee for Integrity had any part to play in this. Harris's understanding was that Gray had initially become involved with Barrett when the latter asked him to search for his wife but 'became alarmed when there was talk of a criminal conspiracy to forge and defraud'. Eventually he accompanied Barrett to Walton Lane police station, where Barrett made his initial statement branding the Diary a fraud. After contacting Maurice Chittenden, the journalist who conducted the *Sunday Times* investigation, in order to learn more about the Diary controversy, Gray was referred to Harris, Chittenden being tied up 'with a complex story'. Since then Gray, Harris said, 'has kept me informed of the many developments in Liverpool, but at no time have I spoken or written to Barrett or offered him any type of inducement to talk'. However, Harris added, Alan Gray was now commissioned by Nick Warren, editor of *Ripperana*, 'to seek out some of the physical evidence that may still be around, but this is quite independent of any police activities'.

Harris also gave his most extensive account yet of the formation of the Committee for Integrity. Named, he said, to counter the degree of misinformation being given to the press by the Diary camp, the committee had been formed after indirect allegations had been made by the Diary camp that Harris, Nick Warren and the document analyser Robert Kuranz had tampered with ink samples of the Diary which were sent to Analysis for Industry. Kuranz had taken the ink-core samples used by Analysis for Industry when he had tested the Diary in August 1993 for the Rendell report. As the media were portraying the argument as a battle between two people, Harris and Feldman, so Kuranz, Warren and Harris decided it was time to 'act as a body and make it clear there was no Lone Ranger involved'.

Despite the publication of the paperback edition of Shirley Harrison's book, there seemed little sign of an end to the ongoing saga of the Diary. Paul Feldman was now planning his own book and another related to it, New Line were developing a film of the Diary and the Diary's critics did not appear to be giving up their campaign either. What would the future hold? That was the theme of a meeting between Robert Smith, Shirley Harrison, Sally Evemy, Paul Begg, Keith Skinner and Doreen Montgomery, held at Smith Gryphon's north London offices on 13 February 1995. Despite Smith's belief that only a major announcement to say the Diary had been proved genuine would affect either the media attitude to it or future sales, it was agreed that cost-effective research would continue to minimise weak areas of the book and establish a solid base for a new edition.

As for Melvin Harris, his own Ripper book, *The True Face of Jack the Ripper*, had met with poor sales and it was agreed not to give him any further platform or opportunity for battle. The aim must be to persuade respected Ripperologists to consider the Diary as an historic document and not as a modern forgery.

If the Diary camp roughly constituted a group gathered around the two teams of Shirley Harrison and Paul Feldman, it was now possible to identify an opposing group of sceptics who also appeared to be linked, albeit tenuously in some cases. Melvin Harris had written that he, Nick Warren and Robert Kuranz of the Rendell team were the basis of the Committee for Integrity, but also that he and Warren were in touch with the Liverpool private detective Alan Gray. The group also seemed to have a supporter in the media, the *Sunday Times* journalist Maurice Chittenden, who had led that paper's investigation into the Diary. It appears that Chittenden, perhaps alerted by Gray, was behind a piece in the 'Quidnunc' column of the *Sunday Times* on 5 February 1995.

The piece was essentially a warning note for hoaxers, illustrated by the cautionary tale of Michael Barrett who had 'tried to fool the *Sunday Times* by forging the Diary of Jack the Ripper'. Barrett, the article revealed, had gained little by his foolhardiness. 'He has lost his wife, his reputation and, last week, his home. A perusal of Barrett's royalty statements for the book shows that up to last September he had earned £26,609.41 in royalties. But legal expenses, researchers, agent's commission and Vat have left him with precisely nothing. Agents, however, are paid to look on the bright side. Barrett's wrote to him reassuring him about the success of the book because of "just how much money has passed through your accounts". To which the reply to the agent should have been that 10 per cent of nothing is nothing.'

In a subsequent letter to Melvin Harris, Robert Smith pointed out that the paper, and Harris, had only drawn attention to one royalty statement. Examination of all the statements would have shown that Barrett had made a considerable amount of money. Ironically, what the *Sunday Times* did not say was that the greatest deduction for Barrett on the one statement they cited (and therefore for Harrison too), over £16,500, had resulted from the action against the *Sunday Times*. Some £2,000 of this represented Barrett's share of the option money that had to be returned to the newspaper, while £14,500 went in legal fees. Approximately £7,000 was also deducted for legal expenses in respect of the film rights, which would nevertheless go on to earn Barrett and Harrison £28,000 each. The fact remained that Barrett had already received over £47,000 before the statement arrived which the *Sunday Times* claimed 'left him with precisely nothing'.

Robert Smith's correspondence with Melvin Harris had not brought the parties any closer together, nor found any avenue in which Diary sceptic and believer could work together. Smith now turned his attention to Nick Warren, whose recent comments, he deduced, indicated he was distancing himself from Harris. He and Shirley Harrison, Smith told Warren, were 'happy to work openly with any bona fide investigator who is prepared to look at the evidence with impartiality'. Indeed, Smith believed that *Ripperana*, which Warren edited, 'can play an important role in reporting new developments to those interested in the Diary'.

Smith, however, was particularly concerned at the determined attempts by 'third parties to interfere with the agreement between New Line Cinema, Duocrave and Smith Gryphon'. He also pointed out that, contrary to speculation, the agreement did not hinge on the Diary being warranted as that of Jack the Ripper. Nor did Anne Barrett's statement form any part of the contractual arrangements with New Line.

Nick Warren's reply, on 24 February 1995, was relatively positive, though as an editor he was highly critical about the threat of censorship from the Diary team. He was also able to shed some light on the vital question as to the identity of the three people Melvin Harris believed had forged the Diary:

Certainly the names are known to me, and to you, so that no surprise can be anticipated. Obviously circumspection is necessary here, but the three constitute –
(a) Someone who composes the text on a WP.
(b) An Amanuensis
(c) A man so embittered against an ex-wife that he always referred to her as 'the whore' (according to a journalist source).

At a later date Warren would feel able to be more precise. As to Smith's chief complaint, that Harris and his colleagues on the committee were attempting to interfere with the New Line agreement, Melvin Harris was back in touch with Smith to put him in the picture. It was, Harris said, New Line themselves who had requested the material on the Diary that had been sent. Initial contact with New Line had come through Paul Gainey, the publicity officer at Ipswich police headquarters, who with his colleague, Ripper expert Stewart Evans, had taken a keen interest in the 'fake Diary'. 'When he heard that yet another lying film was due to be made he [Gainey] lost all patience with the parties involved and rang the States to protest.' Harris, who had not spoken directly to the New Line employee who made the request, had it passed on to him and supplied the material. He had no regrets. 'If they are still unwise enough to go ahead with the film then they need to know that [they] can no longer claim it to be based on an authentic confession. Thus the publicity value of their new acquisition is now nil. They also need to know that they are branding a perfectly innocent man as a sexually perverted serial-killer.'

While the arguments over the authenticity of the Diary continued to rage, the domestic tragedy at the heart of the story was never far away. While there might be dispute over whether Michael Barrett had forged the Diary, the extent of his personal suffering since bringing it to Doreen Montgomery was not in doubt. In the taped meeting of 18 January 1995 he had told Keith Skinner and Shirley Harrison that the motivation for his confession was the heartbreak he felt at losing not just his wife but his daughter Caroline, too. He blamed one man for this state of affairs, Paul Feldman. In a letter to Feldman written on 14 March 1995, Barrett gave full vent to his feelings, accusing Feldman of helping him 'try and destroy the Diary and Anne'.

In this letter Barrett says he has now finally relinquished the bottle and blames Feldman for driving Anne and Caroline, whom he still loves deeply, away from him, by his constant efforts to discredit him to them. He is furious too at the threats of physical intimidation, 'fact not fiction'.

Unable to see his wife and daughter, and because Anne believed all Feldman told her about Barrett, he was 'killed inside'. Now he has stopped drinking 'to try and gain Caroline back at last, also some respect from Anne'. He would love to know how Caroline is and how she was doing at school. It would, he tells Feldman, help him stay off the booze, if only he could hear from them. Barrett has no intention of letting Feldman off the hook: 'If you think your [*sic*] going to destroy me even more by not showing Anne this letter – dont even think about it – As I have photocopied it and will submit it, along with a covering letter to every paper in the land.' He concluded: 'I know you probably show this letter to people to whom you wish to prove the Diary is fact not fiction. So be it.'

Barrett returned to this theme a fortnight later, when he wrote to his agent Doreen Montgomery. It was pure anger, he claimed, that drove his allegation, contained in his affidavit of 5 January 1995, that Anne was responsible for the handwriting in the Diary. She had not only prevented any contact with Caroline, she had even failed to enquire after his health when he was seriously ill. 'Now do you understand why I whanted [*sic*] you all to believe she wrote it, simply to get back at her, and to hurt her the way she hurt me.' While Barrett appears to have no doubt now about Anne's story – 'we all know Tony gave me the Diary' – he is far less convinced about her possible relationship to Florence Maybrick. 'Remember I was the one who researched the Diary. Not Anne. I was the one who spent sleepless nigths [*sic*] over it, Not Anne . . . I was the one who said to her I am going to try and get it published . . . I was the one who discovered it was Maybrick. Not Anne.' Now, eight months after leaving him, she is suddenly a descendant of Florence Maybrick's. It was all too convenient. If Anne wants half the money from him, she has a lot to prove. Otherwise, she will have to fight him in court.

It was certainly true that Anne Graham had kept very much in the background throughout most of the Diary story. She had surfaced briefly and dramatically when giving the new provenance for the Diary, added to so sensationally, and controversially, by her father Billy, and had made a short appearance with Paul Feldman at the

Cloak and Dagger Club. But, overall a very private person, she had stayed out of the spotlight. She had claimed to dislike the Diary and to want nothing to do with it. This situation was about to change in the most unexpected of fashions. Anne Graham, who had ferociously denied any interest in the Diary and laughed at the possibility that she created it, was about to write a book about Florence Maybrick.

There was a suspicion among some Ripperologists that, if the Diary had been created in the Barrett household, then Anne's contribution had been greater than her husband claimed in his affidavit of 5 January 1995. It was not Barrett, it was suggested, who created the Diary, but Anne. Martin Fido, for one, believed she could have concocted the basic story of Maybrick the Ripper 'with one hand tied behind her back'. Writing a book on Florence Maybrick was unlikely to help dampen such speculation. Ironically it was Fido who, with typical generosity of spirit, actually recommended to Headline they go ahead and publish Anne's book.

Anne was more concerned about the impact on Shirley Harrison, Doreen Montgomery and Robert Smith and was worried there might even be legal implications in her participation. 'I am very pleased to be part of this project,' she wrote to Paul Feldman, who had agreed to fund research and find a publisher for the book, on 16 February 1995, 'but I am also aware that my participation in it could cause some "raised eyebrows" in certain quarters and that, considering the amount of money you have already spent on research, I do not want to be the cause of any further unnecessary expenditure, or indeed be the cause of any expensive legal conflicts in the future.' Before proceeding, Anne needed to be sure there would be no problems arising from contractual obligations to either Smith or Harrison. As for the vexed question of Diary ownership, 'Nor do I wish to claim ownership, be it part or whole, of the Diary,' she wrote.

The idea for the book had come from Paul Feldman. With his unflinching belief in the authenticity of the Diary and in Anne's relationship to Florie, the book had an obvious commercial appeal – a book on the wife of Jack the Ripper by her great-granddaughter.

Even at the time of her trial there were those who believed that Florence was the victim of a gross miscarriage of justice. In modern times, when such miscarriages have become a regular occurrence, that belief is shared by many who study the case. Anne Graham, who had become interested in the subject since hearing her father talk, however vaguely, about the family connection, was one of these. As Feldman and Shirley Harrison uncovered more on the Maybricks, Anne, who had increasingly helped with their research, became hooked. In order to inform her agent, Doreen Montgomery, and her publisher, Robert Smith, Anne asked them for a meeting with herself and Paul Feldman in London. Her intention was to iron out any possible conflict of interests, legally and morally, with the Diary. The meeting, which Keith Skinner also attended, was held on 25 April 1995. It was not a success.

The animosity between the two Diary camps has already been well documented. Shirley Harrison, Robert Smith and Doreen Montgomery felt that Feldman, with his much bigger cheque book, had pushed them away from various avenues of research and that he had fouled others by his unprofessional methods. They also believed that the conclusions he claimed as proof were often little more than mere supposition, which reflected badly on the Diary and made Harrison's work of convincing a sceptical public even harder. Now there was a clear sign of conflict ahead. Not only was a book on Florence being mooted, but Feldman had definite plans to write his own book as a 'back-up' to Harrison's. Montgomery was not happy with the situation. 'Anyone is entitled to research, but if they wish to publish, then they have to secure copyright clearance from the copyright owners of the source material.'

While acknowledging the inspirational enthusiasm Feldman had brought to the matter, Montgomery was anxious that his book might invalidate Harrison's:

What is at issue, however, is whether his highly subjective evaluation of the research data represents a purely factual back-up for the veracity of the Diary. You can research the Maybrick background, you can believe Anne to be a descendant of Florie

Maybrick, you can believe that the Johnson brothers have a family connection, but until we have proof, beyond any doubt, reasonable or otherwise, that Maybrick is indeed the Ripper, these matters are almost irrelevant.

Montgomery was worried about the possibility of either book being published without some kind of editorial vetting from her and Shirley Harrison, as, 'in the inflammatory market place situation, each could possibly adversely affect the main property [the Diary]'. She was also curious that Anne should appear 'perfectly content to enjoy a financial benefit from the Florie Maybrick story while, on the other hand, rejecting – until now – revenue from The Diary of Jack the Ripper!' After all, she pointed out, 'there would not be the former, if it were not for the latter'. Now the various parties must work out how to go from here and arrive at a solution that was fair and reasonable.

Anne Graham, who circulated her reply to the others attending the meeting, was not convinced such a solution was possible, or even likely: 'From the tenor of the meeting on the 24th [actually the 25th], which in my humble opinion turned into something of a personality clash of embarrassing proportions between Doreen and Paul – so much so that Robert Smith made a somewhat hasty retreat! That unless the two of them can "bury the hatchet", preferably not in each other's head, I am at a loss to see how anything reasonable and fair can be worked out.'

Anne Graham, who believed her ability as a writer had been impugned by her own agent, was stout in the defence of Paul Feldman, too. While admitting that 'Paul is a victim of his own infectious enthusiasm and his conclusions to some of the research is [sic] on occasion slightly eccentric', her experience was that he was easy to work with: 'I have found that he is perfectly willing and able to listen to opposing views and be influenced by reasonable argument.'

In short, she saw little conflict in either her own book or Feldman's with the Diary, the former being about a woman who had lived for eighty years and was married to James Maybrick for only eight of

194

those. Nor was she happy at the idea of editorial vetting from Montgomery or Harrison. She was angry too at the implication there was something deceitful in her now accepting her share of revenue from the Diary, especially as it was Montgomery and Feldman who had persuaded her to do so at the meeting. 'I have not pursued the financial aspect of the collaboration agreement for reasons of my own which I do not feel the need to justify to anyone,' she wrote.

Those who believed Anne was involved in a forgery hoax might have been surprised to find that as one of the alleged conspirators she had not accepted her share of the royalties over a year and a half after the publication of the hardback edition of *The Diary of Jack the Ripper*. Equally, those who claimed the alleged conspirators did not have the necessary skills for their hoax would find their argument harder to defend as one of the conspirators began work on an historical book about one of the Diary's most important characters. After the research she had conducted for Harrison and Feldman, here was more evidence that Anne could not be lightly dismissed as a potential forger.

That, at least, was the view of Martin Fido, who had recently conducted his first interview with Anne. As he told Keith Skinner in a taped telephone conversation on the night of 1 May 1995, she had failed to convince him her account was completely truthful. She was charming and quick-thinking, and he felt her answers were often evasive and that, when challenged, she would distract with 'stories and laughter'. There were contradictions in her story too, he felt. Why had she given the Diary to Barrett in order to stop his drinking and help with his writing, when she was aware of his lack of writing skills? Her account of when and where she hid the Diary also contained contradictions, and, while Anne had explained that she got the details in her 1994 statement wrong and was now giving a more accurate account, he was surprised the original story contained inaccuracies when she had had time to compose it.

Later that same night Keith Skinner heard Anne's side of the story. Her overall impression had been that Fido was unimpressed with her. She explained to Skinner how confusion had crept into her accounts of the bedrooms at Goldie Street and where she kept the

Diary hidden. Nor could she pin down the dates when her father gave her various bits and pieces, including the Diary. She told Skinner that the Diary was only in the house for a couple of months before she gave it to Tony Devereux to give to Barrett, but acknowledges she is not good at dates. She remembers shoving the Diary behind the cupboard (described in a previous account as a sideboard) before deciding what to do with it. She feels she can't win; if she comes out with an account parrot-fashion, then people will say that is as suspicious as getting it muddled. She also admits that she too was looking for the source of 'O costly intercourse of death' and was very put out that her former husband found it first.

The Diary teams might have decided to try to keep Melvin Harris out of the spotlight, but it was not easy to achieve. Back in January 1995 handwriting expert Reed Hayes had written to Harris expressing some misgivings about the Diary. On 30 May 1995 he wrote again, this time in a very different tone. His previous letter, he said, had been as a result of a message left by Harris on his answerphone asking him to reconsider his opinions about the Diary, based on the 'facts' that Barrett had admitted writing it and that analyses of the ink showed it to be of modern origin. Since then Hayes had learnt that Barrett had made his confession 'under the influence of alcohol' and had since recanted, that 'you yourself supplied the chloroacetamide to the laboratory for the test procedure', and that Leeds University testing had indicated the ink was probably of Victorian origin. Hayes was about to reconsider again, much to the subsequent fury of Melvin Harris.

Now that he had seen a new example of Maybrick's handwriting in the meantime, Hayes did see 'some similarities to the handwriting in the Diary. However, I cannot as yet reach a conclusion regarding authorship of the Diary, since the new Maybrick sample was apparently written some time before he was using drugs, which could account for the differences between his writing at that time and the later Diary writing.'

With the new sample of Maybrick's writing to compare, Hayes now believed there was sufficient evidence to reach a conclusive opinion on the authenticity of the will: 'Having considered the new

Maybrick writing, I am now quite certain that Maybrick did not write the will. As stated to you previously, a man dying of arsenic poisoning would have produced a weak and/or tremulous handwriting, not the firm writing strokes that make up the will and its signature.'

Harris was livid. 'You are being deceived, and deceived mightily,' he wrote back. 'You are also being fed deliberate lies.' He went on to explain that the ink samples were extracted by Robert Kuranz of the Rendell team when Robert Smith had taken the Diary to the US, and placed in non-contaminating gelatine capsules: six ink-cores to each capsule. 'It was only when Feldman refused to test the ink to see if chloroacetamide was present that I made contact with Bob Kuranz. I discovered that he still had two of these capsules in safe-keeping and he agreed to send one of these over for laboratory tests.' This capsule was sent, unopened, by Harris to Dr Diana Simpson, head of Analysis For Industry. Harris also denied sending chloroacetamide to the AFI laboratory. This, he said, was sent by Nick Warren and came from the Diamine laboratories in Liverpool.

As far as Harris was concerned, Hayes was being 'dragged into a dirty, underhanded effort to denigrate both my actions and my reputation'. The letter, which contained most of Harris's arguments for the Diary being a fake, also made some accusations itself: 'the Diary alliance of Smith, Harrison and Feldman is a seedy and uneasy union between people whose sole aim is to make as much money as possible out of this hoax. And it is such a very lucrative venture for them that they will not cooperate in any meaningful way in searching out the origins of this forgery.' Shirley Harrison was singled out for particular scorn: 'Since the Leeds fiasco [the ink tests commissioned by Harrison], Harrison has been promising new tests and keeps posing as someone concerned to reach the truth in this matter, but she is a practised evader and has deliberately drawn things out to the point where I and others no longer believe her promises to be sincere.'

Paul Feldman, who received a copy of the letter from Reed Hayes, was angry enough to revert to his solicitors, Gold, Mann & Co. On 28 June 1995 they wrote to Harris. 'It is clear from the text of the letter that you have expressly and by innuendo stated to Mr Hayes that our client is a liar and a deceiver and party to a "seedy" conspiracy to gain financial advantage from a hoax and a deception.' The letter, they claimed, constituted 'a vicious, malicious and unwarranted attack upon our client's integrity and professional standing'. Concluding that the attack was a 'grave libel upon our client', they made three demands of Harris: a letter to Reed Hayes containing a withdrawal of his accusations; a written assurance not to repeat the allegations, or similar ones; and the payment of Paul Feldman's costs. Harris did not reply. On 6 July, they wrote again, remarking that this failure merely added insult to injury. If they did not hear from him within five business days, their client would have 'no option but to take action through the High Court in order to seek redress'.

Harris did reply, but not until 28 July. Nor was the letter exactly what Gold, Mann & Co. had in mind. Harris set out his store with the letter's title – 'Paul Feldman's libels and slanders' – and began in vintage Harris style, 'Gentlemen, I am sorry to tell you forcibly that you are still being misled, misdirected and deceived by your client Mr Feldman.' Rejecting Feldman's claim that he had been offered the chance to review the results of Feldman's research, Harris declared to the contrary that Feldman had consistently denied him access to 'the very documents that he claims support his case'. These included the evidence that Feldman claims he had shown Harris back in January 1995 to support his argument for the will being false.

Harris believed he had proof that Feldman had defamed him, rather than the other way around, in particular 'spreading his poison' to Reed Hayes, a letter which he quotes from: 'You ought to know that . . . Mr Harris supplied the chloroacetamide to the laboratory himself.' Harris insisted that he had never seen the chloroacetamide and that it was, in fact, sent by Nick Warren, who had been supplied it by Alec Voller, Head Chemist at Diamine Ink. Harris had been quoted in the *London Evening Standard* as promising that the identities of the forgers would be revealed. Thus far they had not, but he gave some clue to his own thinking. 'I have stated in the plainest of plain English so many times, and I repeat it now, MIKE BARRETT DID NOT PEN THOSE PAGES. Whether he had a hand in composing the text, along with others, is another matter, but he had nothing to do with the handwriting.'

Demanding that Feldman send withdrawals of his libellous claims about Harris to a number of documentary programme makers (and also to News International), to safeguard programmes Harris had worked on, he also expected financial compensation. 'Finally my demands for an out-of-court settlement remain unchanged in all important aspects. The letters of withdrawal will have their texts decided on by me alone. While the sum of money demanded remains exactly the same, at £250,000, payable by certified cheque.' That would not quite settle things, though. Feldman, Harris believed, was not deserving of such generosity. 'This revised demand will save your client money, but that is not our intention, so a donation by him of £5,000 to my favourite charity, the NSPCC, will form part of the settlement.'

Gold, Mann & Co. were not impressed. 'The advice given by you concerning how we should conduct our relations with our client,' they replied, 'and the prescription given by you for the administering of a few "calmly directed words" in dealings with our client, is presumptuous and an entirely unwelcome intrusion. Indeed, the ill-temperance revealed in your letters indicates to the writer that such a prescription would be well self-administered.' Their client, it transpired, was considering his position and would instruct them further in relation to his demands of Harris in due course.

Paul Feldman was not the only one criticised by Harris. In a letter to Reed Hayes dated 10 August 1995, Shirley Harrison revealed her astonishment at Harris's 'defamatory attacks on my character and my work'. 'I am confident,' she continued, 'that since you have informed Paul Feldman about the letter you have not, yourself, taken its unwarranted allegations seriously.'

There was, she informed Hayes, no conspiracy, no 'seedy' alliance constructed to profit from fraud. Her prime motivation as a writer on this 'extraordinary project, has been much more the thrill of the chase'. Describing her methods as 'open and straightforward', Harrison claims that 'to suggest that I am a "practised evader" is actionable'. As to Harris's accusations of profiteering, she recommends Hayes look at the cover of Harris's latest Ripper book, which displays a photograph of his suspect, D'Onston Stephenson, 'together with the unequivocal title, "The True Face of Jack the Ripper".' When Harris accuses her of writing for financial gain, is she expected to believe he 'writes as a charitable exercise? Moreover, it is ironic to note that so unproven was his particular Ripper theory, that he, perversely, used the chapter he had devoted to an attack on my book as a publicity vehicle for his own.' 'I sincerely believe the Diary is genuine,' she continued. 'But in my book I make no claim to have PROVED its origin. Research continues on this very difficult task of unravelling the elusive truth.'

Anne Graham had made her own contribution to this research on 31 May 1995, when she met Keith Skinner and the director of the Diary video, Martin Howells. The transcript of the Diary, the discovery of which sceptics believed helped point to a hoax, she told them, had been completed very quickly. Michael Barrett, who claimed he had undertaken the job in order to bring it to London and show Doreen Montgomery, was a poor typist, she said, and she was compelled to retype it, checking back against the original every so often. She had also examined Barrett's research notes and 'tidied' them up on the word processor.

While Michael Barrett's battle continued to reclaim money that he believed Smith Gryphon still owed him, he learnt on 22 June that future payments would have to be shared with his estranged wife. 'What I plan to do,' Doreen Montgomery wrote to him, 'until the circumstances are finally resolved, is to place 25 per cent of monies due, less our commission, into a separate account in Anne's name.' In fact, this arrangement continues to this day.

Another thorny question, that of the Diary ownership, was also addressed by Montgomery, who explained the circumstances surrounding it to Barrett's solicitor, Richard Bark-Jones, on 6 July 1995. 'At that time [March 1993] there was a great fear that the Diary could be considered in the public domain and that Mike and Anne's personal ownership and their vulnerability overall, would not offer the greatest protection. Robert Smith approached the Barretts with this proposition and Mike was more than willing to agree.' However, while this decision was a sound one, Montgomery had insisted on a clause which ensured that 'Smith Gryphon can do nothing without the Barretts' agreement'. On 21 April 1994 Robert Smith, she told Bark-Jones, 'felt it might be safer to transfer the diary to another company, Keychoice Ltd, also owned by him and his wife [the transfer actually took place on 23 May 1994]'. Now the latest accounts had arrived, she added, there would be a gross payment of £59,983.24 to the authors. However, owing to her recent decision, Mike would only receive £15,019.32 before VAT and commission, his share now being divided with Anne.

Barrett was, according to Dawn Shotter of Morecrofts, 'very surprised' at this figure, though he appreciated he would not be receiving Anne's share. Shotter now asked Doreen Montgomery to provide a list of all royalty statements and full statements from her and Smith Gryphon, with all monies received and all deductions taken from the outset of the agreement on 29 July 1992. She also included a list of outstanding expenses claimed by Barrett, who was in 'financial difficulty', which amounted to a sum of £917.00.

Shirley Harrison, who had been given the letter, replied that she and Sally Evemy had given up other work for over two years to produce the book. She had used her £7,000 advance to live on and pay any necessary professional fees. Despite the huge costs involved in interviewing and travelling, she had only billed Barrett for his contractual half of major items, though even this had been delayed. Dozens of smaller expenses were forgotten. Barrett had wanted to help with research and Harrison had tried to make him feel involved, for instance with trips to Liverpool Library. 'Sometimes it was useful but all too often Mike got carried away and did more than I asked. Offset this "work" with all the mayhem and expense he has caused me, after his confession that he "wrote" the Diary, and I think you may feel I have been very gentle.' In short, Harrison felt the money asked for was far too much, suggesting £350 would be a fairer sum.

By this stage it was becoming increasingly difficult to pin down Michael Barrett. Sometimes he was the world's greatest forger. At others he reverted to his original account that he had been given the Diary by Tony Devereux. On 20 July 1995 Paul Feldman paid for him to come down to his Baker Street offices, to try to establish the truth. Over the next few hours Barrett managed to supply both accounts in the space of a single meeting, which was taped.

Initially Barrett announces to Feldman, Martin Howells and Keith Skinner, who are also present, that he has come to prove how he forged the Diary. Furthermore, there is an envelope in Richard Bark-Jones's office, which can only be opened on Barrett's instructions, which will prove this. He has brought a bottle of the same Diamine ink he used and now he just needs a nib to show how he wrote the Diary. He solemnly swears on a Bible that he and Anne forged the Diary together and that Anne has told him that she has both Paul Feldman and Keith Skinner 'by the balls'. Paul Feldman then agrees to go and get a nib and blotting paper for Barrett to prove how he wrote the Diary. Barrett says Anne's story is wrong; she wrote the Diary. Why then, Feldman enquires, does Barrett want the pen, if he did not write the Diary? Barrett evades the question, saying he created the Diary on his word processor and Anne wrote it. The demonstration is called off.

Several attempts are made to call Morecroft Urquhart to confirm Barrett's claim that he lodged a vital piece of evidence with Richard Bark-Jones in 1991, that proves he forged the Diary. The first two numbers offered by Barrett turn out to be Liverpool pubs and when he finds the right number it is discovered that Bark-Jones is on holiday. Dawn Shotter, who also acts for Barrett, can find no information about the said envelope.

Barrett continues for some time with an account of his forgery. Then Feldman asks again about Tony Devereux giving him the Diary. Suddenly Barrett confirms this is the truth. Feldman asks him if he wants to hear Anne explaining to Feldman why she gave Barrett the Diary. Barrett listens to the tape of Anne describing how she got the Diary from her father and where she kept it. He disputes her remark that their marriage was in trouble at the time and talks of a tape *he* possesses in which Feldman threatens him that he would never see his wife and daughter again. Denying this, Feldman suggests he might have said, 'If you carry on the way you are you'll be lucky if you ever see them again', and exhorts Barrett to listen to his tape again.

Feldman calls Howells and Skinner, who have been absent for this discussion, back into the room, in time to hear Barrett say that he now accepts Anne's story. He is getting back at her now because all the years he had the Diary she never told him where it came from. She left him out on a limb as a fall guy. Why did he confess to forging the Diary, Feldman asks? Anne had accused him, falsely, of having a physical relationship with a female friend of his. 'So I said, "Sod it, I wrote the bleedin' diary and to hell with it all".'

One of the most difficult parts of Anne's story to understand is how Tony Devereux managed to withstand so much questioning from Barrett without telling him the Diary came from Anne. According to Barrett's account now, Devereux did crack, eventually telling him to 'look to his family'. He asked his mother, father and sisters, but no one knew anything about it. Finally he thought of Anne and Caroline. He returned to Devereux, who now said, 'Look to your bloody wife.' Why didn't Barrett confront Anne there and then? 'I wouldn't confront Anne because she didn't want to talk about the Diary.' 'Were you frightened to confront her?' Feldman asks. 'Yes.' Asked why was he frightened, he replies that he had been 'nicked' in the past. He was protecting Anne because he thought she wrote it. At the outset of this marathon meeting, Barrett had implied that Richard Bark-Jones had proof the Diary was forged. Now, as the interview winds down, Barrett concludes by suggesting Bark-Jones might be able to confirm that as early as April 1992 Barrett believed the Diary had come from Anne. Barrett says that he first saw Bark-Jones on 17 April 1992, four days after the first meeting with Doreen Montgomery, and told him then that the Diary was genuine and possibly from Anne. From forger to fall guy, even for Michael Barrett, it had been a remarkable interview.

Morecroft Urquhart were trying to discover if Michael Barrett had been paid his full due. According to Robert Smith, who, on 28 July 1995, replied to a letter requesting information from the firm, he had. The solicitors had been particularly surprised at the large legal fee incurred fighting the *Sunday Times*. Though the case had been lost, Smith explained that by delaying the article, Mishcon de Reya, the lawyers employed by Smith Gryphon, had been able to restrict the damage significantly, as 'by then all UK orders had been collected by our reps and the foreign language rights had been sold to about ten publishers. If we had not defended the property the authors would have received no more than the £15,000 advances. As it is, we have paid £188,803.41 inclusive of the advances and net of deductions to the Rupert Crew Agency.'

There had been another area of legal deductions, Smith explained, which was equally important. The same solicitors, with their 'specialised knowledge and expertise in film contracts with Hollywood companies', had been instrumental in bringing to a successful conclusion the prolonged negotiations and contracts relating to the sale of film rights to Duocrave Ltd and the subsequent reversion and resale to New Line Cinema. Without that expertise, Smith estimated, 'we would not have raised the value of the authors' advances against net profits from £70,000, already paid to Smith Gryphon, to over £100,000 if the film is made'.

Though he believed the project had been a considerable economic success for the authors, the publishers, Smith revealed, had fared less well – a state of affairs for which he squarely blamed the various confessions of Michael Barrett. Major outlets like the London Dungeon, Smith said, had refused to stock the paperback edition of the book for this very reason. The hardback had reached number six in the bestseller list but the paperback, which came out after Barrett's confession, had failed to break out of the bottom end of the top fifty. There had also been a large level of returns. The *Sunday Times* story had been picked up around the world, causing the overseas publishers of the book considerable difficulties. Pointing to the fact that he, Doreen Montgomery and Shirley Harrison had all stood by Barrett both personally and financially, despite the huge damage he had done to the Diary, Smith felt that Barrett 'has reason to be satisfied with the way his agent, co-author and publisher have behaved towards him'.

For some months the watch had been pushed to the background as the extraordinary events around the Diary unfolded. Now it would return to the forefront, in the most tragic of circumstances. On 14 August 1995, while on holiday in southern Spain, Robbie Johnson was struck by a motorcycle and killed, aged just forty-five. The younger brother of watch owner Albert Johnson, Robbie had taken the higher profile of the two and was well known to many associated with the Diary. 'He was,' Albert said, 'the best brother anyone could have wished for. He will be badly missed.' The Diary had brought little happiness to those who brought it forward, and now it seemed the watch was equally cursed. Or was it? Soon after Johnson's death, Shirley Harrison reported to Richard Bark-Jones that she had had a call from one Stanley Dangar, an expatriate horologist living in Spain who had taken a keen interest in the 'Maybrick' watch and indeed had travelled to London at his own expense and paid for the Johnsons to bring the watch to meet him. Dangar, who believed the watch was a fake, was now convinced that two people closely connected with the watch had been 'bumped off' in the same week. One, he claimed, was Timothy Dundas, who had repaired the watch before it was sold to Albert Johnson (fortunately, Dundas was very much alive when he made this claim). The other, Dangar believed, was Robbie Johnson.

Over the last months Michael Barrett had wreaked terrible damage to the status of the Diary. Now, it seemed, he was back on track. In an interview on BBC Radio Merseyside on 13 September 1995 (the second instalment of which was broadcast a week later), Barrett firmly denied writing the Diary or knowing who did. He had, he claimed, been drunk when he made his previous confessions. He returned to the original story of being handed the journal by Tony Devereux but, as became apparent in the second instalment, he was not convinced by his former wife's claim that she had handed the Diary to Devereux to give to him. Still bitter at her lack of contact, he does not believe anything will be found to connect the Diary to Anne. Indeed, he maintains the belief he held when Martin Howells interviewed him in 1993, that the Diary was in Knowsley Buildings (where James Maybrick had his office) until 1969 when the building was destroyed. From there, somehow, he surmised, the Diary had come to Tony Devereux.

Just a few weeks later, on 4 October 1995, Anne Graham followed Barrett on to Radio Merseyside, in a series of interviews that would also feature Shirley Harrison and Paul Feldman. Anne's story of the Diary being in her family and her reasons for giving it to Barrett were again recounted, though she appears uncomfortable with the questioning and giggles outright when asked if she forged the Diary. Her disinterest in the Diary, despite the damage it had wreaked in her life, is in contrast to her enthusiasm for her forthcoming book on Florence Maybrick. It was a line from which she would never deviate.

If the Diary were a Victorian document, the ink could not be Diamine, as Michael Barrett had claimed it to be in at least one forgery confession. On 20 October 1995 came a rebuttal of this possibility from a source that could hardly be bettered, Alec Voller, head chemist at Diamine Ink. Examining the Diary at the Kings Cross offices of Smith Gryphon, Voller announced his conclusion after barely two minutes: 'This is not Diamine ink.' The meeting, at which Robert Smith, Shirley Harrison, Sally Evemy, Keith Skinner and Martin Howells were also present, was taped in full, but it is Voller's conclusion that is most significant. 'Certainly the ink did not go on the paper within recent years. . . . you are looking at a document which in my opinion is at least 90 years old and may be older. . . . I came with an open mind and if I thought it was a modern ink I would have said so.'

If the couple who had brought the Diary to public attention now appeared to be back in tandem, at least in their belief in the Diary's authenticity, it would not last long. In a thirteen-page undated letter to Shirley Harrison, in January 1996, Barrett railed against Anne and the claim that she might be Florence Maybrick's great granddaughter: 'She must be sick in the head or doing it for the money.' According to Barrett, Anne had said to him, 'If anyone finds out I'm lying I will make sure you never see Caroline again.' Furthermore, she had allegedly told Barrett's sister Lynn that she had come out with her story of the Diary being in her family because she realised that she had no say in the Diary after leaving him.

By this stage, according to his own estimate, Paul Feldman had spent as much as £150,000 researching the Diary. Now, it appeared, he might get at least part of that sum back. Confirming the interest of Virgin Publishing in a projected Diary book by Feldman, senior editor Rod Green wrote to him on 31 January 1996: 'I firmly believe that you have proved that James Maybrick was the Ripper and that the Diary and the Watch belonged to Maybrick.'

For most of the Diary story, Anne Graham had kept herself as far from the spotlight as possible. When she had emerged, it was usually under the wing of Paul Feldman. As a result there were still areas of her life that Shirley Harrison had not yet investigated. On 12 February 1996, two weeks after reading Michael Barrett's views on his ex-wife, Harrison, with Sally Evemy, took some time to get to know the new star of the Diary story better. Though there would be no startling new information, what did emerge was a much more detailed picture of the couple's life together and the circumstances behind Anne's alleged decision to give the Diary to Barrett.

Anne's father, Billy Graham, had married her mother, Irene Bromilow, in 1946 (three years after Billy said he first saw the tin trunk with the Diary in it). Irene's father had been a professional footballer, as was his brother, and consequently the family had a rather better income than their peers. An only child, Anne had been sent to a private convent school, Broughton Hall Prep, where she felt she was in a 'different class' to the other girls and made no friends, devastating her mother when she failed the scholarship, largely because she didn't want to stay. Life at home wasn't easy either. She hardly saw her father, who was working all the time at Dunlop Tyres, and when Irene contracted tuberculosis she had to spend long periods in a sanatorium. Irene's own mother, a hypochondriac, was also in the house and when Irene started drinking heavily Anne, at the age of twelve, had to look after both of them. After falling off a bike Irene was bedridden for a year and a half, eventually dying of pneumonia on St Valentine's Day 1964 (actually 1965). When Anne was eighteen (actually nineteen), Billy married Maggie Grimes and they moved into a maisonette with Anne. Maggie had three sons from a previous marriage, but Anne recalls that they were not often at home.

Although Anne was very fond of Maggie, whom she had known for many years before the marriage, she wanted to make a life for herself and in 1970, at the age of nineteen, she decided to emigrate to Australia. After completing a nursing course in Canberra, Anne worked in Australia for five years, returning on 4 July 1975. To those sceptics who include Billy Graham in the conspiracy of hoaxers, Anne pointed to the fact that her father did not write one letter to her all this time. 'He could,' she said, 'hardly write.'

Soon after returning to England, she accompanied a girlfriend to the Liverpool Irish club, where she met Michael Barrett, 'nicely dressed, articulate and intelligent', for the first time. On 4 December 1975 they were married by special licence. At fourteen, she learned, Barrett had been run over by a car, leaving him with lifetime kidney problems. Caroline arrived when they were both aged thirty; he would prove to be a 'wonderful dad' and Caroline adored him.

But even before the Diary brought its pressures to bear on their marriage, domestic problems were mounting. Barrett was at home on invalidity pension, and, according to Anne, while he was a good father, he was spending the shopping money with little to show for it. Though she was slower on the uptake than Caroline, she eventually realised the extent of his drinking problem. As she had said many times before, she gave Barrett the Diary to encourage his writing, hoping he would use it as the basis of a fictional book, but now she also painted a picture of a failing relationship into which she was desperately trying to inject some life. The move to Goldie Street didn't help. Anne's stepmother Maggie had recently died, and she wanted to be near her father, with whom she had become very close since her return from Australia. But there was tension between Graham and Barrett and the marriage seemed to be going further downhill.

Why had Anne given the Diary to Tony Devereux, she was asked again? Apart from a few drinking friends downtown, whom he never brought home, Tony was the only friend of Michael's she knew of, even though she had only met him a couple of times and might not even recognise him if she met him on the street. Had she given the Diary to Michael directly, with the full story of the Diary's provenance, there would have been two unwanted repercussions. Her father would have been as remorselessly harassed by Barrett as Devereux was, which, given his failing health, she would not contemplate, and she wanted Barrett to achieve something by himself. Though she had thought of leaving him, here was a more positive option, one that could lead to her regaining a sense of pride in him. Even though she recalls him being happy when reading and researching the Diary, the atmosphere in the house was plummeting. Having given up work with severe arthritis, and losing her own self-esteem in the process, her life was 'absolutely horrendous'.

She was now, she said, at her lowest ebb. She stayed the night at her friend Audrey's, as the thought of coming back into the house at night was 'the complete and utter destroying of my personality'. Even so, she couldn't make the decision to leave Barrett. As for the idea that they could have forged the Diary together with their relationship in tatters, it was impossible: 'We couldn't agree on anything – I couldn't do anything right.' But even though she wanted this to be Barrett's project, she did intervene, retyping the transcript of the journal as he had botched the original attempt. She asked Barrett to read the Diary out to her while she typed, but to tell her the spelling mistakes 'because it should be the same – but whether he did I don't know because he wouldn't have recognised them if they bit him'.

She can't recall whether her failed attempt to destroy the Diary happened before or after Barrett first took the Diary to show to Doreen Montgomery but presumes it was afterwards, as she confidently expected Montgomery to throw her husband and the Diary out. She herself didn't see it as an historical document and assumed no one else would take it seriously either. She remembers feeling 'physically ill' when Barrett, rather than using the book to create his own fictional work, talked of getting a publisher for the Diary. Caroline, she says, remembers how her parents 'argued and fought physically over it [the Diary] on the floor and he won and I didn't see it after that because he had it hidden away – he told me he had it in the piano and I couldn't get the thing open'.

Why was Anne so frightened at the prospect that the Diary would be published? 'People would start investigating it – a serious investigator and it was bound to be found out and what am I going to do? I'm in a worse situation because if Michael found out how could I live with Michael and him finding out, well let's be honest, I've been lying to him – how many months?'

She then talked about the tremendous pressure exerted by Paul Feldman and his insistent harassing of Barrett's family in 1994. After Lynn Barrett (Michael's sister) rang Anne to complain furiously about Feldman, she called him herself and, after much shouting, they calmed down and spoke for four hours on the phone. She then rang Lynn back: 'He's going to give me a million like if I tell him what he wants to know and I said I'll play him along for a bit just to get him off the Barretts' back basically, just didn't have a clue what I was going to do.' When she told her father she would have to tell Feldman about the Diary, he said, 'Do what you like', and reluctantly promised to confirm her story, though she wasn't sure if he would speak to Feldman. Her father by this stage was very ill and didn't care about the Diary being published; indeed, he had never even read it.

Anne Graham's account had never significantly veered from the first time she had told Paul Feldman that the Diary was in her family. Not everyone, it seemed, believed her. At the end of February 1996, just a few days after the final interview with Shirley Harrison and Sally Evemy, Anne received a typed letter from Michael Barrett saying that he wanted half his money back and, while acknowledging his problems with spelling in her absence, reminding her that the Diary is in her handwriting: 'I HAVE THE FUCKED PROFF [*sic*] YOU WROTE IT.' Should she not come to see him by Monday, 'THE WORLD WILL KNOW YOU WROTE IT'.

A few days later another, similar, letter arrived through the post. If anyone thought that the Diary controversy was going to lie down quietly, they hadn't reckoned with Michael Barrett: 'Paul is not going to protect you after what I have done. He asked me to send him the proff [*sic*] . . . no one gets the proff [*sic*], until I'm ready, in other words 14 days from reading this letter.' The proof would be produced in a court hearing, then all would know that Anne Graham wrote the Diary of Jack the Ripper: 'BACK OFF! YOU BITCH. BEFORE I TELL THE WORLD. . . . THEN THERE'S NO MONEY FOR ANYONE. AND MONEY YOUR GOD IS'T [*sic*] IT.'

EIGHT

'Push this one step further
and I will kill you'

The family motto of James Maybrick was 'Time Reveals All'. Sadly, in regard to the Diary claimed as his, time appeared to have no such intention. The Hitler and Mussolini diaries, two of the twentieth century's most notorious forgeries, had been exposed as such in a matter of months, yet as 1996 dawned it was now over two years from the Diary's publication and the truth seemed as elusive as ever. It was over two years, too, since the first scientific tests on both watch and Diary, the first, conflicting, verdicts of ink, paper and handwriting experts and the near-fatal attacks on the Diary's credibility from the Rendell team and the *Sunday Times*. Much time had also elapsed since the crushing blow of Michael Barrett's first confession, and even the detailed account of his alleged forgery, sworn in an affidavit dated 5 January 1995, was a year old. Nor, it seemed, were sceptics any nearer identifying the forgers. Neither believer nor non-believer, in truth, could point to any great degree of progress.

Strangely, given Michael Barrett's regular attempts to incriminate himself, no strong proof had yet materialised to implicate either him or Anne Graham, surely key members of any conspiracy of hoaxers. Barrett's various confessions had been hugely effective in discrediting the Diary, but when examined in detail were found to be riddled with errors. In truth, few now believed Barrett was capable of creating the Diary himself anyway. It was hardly surprising, then, that in some quarters suspicion had shifted to Anne. Her accusers claimed she had introduced the new provenance for the Diary (that it had been in her family) at a suspiciously opportune time, with Paul Feldman poised to conclude a lucrative film deal, before further

212

clouding the issue by embarking on a biography of Maybrick's wife Florence, a leading character in the Diary. If she were capable of creating such a work, the doubters claimed, why not the Diary?

But if Anne Graham were the creative force behind a hoax, what was her motive? The obvious answer would be financial gain, but little in the Diary story is ever obvious. As a letter written to Anne by her agent Doreen Montgomery in late February 1996 confirmed, Anne had shown no interest at all in the spoils of the Diary. Reminding Anne of this, Montgomery wrote:

Not once during this contractual association have you ever asked me to vary the procedure by which, during the period of your marriage, I settled the majority of monies directly to Mike. There were occasions when I was asked by him to make payments to you, and this I did. I recall you told me afterwards that, in fact, you gave them back to Mike! As you know, throughout – including during that meeting at Paul's flat last year – you made it consistently clear that you wanted no part of the Diary or any attendant revenue.

It was only when her marriage to Barrett was over that Montgomery was determined to ensure Anne received 25 per cent of revenue 'against considerable opposition from one particular quarter'. Montgomery continued: 'But I was (and am) deeply concerned for the fairness of the matter, and also that Caroline should derive some benefit for the future. But you have never instructed me to pay monies to you. I have done so, believing that I was fulfilling my duty to you, as my client, in the new circumstances.'

Two and a half years after his report had savaged the Diary, Kenneth Rendell was able to offer some further clarification of his thoughts for Shirley Harrison. Back in September 1993 Robert Smith had voiced his surprise that the Rendell report had not examined the implications of their own scientific testing. Rod McNeil's ion migration test had dated the year ink was put on paper to within twelve years, either way, of 1921. Later he acknowledged that, should a document be kept in certain conditions, that range could be extended to thirty years either way. But, it now emerged, Rendell had only commissioned McNeil's test because 'someone on your side suggested to the publisher that it be done'. Nor did he and his other colleagues agree with the finding. 'I think everybody had the opinion that it was done fairly recently but nobody really thought very much about it because that was not a question that we needed to deal with.' Though amazed that the story was still continuing, Rendell had clearly been keeping in touch with it until June 1994. 'I thought,' he wrote to Harrison on 14 March 1996, 'that someone had admitted forging the diary – the fellow who owned it?'

Relations between the two Diary teams had soured soon after Paul Feldman entered the arena and had never recovered. It was not helping, either, that Feldman appeared unwilling, or unable, to pay the authors of the Diary the money due on the television showing of his documentary. This made it all the more remarkable that, according to Robert Smith, Feldman was hoping that Smith might publish his book, despite an existing offer from Virgin Publishing. On 26 March 1996 Smith was offered a preview of the mountain of research Feldman had now accumulated. It made, the Diary's publisher admitted, 'fascinating viewing', but even so he declined the invitation to publish it.

One of the great disappointments in this long-running dispute was the inability of successive scientific tests to provide conclusive proof either way. Back in 1994, at the prompting of Melvin Harris and others in the Committee for Integrity, the firm Analysis for Industry had tested ink extracts from the Diary, supplied by Robert Kuranz of the Rendell team, and identified the presence of the preservative chloroacetamide, which, it was claimed, could not have been a constituent of Victorian ink (Leeds University, however, had found none). For Harris, here was more proof that the Diary was a forgery. Not so, countered Shirley Harrison. An employee of Dow Chemicals in the US, which manufactures chloroacetamide, told her he had found it in preparations dating back to 1857. Both she and Paul Feldman also wondered if the samples used by Analysis for Industry could have been contaminated somehow. In April 1996 she felt it was worth trying to discover if the chloroacetamide came from the paper, and took the Diary from Robert Smith, who had collected it from its secure place in a bank vault, to the Royal Society of Chemistry's building in London. There she presented it to Diana Simpson, director of Analysis for Industry, who was to take paper samples for further testing. Harrison was not impressed.

Dr Simpson, according to Harrison, produced a brand-new stationery hole punch and presented it to Harrison in its pristine wrapper to indicate it was uncontaminated. The punch, however, was deemed by Harrison far too large for the purpose. 'Robert Smith would kill me if I take it back full of paper punch holes,' she told her. Simpson disappeared and returned, Harrison says, with a 'very thin wire implement'. It was not until halfway through the procedure that Harrison realised that the implement was in fact an unravelled paper clip. 'So much', Harrison concluded, 'for contamination.' AFI's final report stated that no chloroacetamide was found in the paper, the limit of detection being 0.8 part per million.

In March 2003, the authors wrote to Diana Simpson: 'Just to confirm, our understanding is that you examined ink samples from the Diary for the presence of chloroacetamide and gave Shirley Harrison a figure of 6.5 parts per million. (In 1996 you examined paper samples taken from the Diary and found no chloroacetamide). Would you be able to clarify for us exactly what the figure of 6.5 represents? Crucially, we need to know if this figure can help confirm or deny the possibility that the ink you examined is pre-1992 liquid Diamine, which is known to contain 0.26 per cent chloroacetamide, ie: 2,600 parts per million'. Dr Simpson's reply was brief and to the point. 'The results obtained were based on analysis of one or two ink "full stops" and represented 6.5 parts per million of chloroacetamide in the ink. The paper samples did not contain any chloroacetamide because they were blank and, hence, contained no ink.' How could the Diary ink and Diamine be one and the same, if the amounts of this preservative common to both were so different?

If they had failed to deliver the knock-out blow, the sceptics, grouped around Melvin Harris and the Committee for Integrity, were certainly not short of support in their campaign. While most of the flak had been directed at the Diary, Stanley Dangar was now devoting considerable time and money to investigating the Maybrick watch. Not previously interested in Jack the Ripper, Dangar's involvement had begun after reading the references to the watch in Shirley Harrison's book. He soon became convinced that the scratches ('J Maybrick', 'I am Jack' and the initials of the murder victims) were recent additions and from this deduced that the Diary, by association, must also be a hoax. Within a short time Dangar, clearly not a man to do things by halves, was in the thick of things.

Dangar had travelled to London in January 1995 to meet Shirley Harrison (whom he would later invite to Spain) and also arranged for the Johnson brothers to bring the watch down while he was there. Actual sight of the scratches did nothing to deter him from his conviction that they were forged. At the meeting Robbie Johnson discussed a recent letter from the American collector Robert E. Davis, indicating he might be interested in the watch for a figure in the region of $40,000, an offer that the brothers had not taken up. Of the two brothers, Dangar felt Robbie was the most obviously interested in gaining financially from the watch. On hearing of Robbie Johnson's tragic death on holiday in southern Spain, Dangar felt the circumstances merited further investigation.

It is not clear whether Dangar, who died in July 2002, was contacted first by the *Sunday Times* journalist Maurice Chittenden, whose initial investigation into the Diary had done so much damage, or whether he alerted Chittenden to the news. According to Dangar's notes, Chittenden rang him on receiving news of Robbie Johnson's death and asked him to investigate what appeared to him to be a suspicious death. A fax sent by Chittenden on 17 August 1995 suggests it might have been Dangar who first made contact. 'Thank you for your telephone call,' Chittenden wrote. 'I am interested in any possible, suspicious circumstances surrounding the death of Robert Johnson and would be grateful if you could make enquiries on my behalf.'

The next day Dangar faxed back the basic facts:

Death occurred in district Torregudiaro, late evening 14th August 1995. Johnson at this time living in Hotel Patricia, San Roque, a female friend or relative was with him during his stay. This person returned to the UK on night of accident. Johnson was a pedestrian crossing a road when he was struck by a motor-cycle. Cannot investigate the matter further until Monday 21st. when I shall be able to contact the Examining Magistrate. Please pass this on to M.H. [Harris].

Dangar's initial enquiries proved a disappointment as neither the staff at the hotel nor the local police were forthcoming, the latter appearing uninterested in opening a murder investigation. Nor could witnesses to the accident be found, he reported, or any information about the motorcyclist. Learning that the magistrate he needed to speak to would be absent on holiday for some weeks, Dangar returned home and contacted his local police in the hope they could persuade their southern colleagues to open an investigation.

But why did Dangar suspect that Robbie Johnson's death was not an accident? According to a report he compiled for the local police, in which he explained why he believed the Diary and the watch were fakes, Dangar believed there was a possible connection with Paul Feldman that needed to be explored. He wondered if the reason Robbie chose to stay at an otherwise unremarkable hostel in a little-known Spanish town was connected with the presence of a cabinet full of antique watches in the vestibule of the hostel, particularly as he understood the watch had disappeared at this time. Nor could he understand how Johnson had been unaware of a noisy motorbike in a road without obstructions or dangerous corners.

As he noted in the report, he had other concerns too: 'Johnson was staying in this hostel with a young woman named Helen Jane Rutherford. After the "accident" this woman identified the body and disappeared the same night, presumably returning to England. . . . subsequently Helen Rutherford turned up in the house of Paul Feldman . . . who was involved in the Diary of JTR. Up till now, we do not know who this woman is or what her relationship was/is with Paul Feldman.'

The police needed concrete evidence to open an investigation. As Dangar could produce none, and there was no support from the Johnson family, they let the matter rest. But Dangar's interest in the watch and by association the Diary did not wane. Still in contact with Melvin Harris, Dangar employed the Liverpool private detective Alan Gray to make enquiries on his behalf. On 3 July 1996 Gray arranged for the horologist Timothy Dundas to make an affidavit. Dundas had been asked to service the Maybrick watch in 1992 by Ronald Murphy of Stewarts the Jewellers. 'I examined this watch and serviced it and I think I fitted a spring and polished the case,' he said. 'The only markings on this watch at that time were repair markings. A month or so later Mr Stewart [*sic*] contacted me and asked me if I had seen any marks on this watch, relevant to 'Jack the Ripper', and I told Mr Stewart the only marks on the watch were repair marks.' Like Stanley Dangar, Dundas believed the watch to be a lady's watch (one reason why Dangar believed it had not belonged to Maybrick). Dundas had no doubts that any marks relating to Jack the Ripper had been made since his examination of the watch: 'The whole suggestion that this watch belonged to "Jack the Ripper" is completely false,' he wrote.

Gray then spoke to Ronald Murphy (mistakenly referred to as Mr Stewart by Dundas), who gave a different account. Murphy claimed to have polished the watch after it was returned from Timothy Dundas. 'On the rear case, inside, I noticed scratch marks, there were several marks. I did not scrutinise them closely so I am unable to say exactly what they were.' Murphy stated he had put the watch on display in early 1992, and it was subsequently bought by Albert Johnson on 14 July 1992. According to Johnson, it was kept in a drawer for about ten months before he discovered the markings and returned to the jewellers with a number of questions. According to Dundas, Murphy ('Mr Stewart') had contacted him just a month after he examined it in 1992. Someone had got their dates wrong.

In late July and early August 1996 Alan Gray attempted to extract further information from Albert Johnson via a series of phone calls, none of which, according to Gray's letters to Stanley Dangar, was well received. In their first conversation Johnson refused to see Gray and denied there was anything suspicious about his brother's death, allegedly telling Gray that 'it was just one of those things'. Three days later Johnson confirmed that he bought the watch at Stewarts and 'put it in a drawer and forgot about it for a while', but again he refused to see Gray. After another fruitless attempt Gray returned to the fray on 1 August, armed with new information from Dangar about Helen Jane Rutherford, who, Gray insisted, had witnessed the accident. As far as Johnson was aware, his brother was with a young girl called 'Jane', who identified him at the mortuary. Gray tells Johnson that Helen Jane Rutherford left Spain at once before police got the chance to interview her. 'Albert, this matter could get very serious. The watch is a fraud, there is no doubt about that – my report may be passed on to the Police. Now is the time to set matters right.' 'I have the watch and I believe in it,' Johnson replies. 'I am fed up with all this. Jack the Ripper and all the trouble over it. It's only bad luck. I wonder if there's a curse on it and all this.' The conversation is terminated.

Unable to trace Helen Jane Rutherford, Gray reported to Dangar that he had not seen the watch or been able to find Albert Johnson's address yet, but was sure that he had 'been well-briefed by Feldman to avoid me or anyone else making such enquiries. . . . Obviously, he has something to hide.' Along with the affidavits he was sending, Gray enclosed an invoice for his services and a couple of mementoes of his work for Michael Barrett, a bounced cheque for £1,500 and an unpaid account rendered for the second half of 1994 for a further £1,500 owed for services provided – £3,000 in total.

Johnson had relayed Gray's questioning to Paul Feldman, whom Dangar apparently regarded as the 'Mr Big' of the Diary hoax. If he were, it had not yet been much of a coup for him. Thus far, Feldman had invested over £150,000 researching his forgery – an unusual strategy for a hoaxer. It was a sum of money he could not hope to recoup with either video or book and as a result he was now having to placate a growing list of creditors. The consequences of his obsessional pursuit of the Diary had not been purely financial either. Working long hours, seven days a week, his relentless energy fuelled by whisky and cigars, he had driven himself into a state of nervous exhaustion. In early August 1996 Martine Rooney, Feldman's PA, informed Robert Smith that Feldman had taken an overdose, though he had fortunately been found in time to save his life. With her clients still owed money by Feldman, Doreen Montgomery was sympathetic but cautious. His PA would hardly have vouchsafed this information without Feldman's permission, she reasoned. Could this be 'yet another ploy to make Robert feel sorry for him and thus hold off on the demand for the cash he undoubtedly owes us?' (She was referring to an invoice sent to Duocrave in February 1996 for £12,500, payable on transmission of Feldman's documentary on ITV, which Smith had been pursuing for months.)

Shirley Harrison would soon hear at first hand Stanley Dangar's conviction that Paul Feldman was the main architect of the Diary forgery (collaborating, Dangar claimed, with Tony Devereux and Michael Barrett). On the night of 19 August 1996 she received a call from Dangar in Spain, telling her he had been summoned to appear before the Guardia Civil in Gerona in connection with Robbie Johnson's death. He also warned Harrison that Melvin Harris and Alan Gray were actively determined to unmask the Diary fraudsters. Believing Dangar to be 'driven by the need to be associated with major drama and people he sees as "stars"', Harrison sent a memo to Robert Smith, Paul Feldman and Doreen Montgomery urging them to 'treat his information and comments with extreme caution'.

Dangar was back on the telephone to Harrison on 26 September to tell her that the Guardia Civil had just visited him and taken away all his papers relating to the Diary. They were, he claimed, now investigating the 'murder' of Robbie Johnson. Dangar also claimed that he had received a telephone call from Scotland Yard asking him to send all his papers (which apparently included copies of all publishing contracts relating to the Diary and the sale of ownership of the Diary from Michael and Anne Barrett to Robert Smith) to the chief superintendent. Convinced that Paul Feldman had forged the watch scratchings with Robbie Johnson, Dangar also believed he had masterminded the operation that resulted in Johnson's death.

According to Paul Feldman, as he had traversed Hollywood trying to set up a film deal for the Diary, he had been hounded every step of the way by Melvin Harris crying fraud. Now that Virgin Publishing were to publish Feldman's book on the Diary, the same pattern was recurring. On 14 October 1996 Harris wrote to Rod Green, Virgin's commissioning editor, enclosing some material for him to study and warning that it would be impossible to discuss such things with Feldman himself: 'he is the most intolerant and dogmatic man that I have ever met. But that is understandable when you consider that he is used to getting his own way by bawling at and threatening and intimidating his critics. Even his paid henchman, Keith Skinner, states that "In his mind, he [Feldman] is right, everybody else, including myself, is wrong . . .".'

Alan Gray had by now undertaken work concerning the Diary for Nick Warren as well as for Stanley Dangar and Michael Barrett, even writing an affidavit on behalf of the latter when his hand was injured. At this stage Gray appeared to have little doubt as to who were the true villains of the story. 'Be assured,' he wrote to Barrett on 15 October 1996, 'that if we can possibley [*sic*] prove without doubt where you bought the Diary from I can almost guarantee you will make "money". I have a National Newspaper ready to do business, BUT we must get the evidence that will support you. Then watch them jump because your credibility will then be 100 per cent. Feldman is about to release a new book. The time is right to pay these terrible people back. So let's do it. Phone me. . . .'

The main subject of the forgery accusations had never lost touch with the Diary team, even during the most traumatic of times. Shirley Harrison, in particular, had received an endless succession of late night calls and answerphone messages from Michael Barrett, sometimes abusive and threatening, sometimes pleading, often conveying extraordinary pieces of information (he was an MI5 man who had defeated the IRA single-handedly; he was married and going to live in Russia) and requests (could Harrison buy him out of the Diary for £8,000 – including the £4,000 he owed her?). Eventually it became too much. On 28 November 1996 Harrison applied to the Metropolitan Police for a telephone trace, complaining of Barrett's calls annoying her 'constantly day and night'.

As Paul Feldman's book neared completion (it would be delivered some months after his initial deadline), his financial problems showed no signs of easing, despite his earlier optimism. Both Doreen Montgomery and Robert Smith continued to press for delayed payments, now totalling £25,000, including a new invoice for £12,500 owed for the US television showing of his documentary. As 1997 dawned hopes of repayment looked more promising – but at a cost. Feldman's large house in Hertfordshire, where Anne Graham had told him so much of her story, was to be sold. Within 24 hours of completion, set for 14 February, Feldman promised Robert Smith on 3 January, he would 'sort things out', if Smith could extend his deadline accordingly.

Money was also on Doreen Montgomery's mind when she wrote to Michael Barrett on 28 January. Barrett remained angry at the deductions that were still being taken from his royalties. Explaining to Barrett why this was necessary, she reminded him that, at the time of writing, 'YOU HAVE PERSONALLY RECEIVED SUMS FROM US AMOUNTING TO £61,296.19', of which, it would appear, absolutely nothing was left.

If the forgery were as easy as Melvin Harris suggested, could Michael Barrett be telling the truth, or a version of it, in his most detailed confession of 5 January 1995? On 13 February 1997 came more evidence that Barrett's confession might not be all it seemed. Barrett had claimed that his sister, Lynn Richardson, had taken the incriminating evidence of his forgery, including a photograph, compass, discs, pens and ink, to her home, later telling him, when he asked for them back, that she had destroyed them. Having only recently learnt of this, she reacted furiously, issuing a statement through her lawyer:

I wish it to be known that I have never taken or been given anything from Michael Barrett connected in any way with the 'Diary of Jack the Ripper'. Furthermore I have never destroyed anything which belonged to Michael. I have sought legal advice on this matter. As my solicitor advises if this affidavit should be taken to press, we will sue for libel. I have no involvement nor ever had, in the 'Diary'. The only connection I have with Michael Barrett is he is my brother. I have not seen Michael since he stayed with my family in 1994.

Paul Feldman's financial problems showed no signs of easing. By 14 February 1997 Robert Smith was proposing that Feldman instruct Virgin Publishing to pay all monies from his forthcoming book directly to Smith Gryphon until the £25,000 owing to them was paid in full. Another complication had arisen too. Should Feldman be granted the right to reproduce any of the Diary in his book? Doreen Montgomery did not see why such an advantage should go to a rival book, particularly when its author owed them such a considerable amount of money and had caused such large legal bills. In the end Smith gave permission for Feldman to quote up to 1,500 words from the Diary, explaining to Montgomery that, had he refused, Virgin could have quoted it anyway, under fair usage and for purposes of review, 'thereby blowing a hole through our copyright protection'. Shortly afterwards, Duocrave Ltd did go into liquidation, and with it went any prospect of Smith Gryphon seeing a penny of the £25,000 owed.

For many, Anne Graham remained the most unfathomable character in the Diary story. A very private woman, she had initially stayed as much in the background as possible. Then, in July 1994, she emerged centre-stage, with a new provenance for the Diary, one supported by her father, and within a year had announced her intention to write a book on Florence Maybrick. It had been a dramatic personal journey from the ordeal she described of the last years of married life. The Anne Graham that wrote to Shirley Harrison in July 1997 appeared a much stronger character than some might have imagined: 'I have had the tough question,' she wrote, 'here is the tough answer.'

No, she did not know that Robert Smith had been facing a threat from Scotland Yard; she assumed it was her husband being investigated. Nor did she feel any guilt for the huge legal fees resulting from the action against the *Sunday Times*. That was a result of Smith offering the Diary to the one newspaper in England that had been badly mauled by the Hitler Diaries. 'Do you really think that it is likely that they would have accepted my explanation after the event, even with my father's support? There are plenty of people who don't believe it now.' How could she have told anyone else the truth without first telling her husband, who was completely paranoid and drinking heavily, and not telling him was a 'matter of personal survival'. Anne had taped an open letter to Harrison, Montgomery, Smith and Feldman 'out of a sense of responsibility and in an effort to apologise'. A 'normal, fallible human being', Anne Graham clearly felt she had done enough in that department.

A few weeks later Anne's provenance was at the heart of a *Sunday Express* article on 24 August 1997, trailing Paul Feldman's new book, *The Final Chapter*. The writer of the article, which appeared beneath the startling headline 'MASS MURDERER'S DESCENDANTS ARE ACCUSED OF STAGING ELABORATE CHARADE', had clearly had trouble absorbing Feldman's theories. Barrett's confession, the article had Feldman claiming, was triggered by his anger on discovering that the Diary was owned for generations by an illegitimate branch of the Maybrick family, descended from Florence, and that one of them, Anne Graham, had secretly asked a friend to pass the Diary to him. It was then that he falsely claimed the whole episode was a 'scam'.

The wider public would get their own chance to digest Feldman's theories when *The Final Chapter* was published on 18 September 1997. But would the publication merely trigger the end of the Diary story? On 22 September, Melvin Harris told Stephen Ryder, editor of the highly popular Jack the Ripper Casebook website, that his long-awaited unmasking of the Diary's forgers was imminent. He had been holding back in order to read, and subsequently counter, Feldman's arguments.

Paul Feldman was not the only party connected with the Diary to suffer financial problems. On 23 September 1997 Smith Gryphon Ltd, the publishers of Shirley Harrison's book, went into receivership. For a fee of £55,000, the company's assets, including

The Diary of Jack the Ripper, were bought by Blake Publishing Ltd in November 1997. However, while Shirley Harrison's book now had a new home, the physical Diary remained with Robert Smith. On 7 July 1998 Smith also purchased the copyright in the Diary from the receivers, much to the fury of Doreen Montgomery, who only learnt of the deal after its completion. She was already angry that Smith had written to Anne Graham's publishers, Headline, asking for a fee for allowing her to quote from the Diary in *The Last Victim*, her biography of Florence Maybrick (for which Montgomery did not represent her). Nevertheless Headline did pay Smith a small reproduction fee and published an acknowledgement of his copyright ownership. Montgomery wrote later, 'they [Blake] consult with Robert as the "owner" of both diary and copyright therein. I personally find it iniquitous that he should be either and I am just wondering whether there is any illegality here that could restore the status quo.'

Having acquired Shirley Harrison's book, Blake were now anxious to put out a revised edition. This would boast an intriguing foreword. David Canter, a professor of psychology at the University of Liverpool, and a criminologist who had helped pioneer offender profiling, had become fascinated by the Diary, whether it was genuine or not. Canter's ruminations on the Diary had been helped by one who had no doubt it was the latter. On 13 December 1997 Canter wrote to Melvin Harris thanking him for taking the trouble to send his detailed notes on the subject. Harris would certainly have no disagreement with Canter's reason for not getting involved earlier – Paul Feldman. 'I found,' Canter wrote, 'his whole style and approach to be the total antithesis of reasoned argument and serious examination.' Canter's intention, he told Harris, was to draw up a psychological profile of the author of the Diary, 'in order to leave the reader to judge whether this better fits a faker or JTR'. Harris would not, however, have agreed with Canter's next contention. 'If it is the fake you suggest then it must stand as one of the most inventively constructed fakes of all time.'

If that were the case, then was Michael Barrett, as he once claimed himself, one of the greatest forgers of all time? A one-time champion, it seemed, had now changed his mind. Barrett's credibility had been stoutly defended by the Liverpool private detective Alan Gray since he first became embroiled in the story, supporting him against what he perceived was a conspiracy to defraud Barrett of money and credit by those in the Diary teams. But unpaid accounts and Barrett's erratic behaviour had destroyed the relationship. By the beginning of 1998 Gray felt so strongly about his former employer that he felt compelled to swear an affidavit describing a meeting in Liverpool with him. By now his disillusionment was total.

Noting that Barrett was clearly under the influence of drink, Gray tells him that he has tried for years to get to the truth of the Diary: 'I have protected you and looked out for you, been bodyguard and friend over a long period of time in which you run up a bill with me of over £3,000.' Gray describes Barrett as a 'Rat, Scum and the biggest liar I have ever met.' 'Well, Alan,' Barrett allegedly replied. 'You have to tell the tale right, it's just like fishing, you play the line then just pull them in. I told you just what you wanted to know. I knew what you wanted to hear and then I had you believing.'

Though still convinced that the Diary is a fraud, Gray no longer believes Barrett could have been its creator, being 'to [*sic*] thick' and 'to [*sic*] drunk'. Gray's current theory, he tells Barrett, is that Tony Devereux composed the storylines and Anne Graham wrote the Diary. 'Anne sold you out all the way down the line, before you had finished your early morning drink.' Barrett counters that he did indeed write the Diary, 'with a little bit of help from Devereux – he was a knowledgeable man, very intelligent and Anne Barrett wrote it down'. Gray is not impressed: 'Michael you can't write, you can't even lie properly these days, your [*sic*] pathetic. You made an attempt with a story – 'Daniel the Dolphin Boy' – what a load of rubbish.' Apparently believing the Diary to be a conspiracy of hoaxers involving Paul Feldman as well as Anne and Devereux, Gray takes some pleasure in 'seeing Liverpool's best con-man conned, that's the funny part. They had the money, you had the promises.'

Gray is particularly incensed after Barrett tells him he was promised money he never received but will pay Gray back when he can: 'Michael, another lie, you received over £11,000 on one occasion and your solicitor kept the lot you said, but again you had your share and you paid nothing off your debts. I have to tell you don't call me as a witness, I'll help you down. You are a liar and a cheat and if I had my way, you would be charged with conspiracy. I have no intention of doing anything for you, giving evidence or being of any assistance.' 'Ha, ha, ha,' Barrett replies, 'I give my name to history, what love can do to a gentleman born.' 'Don't ring me any more or contact me,' Gray warns finally. 'I am going now before I kick the shit out of you.' 'I then left the area,' he notes.

The threat of violence had not just been used against Michael Barrett. Since the final breakdown of their marriage in January 1994, when she took their daughter Caroline from the family home, Anne Graham had reported a series of intimidating visits made by him. On 29 August 1997 came the final straw. According to the account she gave police, Barrett had banged loudly on her front door, shouting threats. If this claim was open to challenge, the note he pushed under the door was not. It read: 'So help me God, push this one step further and I will kill you. I want you to know you can never walk the streets in safety. If you use Caroline and label her a Maybrick I'll blow your head off – and I mean it.' Barrett was charged with threatening to kill her.

But when the case reached Liverpool Crown Court over a year later, on 11 September 1998, the case seemed to centre as much on the Diary of Jack the Ripper as on the specific charge. The impetus for his anger, Barrett claimed, was the article in the *Sunday Express* publicising Paul Feldman's book *The Final Chapter* and its assertion that Anne, and therefore Caroline, were descendants of Florence Maybrick. All Barrett cared about, he told the court, was protecting his daughter's name and proving she was not related to Jack the Ripper. Worse, Florence Maybrick was convicted of the murder of her husband, so that linked his daughter to two murderers. Barrett seemed unaware that Feldman had not claimed a relationship between Anne and James Maybrick but rather suggested that she was descended from an illegitimate child of Florence Maybrick. It seemed to make little difference.

227

Admitting to being an alcoholic, Barrett told the court he was drunk when he wrote the note in a taxi on the way to Anne's house and was horrified when, sober, he later read it. 'Totally upset and angry', after seeing the *Sunday Express* article, he had, he claimed, only wanted to see his daughter and assumed Anne would take the note 'with a pinch of salt'. Asked if he had really intended to kill her, he replied, 'No, not in a million years.' He described to the court how he and Anne had forged the Diary, using an old photo journal, with he composing the text and she writing it. 'I regret the day Anne and I carried it out. It was a Frankenstein monster.' Claiming he had not made any money from the Diary, and was even homeless at one stage, he blamed his worsening drink problem on the stress caused by the Diary.

The forgery claim was denied as ridiculous by Anne, who said neither of them was involved. She told the court that her ex-husband had begun drinking heavily in 1988 and had been abusive and violent, harassing her after she moved out of the family home. The jury deliberated for an hour before deciding that Barrett was innocent of the charge. Outside, Barrett told the waiting media he was 'delighted. It proves I am not a violent man.' He continued, 'This should prove the case about the Diary of Jack the Ripper. I stopped the fraud, but nobody believed me. I feel totally vindicated. I've gone through five years of hell. I've cleared my name and it's come out in court that my daughter is not related to Jack the Ripper. I'm not the father everyone thinks I am. All I cared about was to protect my daughter's name. One day,' he concluded, 'she will appreciate that I have saved her from the stigma of Jack the Ripper.'

The Blake edition of Shirley Harrison's book was to be published on 1 October 1998. A fortnight before, on 15 September, the Diary was granted a rare accolade. As part of the Fifth International Psychology Conference at the University of Liverpool, Professor Canter, author of the new edition's foreword, was to discuss the Diary with Shirley Harrison and Keith Skinner. Canter introduced his thesis under the mischievous title, 'Was Jack the Ripper a Scouser?' The best test of authenticity when judging a disputed diary, Canter claimed, was the persona that emerges from such a document. The Hitler that emerged from the discredited Hitler Diaries, he contended, was simply not believable. 'By contrast the "Jack the Ripper" diary creates a character that is remarkably convincing.'

The discussion was aimed not at asking whether the author of the Diary was Jack the Ripper but if it could be the work of a consummate craftsman and creative conman or a lucky amateur hoaxer? 'Or does it, indeed, reflect a killer's tormented spirit?' The Maybrick Diary, Canter believed, had not been given a fair hearing. 'As Conan Doyle pointed out, when the implausible has been dismissed you are left with the only possibility. Who is the most plausible author of the "Jack the Ripper" diaries?'

There was one man present who insisted that he knew the answer. Making an unscheduled appearance, Michael Barrett took the floor and gave an account, lasting about ten minutes, of just how he had forged the Diary, earning himself a generous round of applause from the conference delegates in the process. As a result of his claims, Professor Canter assigned one of his students to make a linguistic comparison study between Barrett and the Diary, 'to assess the likelihood of Michael Barrett being the author of the "Jack the Ripper Diary"'. The conclusion, revealed six months later, was 'very low'.

There were some people who believed the author might be not Barrett but his ex-wife Anne Graham, pointing to the biography she was co-writing with researcher Carol Emmas on Florence Maybrick as evidence that she might have the literary and research skills necessary for the forger. Now they could judge for themselves. At the beginning of February 1999 *The Last Victim*, the story of Florence Maybrick, was published by Headline and Anne was once more in the spotlight. In the introduction to the book, Anne described how her father first saw the Diary in 1950, though he claimed to have heard about it as early as 1943, and her own first sight of it in 1968. As to her decision to hand it over to her then husband as a means of encouraging him to write, it was a matter of great regret: 'My foolish actions had unhappily and unwittingly touched a great many lives, causing anger and misery.'

There was, for once, some positive publicity coming Anne's way, too. In an interview in the *Telegraph* magazine of 6 February 1999, Anne talked about how her eighteen months' work on the book had helped her recover from the trauma of her marriage break-up and the resulting loss of self-confidence. Despite her complete indifference to Jack the Ripper, she became gradually more interested in Florence after her father's suggestion that they might be descended from her, and became more and more convinced of her innocence of the murder of James Maybrick. Despite the amount of research material – largely 425 Home Office files relating to the case, and copies of the extensive collection of notes and papers of American author Trevor L. Christie – she managed the daunting task of writing the book while working part-time as an archivist to bring in the rent.

She found the work had helped restore the confidence she lost after the split with Barrett, when she describes walking around as if in a dream: 'It left me in pieces and I lost all my self-esteem. I could not even make a decision about cooking a meal. One day,' she says, 'I awoke feeling happy. It's wonderful but it takes a long time to reach that stage.' Now halfway through an honours degree in health at Liverpool's John Moore University, she was not, the magazine reported, looking too far ahead. 'I've never expected a huge amount of happiness,' she says, 'there's no such thing – being content is what is important.'

The signature of Gerard Kane, witnessing Tony Devereux's will, which alerted Melvin Harris to the possibility he might have written the Diary. (The witness A. Graham has no connection with Anne Graham.)

During all of this time Stanley Dangar had maintained his active interest in the Diary and watch. Now, with the help of Alan Gray, he turned his attention to the question of who was responsible for the handwriting. As early as 1993 Melvin Harris believed he had discovered a likely candidate. The man who had witnessed the will of Tony Devereux, his friend cabinet-maker Gerard Kane, possessed, Harris believed, handwriting that bore an uncanny resemblance to the writing in the Diary. Harris, though, had no evidence other than the signature and it proved difficult to find more. Until the arrival on the scene of Stanley Dangar, and more specifically Gray, it appeared unlikely anyone would alter this state of affairs. But, working on behalf of Dangar, Gray was able to obtain, in February 1999, the following sample of writing from Kane:

Dear Sir, This is Mr Kane writing to say that I am sick to death of you people. You come to my house to sign a form which I did you said I wouldn't hear no more. Signed G Kane. PS Sorry about the writing.

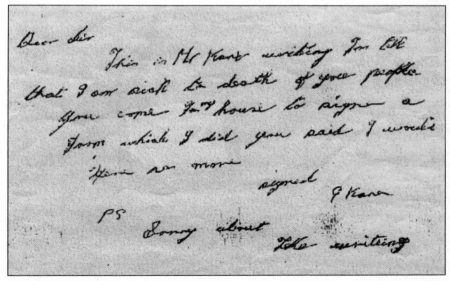

Private detective Alan Gray obtained this sample of Gerard Kane's handwriting in February 1999.

I do not have the courage to take my life. I pray each night I will find the strength to do so, but the courage alludes me. I pray constantly all will forgive. I deeply regret striking her, I have found it in my heart to forgive her for her lovers.

I believe I will tell her all, ask her to forgive me as I have forgiven her. I pray to God she will understand what she has done to me. Tonight I will pray for the women I have slaughtered. May God forgive me for the deeds I committed on Kelly, no heart no heart

Journalist Stephen Grey, like Melvin Harris, sees similarities between Gerard Kane's handwriting and the Diary, and refers to the idiosyncratic K in Kane's signature. This excerpt shows how its author writes the K of Kelly.

Dangar's fervour to expose the Diary and watch now matched that of the most prominent and long-standing sceptic, Melvin Harris. It should have been no surprise when the two announced their intention to collaborate on a book exposing the double hoax of which they were so convinced. To the research already carried out by Harris and Alan Gray could be added Dangar's informed opinions regarding the watch. To this end he had written to both Dr Wild and Dr Turgoose, believing their findings had been misrepresented in both Shirley Harrison's and Paul Feldman's books. He had also arranged for reports on the watch by colleagues at the universities of Cologne and Barcelona. According to Janet Dangar, Stanley's widow, a breakdown in communication led to a synopsis of their idea being circulated to publishers by a literary agent friend of Dangar's, David Cobb of Equinox agencies, apparently without the knowledge of either. His choice of recipients could not have been more unfortunate.

On 11 March 1999 Cobb decided to send a copy of the synopsis of 'The Jack the Ripper Diary' by Melvin Harris and Stanley Dangar to, of all people, Robert Smith at the former offices of the now-defunct Smith Gryphon, original publishers of *The Diary of Jack the Ripper*. From Smith's point of view, the outline synopsis (prepared by Melvin Harris, according to Stanley Dangar's widow) could not have seemed particularly tempting. It pulled no punches regarding the Diary and those who promoted it: 'But it [the Diary] was handwritten in an old-fashioned scrapbook and that was enough to allow one agency and one publisher to suspend caution and market this Diary as an authentic confession. To make this happen they were even prepared to brand Maybrick's legitimate will as a fake! A big market and big money beckoned!'

The Diary, the authors believed, had been constructed 'from the material used in two popular modern Ripper paperbacks of 1987. And all the extra Maybrick material can be shown to be derived from just one popular Penguin paperback of 1989.' Presumably Melvin Harris would be responsible for disproving the Diary. Stanley Dangar, who had reports from the universities of Cologne and Barcelona (though they had not actually seen the watch) which showed 'that the claims made for the watch tests cannot be substantiated', would attend to the watch.

'Every hoax,' the synopsis concluded, 'contaminates the fields of honest research and this one will not die overnight. Its time-wasting stupidities may linger on to dog some historians for years to come. But the book we propose will provide the essential documents and analyses that every enquiring, rational reader needs. And it will ultimately give the death-blow to the unwelcome impostor.'

As Smith explained in the June 1999 edition of *Ripperologist*, he was a little surprised to be the recipient of such a proposal, given that one intention of the new book was to show how gullible Smith Gryphon had been in being taken in by such a hoax, though as Smith pointed out, 'not so insane, surely, as to publish a book purporting to expose the Diary they published'. The synopsis had also been sent to Blake Publishing, the current publishers of the Diary, who were no more likely to consider such a book.

The Dangar/Harris partnership was not to survive long enough for the proposal to be taken up. Harris, Dangar informed Shirley Harrison on 20 May 1999, had given him the sack, furious that Dangar's agent had been telling people about the book. According to Harrison's memo of the call, Dangar told her that Harris 'was going to name the forgers – but he can't because there is absolutely no proof at all that this is a modern forgery'. Contrary to the suggestion in the synopsis, Dangar also told Harrison that Barcelona University had actually confirmed the two reports on the watch. 'It is quite clear the watch is not a modern forgery but it can't be accurately dated. I want this to go into your next edition with my blessing.' According to Harrison, Dangar was to send her all his, by now extensive, material on the Diary and watch, including a letter which he claimed supported Anne's story that the Diary came from her, from someone who saw her father's trunk being moved from his house. The material did not arrive.

After a long period out of the public eye, the man at the centre of the Diary story was back on the scene and he was back with his forger's hat on. On Friday 11 April 1999 Michael Barrett arrived in London to explain how he had gone about his hoax. It was to be a rare case of the chief defendant putting the case for the prosecution. But which particular version would he give? By now Barrett had offered various accounts of how the Diary was forged and who was involved, as well as at various stages reverting to the original story that it had been handed to him by Tony Devereux. After seven years it was felt that the Ripperologist fraternity, for which the Diary debate had remained one of central interest, was due an explanation from the horse's mouth.

Barrett began his London tour at the Portobello house of crime bookseller Camille Wolff, who arranged what would be the last of her legendary true crime lunches to honour him. A minder from among the ranks of Ripperologists, Andy Aliffe, was assigned to keep Barrett in check, at least until his talk at the Cloak and Dagger Club the next evening, warning the other guests against any provocative questioning that might result in him storming out. This had nearly happened that morning, when television presenter and true crime enthusiast Jeremy Beadle, on being introduced to Barrett, had mentioned the syndrome whereby confidence tricksters begin to believe their own web of deceit. Barrett, assuming this was an attack on his own integrity, had to be pulled away and led outside to cool down. When he returned, Beadle had left.

In the event the lunch, which went on until early evening, passed peacefully, with some significant pointers emerging to Barrett's current thinking. Guests, including Keith Skinner and the then editor of *Ripperologist* Paul Daniel, heard him relate that he had always believed James Maybrick *was* Jack the Ripper and had forged the Diary in order to draw attention to this fact. There was another interesting deviation from earlier accounts. Barrett told the assembled guests that he had contacted Doreen Montgomery *before* he had actually forged the Diary. When the agent took the bait, Barrett claimed, he found himself with just eleven days before their meeting to actually produce the Diary.

Writing in the June 1999 issue of *Ripperologist*, Paul Daniel was not convinced by Barrett's account: 'Mike has now had many years to arrange his "defence" of having created the journal, and it appeared to me that over those years he must have prepared and learnt a script, held in his mind's eye, that covered all contingencies and contained stock answers to any questions he might be asked. Though when taken out of chronology, or context, he floundered, and bluffed and blustered.'

The City Darts pub in Whitechapel, a stone's throw from the locations of the Ripper murders, was at this point the venue for the bi-monthly public meetings of the Cloak and Dagger Club, which was affiliated to the *Ripperologist* magazine. The next evening, in the packed upstairs room of the pub, Barrett was interviewed on stage by Keith Skinner, hoping, in his own words, to finally 'Kill the Diary'. Alongside the regular club members, Shirley Harrison and Robert Smith were in attendance, as well as Jeremy Beadle and a number of Ripper experts, including Martin Fido and Stewart Evans, who were adamant that the Diary was a modern hoax. It soon became evident that Keith Skinner's attempt to keep the interview along chronological lines would not be successful – Barrett was not to be restrained. Frequently during the evening, as at lunch the previous day, Barrett lashed out at his ex-wife for keeping their daughter from him and at Shirley Harrison for printing inaccuracies about him.

The evening was not without significant new claims, however. Barrett insisted the Diary had been written by Anne but created by him. Pressed by Skinner to explain why the writing was not similar to Anne's, Barrett announced that this was because Anne suffered from a multi-personality disorder, quoting Anna Koren's analysis of the handwriting in the Diary as evidence. Barrett returned to the matter of the red Victorian diary again, claiming he had bought it after contacting Doreen Montgomery. However, realising it was too small (not to mention the fact it was for 1891, two years after Maybrick's death), he then claimed to have bought a larger, black ledger from Liverpool auctioneers Outhwaite & Litherland. Before the meeting Barrett had claimed he would produce the lot receipt, which he was keeping in his pocket and which, all agreed, would certainly kill off the Diary once and for all. As the audience waited expectantly for the final demise of the Diary, Skinner asked Barrett if he had the receipt with him. 'Yes,' came the reply. Would he produce it? 'No.' The night's great moment of drama had misfired.

After the meeting Barrett confided he had been terrified of producing the receipt in front of so many people and being arrested for his involvement with forgery. Instead he promised to post it to Andy Aliffe. Aliffe is still waiting. The evening came to a premature close when a member of the audience mentioned Barrett's daughter Caroline in the course of asking a question. Barrett grabbed the microphone, leapt off the stage and threatened to attack the questioner. Though violence was averted, the public session was over.

According to Paul Daniel, the evening was a missed opportunity, and 'the majority of the audience went away unable to accept that Mike Barrett could possibly have forged the Diary'. The result of the meeting in which it was hoped to clear up the provenance of the Diary once and for all, Daniel concluded, 'was that it has been left in possibly more confusion than before'. There was an important point in all of this. As Shirley Harrison relayed in the letters column of *Ripperologist*, others would now understand the problems associated with trying to get a coherent and true account from Michael Barrett. Should not the same standards apply, she asked, to those who asserted Barrett was the forger as to those like herself, who believed the Diary was the work of James Maybrick. 'It puzzles me,' Harrison wrote, 'that even now some serious historians of the Ripper world – who demand documentary support of every fact from me – are prepared to state categorically that Michael and Anne collaborated in the forgery of the Diary. Where is THEIR proof?'

Once again the red diary had been cited by Barrett as proof of his forgery, only now it was bought *after* his first call to Doreen Montgomery on 9 March 1992 and rejected in time for him to then acquire the black ledger and forge the diary before his meeting with Montgomery on 13 April. Anne Graham's explanation has always been that Barrett sent away for the red diary when he was already in possession of the Diary, in order to confirm what a Victorian diary actually looked like. In August 1995 Keith Skinner had investigated the matter and, with Anne's cooperation, traced the cheque Anne had paid with from Lloyds Bank. Anne also gave him the diary itself, a maroon fabric-covered book, about 3 by 2 inches. Skinner's investigation revealed that the company, H.P. Bookfinders of Buckinghamshire, had received a telephone inquiry from a Mr Barrett asking them to locate a Victorian diary, which struck them as an unusual request. However, the 1891 diary was duly located and sent to Barrett's home address on 26 March 1992, reaching him, presumably, by Saturday, 28 March. The bill, for £25.00, was not paid until 18 May 1992, resulting in the company marking Barrett as a 'late payer'. According to Barrett's testimony, this would have left him barely two weeks to have rejected the maroon diary, seen the black ledger at an auction at Outhwaite & Litherland, put in a successful bid, and then completed the forgery.

Ten weeks after the public meeting at the Cloak and Dagger Club, Michael Barrett was back in touch with Shirley Harrison on 21 June

1999, requesting that the following (summarised) statement be inserted in the next paperback version of her book:

> I am not an alcoholic. I have got my life back on track and I am not on invalidity pension any more because I am fit. You must say that Anne (Graham) wrote the Diary – she wrote it with Billy Graham (her father). When Anne left me I turned around and said 'I know you wrote the Diary, love, but I will take all the blame.' I took all the blame because I didn't want to see her go to prison and my Caroline not have a mother. I loved her pure and simple. I said 'I'll go to prison for you', and I dug myself a hole deeper and deeper. I told so many lies it wasn't true . . . lie upon lie and it destroyed me. . . . Anne is a wicked schizophrenic; the Diary is in her handwriting. . . .

On more than one occasion over the previous five years Melvin Harris had indicated that the waiting public would soon be put out of their misery and be told the identities of those involved in the forgery conspiracy. The public were still waiting. Nick Warren, according to Harris a founder member of the Committee for Integrity, wrote to Shirley Harrison on 4 September 1999 to confirm who he believed were the trio Harris had in mind. Harris, he told Harrison, had always believed that Anne Graham composed the Diary text, while Barrett was her risk-taking leg-man. But he had identified someone else as the actual amanuensis of the prepared text – 'Tony Devereux's best mate from ——' – here Warren gave Gerard Kane's address.

On 2 October 1999 Warren was back in touch with Shirley Harrison to inform her that he had contacted Professor William Rubinstein of the University of Aberystwyth in Wales, who had recently become interested in the Diary and had declared himself 'more than 90 per cent convinced' that Maybrick was the Ripper. One of Rubinstein's arguments for believing the Diary was genuine was that if it were a modern forgery, the protagonists would have been identified by this point through gossip. Warren believed the answer to this was obvious, giving his own 'Roll of Honour' of forgers and explanations for why they had not been identified through this means: 'BG (deceased) TD (deceased) MB (irreversibly amnesic/ Korsakov's Syndrome)'.

The story of the Diary had developed at the same time as the dramatic increase in the use of the worldwide net. Given the staggering levels of interest in Jack the Ripper around the world, not to mention the controversy aroused by the Diary, it is hardly surprising that both would become huge favourites for internet debate. It also meant that information, theories and ideas criss-crossed the world in abundance, however odd they might seem. For a while in late 1999 and early 2000 it appeared that one such source might provide the crucial breakthrough Diary watchers had been waiting for.

On 4 October 1999 Ripperologist Andy Aliffe received an email with an interesting aside. Writing on a non-Ripper-related matter, Australian Steve Powell added, almost as an afterthought, that he recalled hearing about an English nurse in Sydney, sometime between 1967 and 1971, who had talked to other nurses about a Jack the Ripper Diary or letters that had come from her father. Long interested in the Ripper, Powell had wanted to see her but was told she had 'suddenly gone home to England'. It was not classified information that Anne had worked as a nurse in Australia and Paul Feldman's book, published two years earlier, had given the correct year of departure for her stay in Australia, 1970 (she returned to England in 1975). But Powell could not have read anywhere that she worked in Sydney or had returned abruptly to England. In theory, the nurse he referred to could have been Anne and, though it is curious that she hadn't mentioned it herself, it could provide much-needed corroboration for her testimony. Or so it seemed at this stage.

As interest in the matter grew, Powell sent a further email to Melvyn Fairclough, a Ripper author and researcher who had worked on Paul Feldman's book, and to Ripper author and historian Paul Begg, who was asked to forward it to Shirley Harrison. Powell's story was not merely fleshed out in this second email, it had completely changed. Now, it appeared, Powell did not merely suspect that the nurse in question might have been Anne Graham, he was able to recall a detailed account of a 'fiery meeting' with her, despite having claimed in the first email that she had returned to England before such a meeting could be arranged. According to Powell, the nurse said the Diary was real one minute, a forgery created by her father the next. She also said there were people who did not want anything about the Diary to be revealed. Powell said the meeting ended with him telling her that if she ever wrote about the Diary, he would 'shout from the rooftops that it was a lie, thought up by her and her father'. He claimed he was told by other nurses that, soon after the meeting, she had suddenly left for England and that some 'heavy officials' had told everyone 'to forget what they heard' and took all the nurses' records from the hospital.

The fact that Powell, in the space of two emails, had so dramatically changed his story was a warning, but those on both sides of the Diary divide still felt his story should not be dismissed out of hand. Powell himself offered to try to find corroboration. He had been in a rock band at the time and promised to find contact numbers for ex-members who would have known about the nurse and also an ex-girlfriend of his who had been a friend of hers. Both Shirley Harrison and Professor Rubinstein, who had contacted Powell when in Australia, felt this attempt to find corroboration showed his intentions, at least, were honest. Indeed, an ex-girlfriend was contacted, initially by Powell himself, and she recalled the possibility of knowing Anne. By this time, however, Powell's story had progressed to helping Anne and her alleged boyfriend at the time, an Australian-based Liverpudlian, forge the Diary itself. Credibility, or lack of it, now became a serious issue. It had been a long and distracting diversion, but was a good illustration of how theories could grow, take life and seriously impact on the Diary without any apparent foundation in fact at all.

As the web war intensified, with the majority of combatants convinced the Diary was a modern hoax, most of the central characters in the long-running war joined battle on the boards. One of the most important of these was Melvin Harris, whose writings on the Diary became the basis for many arguments on the net. In March 2000 Harris was interviewed for the American Ripper magazine *Ripper Notes* by its then editor, Christopher George. It provided an interesting insight into the background of the man who had led the crusade against the Diary from the outset. Telling George that he prefers to be described as a professional investigator rather than a writer and researcher, Harris reveals he has now worked on thirty-eight of the Arthur C. Clarke *World of Strange Powers* programmes as well as publishing a number of books debunking myths, among them *Investigating the Unexplained* and *Sorry – You've Been Duped.*

As early as age thirteen, Harris explained, he had become 'aware of the stranglehold that myths, lies and illusions had over the mind of adults. After that, I never took anything on trust and I learned how to ask the right questions and where to go for answers.' He blames journalists for introducing the rampant dishonesty into the story of the Ripper, whether it was inventing the 'Dear Boss' letters or the many subsequent hoaxes and legends that purported to solve the mystery. While journalists could not be blamed for creating the Diary, Harris (following a stout defence of his own Ripper suspect, Roslyn D'Onston) has no doubts whatsoever that it was a hoax. He is not, however, of the opinion that it was created by Michael Barrett: 'I've seen Mike's writings. He did not compose the Diary text. He does not have that capacity.'

He did, however, help with the research, Harris is convinced. As far as he is concerned, the lines in the Diary taken from the poet Richard Crashaw ('O costly intercourse of death . . .') are one obvious indication of this. Barrett's revelation of these lines on 30 September 1994 had created yet another battleground between modern hoax theorists and those who believed the Diary to be, at the very least, a decades-old document. The crux of the argument was how Barrett had discovered a line (and not a first line, which would be indexed in any collection) from an obscure poem. Harris believed he had the answer. Having seen Barrett's own copy of Volume Two of the *Sphere History of Literature* (republished in

241

1986), Harris can confirm Barrett's claim that the book fell open at just the right place:

> This does not mean that Mike wrote the Diary, but my examination of his copy of the book proves that he is right on one score: the book DOES FALL OPEN at the right page. The reason for that is simple. The copy is a substandard one with binding defects on pages 128, 112 and 183–4. The defects on the linked pages 183 and 184 biases the volume to open up on those pages and at the foot of page 184 are four lines of verse; the only such lines on that page. They open: "O costly intercourse/of deaths, & worse,/ Divided loves . . ." etc. The Diary entry is a slight variation of the first five words. Five words that gave the game away!

(Former publisher Robert Smith gave an alternative explanation to the authors in January 2003: 'Although Harris would not agree to release Mike's copy for an independent assessment, I have examined two copies of Volume Two of the Sphere book from Liverpool Library, where Mike claimed he discovered the quote. I found pages 112 and 128 to be perfectly normal. So were the relevant pages with the quote, 183–4, which are at the beginning of a new (16-page) section. Sewn hardback books have a natural tendency to open at such points, because of glue being applied between the sections to strengthen the binding. As Harris himself admitted in May 2001 on the Casebook message boards, "The book does not always fall open at page 184", and he cites page 196 and pages 478–9 as further examples, both being at the end or beginning of new sections. The two copies I examined behaved in a similar fashion. It is not surprising that the book should tend to fall open at these pages, and it might explain how Barrett came to find the quote in the library. There is no question of the book's production being substandard or of Mike's copy being defective.' The authors, for whom one of the two copies in Liverpool Library also opened at the right page, feel it should be noted that, if this book was the one photocopied for Shirley Harrison, it would have developed a bias after being pressed flat. However, the experience of forensic genealogist Peter Birchwood, who reported that a copy of the book he bought in July 2002 in a second-hand shop in Welshpool also opened at the right page, has to be taken into account.)

The Diary, Harris concludes, had been a great waster of time but was no block to valid investigations of other suspects. The hunt for the true Ripper could go on. But it had, he believes, shown up the weaknesses of some of the people who became entangled with it. 'Not a pretty sight! But there is always the chance of repentance!'

However much its critics might wish, the Diary of Jack the Ripper would not go away. On 17 June 2000 it even made the property section of the *Daily Telegraph*, when writer Roger Wilkes profiled Battlecrease House, the home James and Florence had rented during the period covered by the Diary. Interviewing the current owner Paul Dodd, whose father had bought the property after the war for £2,000, Wilkes described the 'sunny sitting-room, overlooking Liverpool Cricket Club', which in 1889 was the darkened bedroom where James Maybrick died. Since the trial of Florence Maybrick, the house had been a Mecca for murder devotees, 'three coachloads a day', according to Paul Dodd, not to mention '50 people wandering in the garden'. But in recent years, Wilkes reported, 'a new generation of crime crawlers makes the trek to Riversdale Road: Ripperologists'. Dodd himself admitted to becoming caught up in 'the Ripper thing' when the Diary first surfaced in public, 'but with different people claiming different things and the whole media ferment, it all became stressful'. Now, Dodd said, he was merely 'befuddled' by it all. As for Florence, the original Battlecrease murder suspect, Wilkes quoted no less an authority than crime writing legend Raymond Chandler. 'I'm pretty well convinced that the dame was guilty,' he said.

A few days later, on 28 June 2000, the Diary was back in the news, this time with the *Independent* announcing William Friedkin's forthcoming Diary film *Battlecrease* and *London Today* running a lunchtime television interview with Shirley Harrison on the same subject. No more details on the projected film have been forthcoming since, but the Diary itself has remained the subject of continuing speculation. In September 2001 Ripperologists from all over the world descended on Bournemouth for the third Jack the Ripper conference to be held in the UK since 1996. There they were treated to a Ripper musical (*Jack*), tours of Ripper-related sites and a talk by Joseph Sickert (who died on 9 January 2003), who claimed to be the illegitimate son of Walter Sickert, the Ripper suspect named by Patricia Cornwell. They were also able to meet Albert Johnson and view the Maybrick watch (the Diary was also on view) and question a panel including Shirley Harrison and Robert Smith. A few months later, on 24 February 2002, the Discovery Channel aired its *Trial of Jack the Ripper* (with Jeremy Beadle as the advocate for James Maybrick). Maybrick convincingly beat off the three other suspects in both the studio and public polls.

The growing speculation on the internet, especially on the 'Jack the Ripper Casebook' message boards, rarely took into account the feelings of those being speculated about. Normally this was not a matter of concern. None of the main characters in the Diary or watch story appeared interested in accessing the site. But as the furore over Robbie Johnson's role in the Maybrick watch continued, his surviving brother Albert asked Shirley Harrison to pass on the messages to him by post. Reporting back to the message board, she felt it only fair to record his genuine distress. She also passed on the following message from Albert Johnson on 17 February 2001:

How dare these people who don't know me and never knew Robbie and haven't seen the watch either make up all this stuff about us. Robbie was not a bad man – he did some silly things – but I loved him very much . . . as soon as we knew about the scratches I rang him and he shot over because he was so excited. After I rang the *Post* [the *Liverpool Daily Post*] and they gave me Robert Smith's telephone number we realised the watch could be valuable so we asked a solicitor to look after us. We went back to Mr Murphy's shop too and then up to Lancaster to see if Mrs Murphy's father's shop was there. Would we have done all that if we knew it was a forgery? Would I have invested all that money in laboratory tests, with Robbie's full support, if we had known it was forged? It's just ridiculous. None of it makes sense.

Back in September 1999 Nick Warren had outlined the trio he
believed Melvin Harris had identified as the Diary forgers. By April
2001, however, he appeared to have a slightly different
understanding of Harris's line-up. Writing to Keith Skinner about
Harris's 'three guilty men', he now had Barrett and Tony Devereux
composing the Diary. Because it seemed to have been composed on a
word processor, Anne Graham's secretarial skills may have been
involved, but Harris apparently doubted her active participation in
the forgery. The penman was, again, Devereux's friend, 'who was
very nervous' when duly interviewed by a *Daily Express* reporter –
behaviour that Harris, Warren said, found suspicious. The *Express*,
Warren reported, spiked the story. Harris, already hit by Feldman's
libel suit, 'got very scared and dried up'.

Perhaps the clearest account of Harris's own thinking on the
matter came in a message to the Casebook message boards on 19
October 2000:

Feldman claims that I had examined Devereux's Will and
'concluded that Mr Cain, one of the witnesses, was the forger'
and he had mysteriously 'disappeared around the time that the
diary became public'. This misrepresents my views in two ways.
The idea that Mr Kane (the real spelling) had disappeared was not
mine, but was the conclusion of a newspaper reporter who tried
to trace him. And I have never identified Mr Kane as the forger.
What I did say, and stand by, is that his handwriting on the Will
bore an uncanny resemblance to the writing in the Diary. But it
was only a small sample; too small to indict anyone [see
illustration on p. 230].

Every competent investigator has a duty to clear people of
suspicion, and it was in that spirit that an attempt was made to
secure lengthy samples of Mr Kane's handwriting. This was not
undertaken by me, but by a reporter known to me. Unfortunately,
and rather foolishly, Kane drew suspicion upon himself by first
denying that the writing on the Will was his; then by refusing to
show a single sample of his handwriting. Later on, when
interviewed by DS Thomas, he finally admitted that the Will

writing was his. But this man's health is so poor that no further enquiries were made by me, or by the police, and he was never pressured into supplying samples of his writing.

Having spoken to Harold Brough, the senior of three reporters who covered the Diary story for the *Liverpool Daily Post*, we discovered that he and Amanda Williamson (the other reporter was Steve Brauner) had tried to locate Kane but did not find him at the address they had. Brough believes now that it was neighbours at the block of flats they visited who first revealed to him Kane's poor state of health. However, it is likely that Brough, who recalls being in contact with Harris during this period, had visited Kane at the address identified on Tony Devereux's will, and was unaware that he had since moved to a bungalow for reasons of health.

Harris had revealed more information regarding his alleged penman in a message sent to the Casebook message boards on 30 June 2000: 'an investigation was carried out in Liverpool in 1993/4 by a daily paper (not in the Murdoch Group). That paper, as an act of courtesy, made their discoveries known to me. But they decided to sit on their material until there were fresh developments. They had the talked-about film in mind. I had supplied their reporters with some documents, but I was not paid by them. Even so, I stay silent because I endorse the professional code that we both operate under.'

Nine months later Shirley Harrison attempted to enlist Harris's help in obtaining access to these discoveries by passing on a letter to the newspaper editor concerned. In a message to Harris on the boards on 1 March 2001, she wrote:

I have understood that you will not publicly name your journalists but there is no reason not to name the newspaper concerned. You of all people, with your pedigree, must surely understand that it is just not good enough to tell us we must accept your reported version of what the newspaper editor has said. I need to be told first hand that he will not discuss the fact that he is holding the information which would conclusively condemn the diary as a modern forgery but will not reveal what it is. So please Melvin, I do hope you will pass my letter on.

Her request does not appear to have been met. On 3 May 2001 Shirley Harrison included Harris's Casebook message of 30 June 2000 in a letter to Christopher Williams, the current editor of the *Daily Express*, which she believed was the paper in question. Would Williams confirm or deny this and would he discuss this embargoed material with Harrison, a research colleague and an independent witness? There was no reply.

In view of Melvin Harris's reluctance to name the journalist responsible, we decided to try to find the most likely person ourselves. We began by tracing the journalists from non-Murdoch newspapers who had covered the Scotland Yard investigation into the Diary. Eventually we tracked down Stephen Grey, who, while working for the *Daily Express*, had travelled to Liverpool and interviewed Gerard Kane. Today, ironically, he is editor of the *Sunday Times* Insight team, for whom Maurice Chittenden was working when he conducted the original *Sunday Times* investigation into the Diary, published in September 1993 (Chittenden still works for the paper). On 20 June 2002 we met Grey at a pub in London's Docklands, near the *Sunday Times* offices. Grey was not only able to recall the details of his trip to Liverpool, he also brought with him the full draft of the article he had written about his investigation. Only the first few lines of the original draft had made it into the *Express* on 26 November 1993 (see Chapter Three). But what about evidence on the handwriting that might have been suppressed?

There was, indeed, a passage in the draft article which referred to (but did not name) Gerard Kane and had not been published in the paper:

Investigators at one stage puzzled over the handwriting of a retired cabinet maker who was at one stage a close friend of Tony Devereux. A witness to Devereux's will, this man's handwriting bears a very strong resemblance to the handwriting used throughout the 'Ripper diaries'. Both contain letter 'K's which each contain a tiny letter 'z' inside – a rare style. But the man, who has been interviewed by the *Daily Express*, has denied any knowledge of the diaries. Detectives believed the handwriting resemblance is simply a 'strange coincidence'. Instead, the likelihood is that the diaries had no connection with Devereux at all – and are simply a modern hoax or practical joke.

There was, Grey told us, no sinister reason for the editing. It was, quite simply, that he had no proof. 'What readers wanted to know is the real concrete theory and if I'm saying, "maybe this" and "maybe that", it's not as interesting as being very definite about it.'

Grey's interest in the Diary had begun when he had been sent to report on the launch of Shirley Harrison's book, where he witnessed Melvin Harris's unscheduled attack on the authenticity of the Diary (though he can't recall if he actually spoke to Harris there). He was, however, in touch with DS Thomas, the senior officer conducting the Scotland Yard investigation into the Diary. Grey decided 'it would be interesting to try to prove whether or not the diaries were fake or genuine'. First, he checked Tony Devereux's will in Somerset House, where, he says, he noticed the same stylistic idiosyncrasy (the way the letter 'K' is written) in Kane's signature as in the writing in the Diary. However, it is self-evident from the illustration on page 232 that there is no such idiosyncrasy in the Diary.

As far as Grey can recall, he had just one day in Liverpool, during which time he also interviewed Nancy Steele and visited Liverpool Library to locate Gerard Kane's current address from the Electoral Roll. Grey, who recalls Kane's poor health and age as being reasons for not pursuing his investigation further, regrets now that he was forced into doorstepping the cabinet maker owing to his limited time in the city. Kane was unhappy at the intrusion and Grey received no sample of writing or any kind of evidence. Though Grey believes he did get inside Kane's house, it was a difficult situation. 'I think he just didn't want to talk about it. He said he didn't know anything about it . . . he didn't make me feel he was innocent or guilty . . . he could either have genuinely not known anything about it or could be covering up.'

After the article Grey, who recalls that his news editor was not particularly interested in the subject, let the matter drop. He can shed no light on whether Melvin Harris is referring to him but certainly has no recollection of 'talking about any kind of film or sitting on any kind of sensational evidence.' It is possible, he says, that Melvin Harris is talking about someone else and he has 'no reason to doubt that what he says is correct'.

To ensure Melvin Harris's position was being correctly and fairly represented, the authors twice offered to meet with him during the preparation of this book. Regrettably Harris showed no inclination for any such meeting. As part of our research for the book we also wrote to Gerard Kane to inform him of the speculation that was taking place, largely on the internet, and asked if he would help us resolve this matter once and for all. He did not answer our letters. However, we understand from a third party that he has a heart condition which dates back to the 1980s, when the modern hoax theorists claim the Diary was written, and remains in very poor health. Informing us that the speculation about his involvement in a forgery was 'laughable', the third party told us that Kane had become very distressed to learn of the continuing furore. As such, the authors confirm that they, like DS Thomas of Scotland Yard, have found no evidence whatsoever to support the theory that Gerard Kane is responsible for the handwriting in the Diary of Jack the Ripper.

NINE

'I want a future'

6 I 've got Jack the Ripper's diary, would you be interested in seeing
it?' A decade had passed since Michael Barrett, using the
pseudonym Williams, had rung Doreen Montgomery in March 1992
from Liverpool. The intervening years had been marked by the
break-up of the Barretts' marriage, dramatic confessions and
retractions, bitter personal feuds and the acrimonious trading of
claim and counter-claim between pro- and anti-Diary camps. There
had been lawsuits, police and private investigations, allegations of
forgery conspiracies and even accusations of murder. Ten years on,
the authors of this book visited Liverpool to bring their investigation
up to date and attempt to resolve some of the outstanding issues.

'I may return to Battlecrease and take the unfaithfull [*sic*] bitch.' It
was this reference, Barrett once claimed, that alerted him to the
purported author of the Diary, cotton merchant James Maybrick. In
January 2003 we visited the house in Liverpool which the
Maybricks rented during the period when James Maybrick,
according to the Diary, conducted the Ripper murders some 200
miles away in London, and where his death would lead to the trial
and conviction of his young American wife Florence for murder.

Now known rather less evocatively as 7 Riversdale Road, the
house and its adjoining neighbour (the houses, built in the 1830s,
have occasionally been used as one, though not in the Maybricks'
time) are the last survivors of the street's Victorian era. The other
houses which the Maybricks would have recognised on the long
street, which is bordered at one end by a busy dual carriageway and
at the other by the Mersey river, have long since succumbed to
bomb damage or decay and given way to nondescript modern
architecture.

According to Paul Dodd, whose family have owned Battlecrease since 1946, the house was fortunate to survive. When his father bought it for £1,900, it had been condemned after suffering damage from the wartime bomb that destroyed the nearby railway bridge. Dodd points out a cinder track that begins near the bridge's replacement, and runs along by the railway lines to the old Mersey Road and Aigburth station, where, he understands, James Maybrick would have caught the train through to London's St Pancras station for his business visits to the city (and, believers in the Diary would claim, other activities too). Maybrick would have reached the cinder track through the apple orchard, since replaced by private houses, that covered much of the original grounds of Battlecrease.

Inside the four-storey house, now converted to flats, we are guided through to the adjacent first-floor bedrooms of Florie and James (they slept separately, it was claimed, since Florie first discovered her husband's adultery), with large sash windows overlooking the Liverpool Cricket and Sports Club grounds on the other side of the road. Maybrick's bedroom still has the small adjoining ante-room which he used as a dressing room and which was otherwise locked, with access prohibited to all.

As we look around, Dodd, who now lives next door, tells us his doubts as to the possibility of a Battlecrease provenance for the Diary (as to whether it is genuine or a hoax, he remains agnostic). He believes that far too much was made of this theory and allows a less than 1 per cent chance of the Diary being found when floorboards were lifted in the late 1980s/early 1990s. Despite the claims made by Paul Feldman in his book, Dodd says the floorboards had been lifted a number of times since 1946 and nothing found (in fact, Dodd says, very few floorboards were actually raised during the period Feldman investigated). Though unwilling to disclose his source, he has since heard that there had been no substance at all to the claims made of finding the Diary at Battlecrease. Feldman, he understands, had been the victim of a scam.

Dodd has clear memories, from his childhood onwards, of the coachloads of visitors that would arrive three times a week to view the Maybricks' house. Then, signalled by the first visit of an excited

Michael Barrett, who arrived with many questions about Maybrick (Dodd recalls this as being when Barrett was first in contact with Shirley Harrison), came the Ripper period. Since then there have been thousands of visitors, either participants in the story, national and international media or sightseers. It is, perhaps, not surprising that Dodd, a deputy headteacher, is considering selling the famous house prior to his retirement.

Liverpool Central Library, near the city centre (and a stone's throw from St George's Hall, where court Number One is barely changed from when Florie was tried and convicted there of murder), has been the source of much research into the Diary. It was also at the centre of one of the most contentious debates between modern hoax theorists and those who believe the Diary to be old, if not necessarily genuine. The argument revolved around Michael Barrett's revelation of the source of the quote used in the Diary, 'Oh costly intercourse of death,' a source that had long baffled both Shirley Harrison and Paul Feldman's teams and which, Harrison says, she asked Barrett to look for in Liverpool Library. On 30 September 1994 Barrett had rung Feldman's PA Martine Rooney to announce that he had found it. Barrett soon confirmed the quote was from Volume Two of the *Sphere History of Literature*. A few days later, and not unusually with the Diary, things became a little more complicated, with Barrett revealing that he already owned a copy of the Sphere edition in which he had found the quote. What is more, he claimed to Shirley Harrison on 12 October (having initially told her he had found it in the library), it was to be lodged with his solicitor that very day as proof of the fact he had forged the Diary.

It was not the arcane matter it first appeared and others would claim a very different timing for this crucial action. According to Melvin Harris, Barrett had told private investigator Alan Gray that he had lodged the book with his solicitor, Richard Bark-Jones of Morecroft, Dawson & Garnett of Dale Street, prior to his confession of 24 June 1994, as a piece of vital evidence to prove his forgery.

On 19 October 2000 Harris claimed on the 'Casebook' message boards that Barrett had told Alan Gray of the story behind the quote in September, 1994: 'NOTE WELL: the Sphere volume had been left with Mike's solicitor LONG BEFORE the break with his wife and the "confession".' Harris furnished further details in April 2002, after prompting on the message boards: 'GRAY HAS A RECORD MADE IN THE FIRST WEEK OF SEPTEMBER 1994, WHEN HE WAS GIVEN A NEW SET OF INSTRUCTIONS. Those instructions listed the "evidence" that Mike claimed he could produce to back up his story. The full list has not yet been published, but it included a copy of a book used to provide a quotation found in the Diary. The quote was highlighted and its source identified as the Sphere book, then said to be with his solicitor.'

But had Alan Gray been aware of the quote, its source and significance in the first week of September 1994? Indeed, had he written down the 'full list', said to include the Sphere book? The taped conversation between Barrett and Gray on 7 November 1994 indicates that Gray is hearing about the quote, and the fact that it is lodged at Barrett's solicitor, for the first time. Gray wrote to us on 20 January 2003 to help us clear this matter up: 'If the tape you refer to as being made in early November,' he wrote, 'shows indifference on my part to the Sphere book, this is no surprise because at that time no person had ever mentioned that it could be of great importance and that includes Mr Melvin Harris.' Gray also confirms that, 'As far as my September instructions were concerned I did not need to keep a written account of the briefing . . .' In a letter written to Keith Skinner on 29 January 2003, Harris apologised for any confusion he may have caused in this regard. It was, he wrote, a simple misunderstanding: 'When I wrote of a list I was merely using the term colloquially, to indicate that Mike had passed on to Alan a number of bits of information for him to digest and maybe act on. As you can now see the information was very sparse, easily understood and memorised and did not warrant writing down, as Alan has explained.'

According to Gray, Michael Barrett had retrieved the book from Morecroft's offices on 6 December 1994 and handed it to him outside. In his letter of 29 January 2003 to Keith Skinner, Harris commented that the timing of the lodging of the Sphere book with

Barrett's solicitors had not been significant. 'I did not ask Alan to check on the date when the book was placed with the solicitors,' he wrote. 'This was of no importance to me.' For the authors of this book, it had always been critical. If Harris's dates were correct, Michael Barrett had deposited a highly damning piece of hard evidence with his solicitor prior to his newspaper 'confession' of 24 June 1994 – but had bizarrely failed to make any use of it. Our investigations had also confirmed that, despite earlier indications, neither Melvin Harris nor Alan Gray had been aware of the quote before 7 November 1994, which meant there was no contradiction with Barrett having found the quote in Liverpool Library on 30 September 1994.

Back in October 2000 Harris had discouraged people from contacting Barrett's solicitors by writing: 'The only person who can give the exact day and month of the lodgement is the solicitor used by Mike. But he has not been paid and is owed large sums, therefore he has no incentive to waste any more time on inquisitive Ripperologists!' Undaunted by this advice, and armed with a letter of permission from Michael Barrett to access his files, we were able to arrange an appointment to meet Richard Bark-Jones at Morecroft's offices on 22 January 2003.

Although it had been some years since Barrett had been a client there, the subject of the Diary, and Barrett's involvement with it, was not one Mr Bark-Jones was likely to forget. He confirmed from his files that Barrett had first attended his offices on 18 June 1992. Contrary to expectations, Barrett said he was not interested in advice on the publishing agreement he was to sign with Smith Gryphon Ltd; his sole concern, Bark-Jones notes, was whether Scotland Yard could claim the Diary as an original murder exhibit if their forensic unit was asked to test the ink, as was apparently being proposed. Bark-Jones also recalled the retraction he issued after Barrett's confession of 24 June 1994. A few days after first telling local journalist Harold Brough he had forged the Diary, Barrett was taken to Fazakerley Hospital for treatment for alcoholism. There Dr Miller informed Bark-Jones of Barrett's tendency towards confabulation (where gaps in memory are filled by stories the person believes to be real). Contrary to Paul Feldman's belief, it was this – and not because he held evidence to prove the Diary was genuine – that prompted the solicitor's retraction. Though he would not have represented Barrett if he felt the Diary were a modern hoax, Mr Bark-Jones confirmed to us that Barrett had never lodged anything with him to prove the Diary was genuine.

Or, it seemed, a modern hoax. There is, it transpires, no record of the Sphere book being lodged or withdrawn on any date. Bark-Jones cannot recall it, nor can his then assistant Liz Winter, nor can Dawn Shotter, who also dealt with Barrett during this period. It is possible, Bark-Jones concedes, that there might be circumstances in which a lodgement or withdrawal could be made without record, though he considers it unlikely. Nor is there any record of Barrett attending the offices between 25 August 1994 and 9 January 1995, though there are numerous telephone conversations logged. One of these makes the only allusion to the matter that Bark-Jones could find. In the notes made by Liz Winter of a thirty-minute telephone call with Michael Barrett on 13 October 1994, she has recorded the following: ' "O sweet [*sic*] intercourse of death", Vol 2 P 184. In diary. Santa [*sic*] Maria 1643–1652. Found phrase in library.'

There is another book which some believe supports the modern hoax theory. In September 1993 Tony Devereux's three daughters had told Martin Howells that their father had borrowed a copy of the Richard Whittington-Egan book *Tales of Liverpool – Murder, Mayhem and Mystery* from Michael Barrett and that they had in turn borrowed it from their father. While conducting their investigation in late October 1993, the Scotland Yard detectives had taken this book from the sisters. It had been *Murder, Mayhem and Mystery*, Barrett claimed, which first alerted him to the Maybrick connection in the Diary. Hoax theorists suggested the book had, instead, provided valuable material for a forgery. Again timing was important. Barrett had claimed he bought the book in WH Smith's just prior to commencing his research on the Diary, which by his own account is likely to have begun after Tony Devereux's death on 8 August 1991.

Over the years confusion had grown up over just which sister had borrowed the book and, more crucially, when. We were able to confirm with Nancy Steele, the eldest, that it was her sister Janet who had borrowed the book. Janet, she told us, had been pregnant at the time and was bored, having recently left work to begin maternity leave. Having seen the book at her father's, she thought it would be interesting to read and asked to borrow it. She was told it had to be returned as it belonged to 'Bongo', Devereux's name for Barrett. As Janet's son was subsequently born on 27 November 1991, the sisters believe it must have been in the summer, probably late July or early August, just before their father's death, that Janet would have borrowed the book. When the two Scotland Yard detectives called on Nancy, only her other sister Caroline was present. They subsequently visited Janet. As they were leaving, Janet asked if they wanted the copy of *Murder, Mayhem and Mystery*, which was still in her possession. The detectives had this copy in the boot of their car when they interviewed Michael Barrett.

Mrs Steele's original interviews, both with Martin Howells and with Nick Warren, had cast considerable doubt on Michael Barrett's claim that the Diary had been given to him by their father (though they fiercely denied the possibility that their father could have taken part in a forgery). But the years have changed Nancy's view and she now believes that the account given by Anne Graham of handing the Diary to her father to give to Barrett is plausible, though she still cannot understand why her father didn't tell them about it. She had assumed that Anne had given the Diary to her father during the last days of his life when he was taking medication and had become forgetful, and was surprised at the timing Barrett had given of receiving the Diary in late May or June 1991 (Anne Graham has never been able to date her account). She also points out that if Barrett were constantly badgering her father about the Diary, which he originally claimed was the case, he could hardly have forgotten about it. Unlike her two sisters, she retains some curiosity about the Diary, but is convinced it will always remain a mystery.

Liverpool had not just given birth, one way or another, to the Diary. It was also the home of the Maybrick watch. When it first arrived on the scene in June 1993, the watch had been a most unwelcome development for Shirley Harrison and the Diary camp. Then they had feared the first signs of bandwagon-jumping, but later, after positive tests by Drs Turgoose and Wild, the watch had become part of the armoury of the Diary believers. Even so, speculation of forgery had continued to grow here too and unanswered questions remained, not least about the death of Robbie Johnson, younger brother of Albert, the owner of the watch since July 1992.

It had been suggested that of the two brothers, Robbie was much the more likely forger and even that he had managed to put the scratchings there without his elder brother's knowledge. It is a theory that Albert Johnson, whom we met with his wife Val, dismisses out of hand. Acknowledging that Robbie served eighteen months of a two-year sentence, in an open prison, for possession of cannabis (he was released on 17 July 1992), Johnson describes his younger brother as 'basically a good lad, whom I loved'. He says that Robbie did not know of the watch's existence until the day after a journalist at the *Liverpool Echo* had been round to inspect the scratchings. Had either, or both, brothers been responsible for these, their starting point would have to be the *Liverpool Daily Post* of 22 April 1993, when the purported author of the Diary was revealed publicly for the first time. Albert Johnson's call to Robert Smith, telling him of the scratchings, was made on 4 June 1993.

Albert Johnson's reaction to the forgery allegation is to ask a question. If this were true, why would he risk approximately a thousand pounds submitting the watch to two examinations likely to reveal it to be a hoax? He still vividly recalls the day he bought the watch. He had walked by the shop on a number of occasions trying to pluck up the courage to pay the required £250. Finally on 14 July 1992, emboldened by a win on the horses, he haggled the price down to £225 and bought it. As to the current ownership, it is our understanding that Johnson, his wife Valerie, their daughter Tracy and their solicitor Richard Nicholas all own shares in the watch. We also understand that there may be another share in existence, one originally owned, then sold, by Robbie. Thus far,

Albert Johnson claims to have actually lost money on the watch, which he remains convinced belonged to James Maybrick. As for selling it, he is wary of disclosing information, but acknowledges that, though there have been further offers from the Texan collector Robert E. Davis over the years, the watch remains in his possession.

Clearly the death of his only brother affected Johnson deeply and he reacts with scorn to the theory proposed by Stanley Dangar that Robbie had been 'bumped off'. The watch, contrary to Dangar's belief, had not disappeared at this time and had always been in Johnson's possession or that of his solicitor. But he does wonder, as he mentioned to Alan Gray, whether there is a curse on the watch and whether his brother would be alive today if he hadn't bought it.

We would get more reaction to Dangar's theory from another Liverpudlian, Robbie's closest friend from the age of seven, Charlie Pulford. It had been Dangar's belief that Robbie's death was part of a conspiracy, orchestrated by Paul Feldman, involving the watch. However, what we were told by Pulford, who was closely involved in the aftermath of his friend's death, contradicted Dangar's assertions. Robbie, he says, had gone to Spain not on holiday but to work in a time-share business. He had anyway sold his share in the watch, for £15,000, by this stage. His death, says Pulford, was nothing more than a tragic accident. Yes, Robbie did stay at the Hotel Patricia in San Roque and a female friend was with him during his stay, as Dangar had initially reported to Maurice Chittenden of the *Sunday Times*. But this person, actually his girlfriend Helen Rutherford, did not, as Dangar asserts, return to the UK on the night of the accident (nor would she end up with Paul Feldman, as he made clear to us later). The facts, he says, were these: Robbie had only been in Spain for two days when he left his rooms to change some money across the road. He walked out between two parked vehicles and, perhaps as a consequence of being abroad, looked the wrong way. He was killed instantly. The bike rider, who sustained minor injuries, was not prosecuted. Helen Rutherford did not disappear. Heavily sedated, she remained for over a week in the house of the paramedic who had attended the scene, being looked after by his English wife. Meanwhile, Pulford and another friend were desperately trying to raise the money for Robbie's body to be flown home for a funeral in Liverpool. By Spanish law they had just four days before the body was cremated. They just made it. It had been a terrible ordeal for all concerned. It had not been murder. It was a typical instance of the way wild speculation could grow around the Diary and watch. Albert Johnson refers to those who indulge in it as suffering from CRS, or 'Chronic Ripper Syndrome'.

Robbie Johnson suffered from scoliosis, a spine curvature condition, which grew worse towards the end of his life and prevented him from enjoying a normal working life, though being a great music lover he did manage a couple of bands. Pulford recalls Robbie being initially sceptical about the watch and only growing excited about it later. What about the accusation that Robbie forged the scratchings? Pulford lists a number of reasons why he believes this unlikely. Having journeyed to Bristol with both brothers for Dr Wild's testing on the watch, Pulford recalls that neither showed any surprise at his conclusion that it could be many years old. He also claims that, had he been considering a forgery, Robbie would have asked Pulford to do the scratchings for him and says that, as the brothers were so close, it would have been unthinkable anyway for Robbie to have done such a thing behind Albert's back. The suggestion that Pulford might have been taken in by his friend is wryly dismissed: 'I know what he was,' Pulford says, 'and I know what he wasn't.'

Paul Feldman's involvement with the Diary, and his relentless pursuit to prove it was written by James Maybrick, would dramatically change the course of the story and change lives, not least his own, earning him the enmity not only of the man at the centre of the story, Michael Barrett, but many sceptics as well. Feldman had amassed a wealth of research material on James and Florence Maybrick and on Jack the Ripper, but had been accused of polluting the research waters and presenting as hard proof evidence that was merely circumstantial.

Feldman, today, though still able to speak passionately about the Diary, is not the relentless dynamo of the early years, rehearsing theories at a hundred miles an hour. The years of ill health that followed the publication of his book have slightly dimmed that extraordinary energy, though the familiar cigar remains ever present. Now living near Elstree in North London in a modest house, he is also getting back on his feet in business after the crippling financial legacy of his pursuit. Asked how much he really spent, he smiles: 'When I used to do the numbers I would start at £150,000 and work up. That's if I lie to myself. The highest estimate would be £250,000.' Nor will he make it back. *The Final Chapter*, he says, has sold in excess of 50,000 in total. The video, now a DVD too, has sold approximately 20,000 copies but not nearly enough to repay the money spent on it.

He and leading sceptic Melvin Harris became almost the public *personae* of the pro- and anti-Diary camps, somewhat misleadingly as there were many shades of opinion in between, and their clash of personalities as well as theories coloured the debate for many years. Feldman has not tempered his opinion of his rival in the intervening years. After our meeting Feldman sent us the following statement:

> Melvin Harris has been challenged to replicate the diary on so many fronts but has failed miserably to do so. The only thing that can be explained is that his behaviour towards this and no other Ripper theory is that of a desperate man. He jumped in with both feet before examining any of the facts – he didn't realise there was an anchor tied to his legs at the time.

Feldman says he first contacted Harris with the intention of his taking part in a wide-ranging debate on the Diary among Ripper experts. After a meeting at Feldman's house, he says he paid Harris to produce a report on the Diary, a photocopied transcript of which he was given by Feldman. The report, Feldman claims, was 'shallow', mainly listing the books where the instigator of a forgery, as Harris was by now sure it was, could have got his material. It would be downhill from there. (Harris dates his first sighting of the Diary to 13 May 1993. In his letter of 29 January 2003 to Keith

Skinner, he writes, 'By that time it was far too late for sound counsel to be heeded. The book was finished and the various Rights had been sold and I was told by Feldman that I had not been invited to view the Diary earlier because I "lacked integrity", according to some of his team. The detractors were never named!')

Melvin Harris had asserted that the main, though not only, proof that the Diary is a modern hoax is the clear discrepancy between the writing in it and in Maybrick's handwritten will. (Indeed he continues to maintain this position today, accusing Keith Skinner of disingenuously endorsing the claims made by Paul Feldman regarding the will.) Feldman's belief that the will was not written by Maybrick was the battleground of their legendary confrontation at Camille Wolff's. Unexpectedly, Feldman now concedes that he no longer believes the will is a forgery, though he suspects that its anomalies (such as Maybrick twice misspelling his daughter's name) indicate it was tampered with. He says the similarity in handwriting between a letter written by Maybrick aboard the SS *Baltic* in March 1881 (discovered by Anne Graham) and a 'Ripper letter' from the Scotland Yard files, written from Galashiels in Scotland in October 1888, means that the will does not matter. In fact, Feldman believes that Maybrick even used the same nib on the Galashiels letter as on the one written from the *Baltic*.

Feldman also now supports Paul Dodd's belief that the alleged Battlecrease provenance for the Diary was, in effect, a scam. He confirms that some electricians had taken documents found at Battlecrease to Liverpool University but says he discovered they were letters unrelated to the Diary. That, he says, was the end of his interest. The motive for these stories? – 'A lot of people were trying to get money out of me.'

As to the accusation that the provenance given to the Diary by Anne Graham was suspiciously convenient, at a time when Feldman was frantically trying to secure a lucrative film deal for the Diary, he does concede to having been 'up shit creek without a paddle', but says that 'she contacted me, not the other way around'. In fact, he says, Anne's fateful telephone call in July 1994 began in an atmosphere of great hostility. 'Given my language she was entitled to tell me to "piss off". She gave as good as she got.' There are also many who doubt the conviction of Billy Graham's memory of a family link to Florence Maybrick, believing it nothing more than conjecture. Again Feldman remains certain. 'I was pretty sure when I met Billy what was going to come back was a connection to James not Florence. . . . I think Billy brought me there for a purpose, and that purpose is . . . there's a point on the tape where I start talking and he says "be quiet" or "shut up". He's going to tell me. I think he felt it had to be known.'

He also dismisses Stanley Dangar's theory about the death of Robbie Johnson. He had met Helen Jane Rutherford occasionally before and (some time) after Johnson's death but refutes absolutely the idea that she came to him directly afterwards. He has no more time for the idea that Anne Graham's biography of Florie reveals her ability to be a potential forger, saying it is precisely why it couldn't have been her. 'Anne is an extremely bright lady who lived in a terrible environment. I underestimated her literary ability but was the first to see the glint in her eye. . . . If you are a forger you don't sit down and write that book.'

On numerous occasions, both to Feldman's face and also in affidavits, Michael Barrett alleged that his life was threatened by Feldman. While admitting he would have used strong language at times, Feldman laughs off such suggestions. 'I wouldn't have physically threatened him. He used to turn around to me and say, "Just because you know the Krays doesn't give you the right to hassle my family" (he thought I knew the Krays because of the film). But there was nothing he could have misinterpreted. It's a total invention and not my style. Physical violence ain't me.' Deep down, Feldman claims, he had a 'genuine liking for the guy and felt sorry for him. The more I knew about their background I felt this guy has never really had a break.'

With financial problems mounting and early signs of his health failing, it appeared in 1996 that Paul Feldman had tried to take his own life. That was certainly the picture given to Doreen Montgomery by his PA, Martine Rooney. Feldman is not so sure. 'I know that was other people's perceptions of what I'd done and that's what I was told I'd done but I'm not convinced. I just think I took a few pills to escape from the situation I was in at the time . . . the Ripper and what had gone on in my life.' The impact of his pursuit (he won't accept the description of it as an obsession) of the Diary was also considerable on his marriage, which broke up soon after. 'I worked five days and nights and then Friday night off to Liverpool.' Researching in Liverpool all weekend, he returned home, often on Monday morning. 'Which is why I got the information I did and no one else did. I was like a pain-in-the-arse journalist kicking butt . . .'

Following the publication of *The Final Chapter* in 1997, his health worsened considerably. He was seriously ill for a period of over two years but is unsure if it was connected to the Diary. 'I've burned the candle at both ends, worked hard and played hard all my life.' Still resentful at many experts 'for their unbelievable ignorance', and the inability of Diary critics to deal with the important issues he has raised, Feldman has no regrets about his involvement or doubts about his achievement. 'I think I have the evidence in my book that it [the Diary] was written by James Maybrick. What's worse is that no one has attempted to disprove anything I've written.' He talks of 'an incredible peak and trough of emotions for five years', but doesn't believe his work will be recognised until there is a film on the Diary, when people will see the truth on screen in a way they can understand. Now his interest has waned ('Jack the Ripper has always bored the pants off me'), he says that the only way it will be reignited is if someone wants him to work for them on the film script.

If any one person can be said to hold the key to the Diary, it is the woman who called Paul Feldman that evening in July 1994 and changed the Diary story forever. Unlike that of her ex-husband, Anne Graham's account, belated in its telling though it was, has remained substantially the same over the years, but there are areas of her story we still wanted to probe.

Of all the major players in the Diary story, none has changed more dramatically over the last ten years than Anne Graham.

Friendly, if a little guarded, she appears now a much stronger and more determined character than the desperate woman she describes giving the Diary to her then husband. She is, though, a very private person and, as Paul Feldman had discovered on his meeting with her in July 1994, when he first heard of her account, remains adamant that she will not be interviewed at home. We meet instead in a quiet Liverpool city centre pub.

Even as we meet, there is disappointment. Michael Barrett had described their daughter Caroline, then nine years old, as a witness to him bringing the Diary back and unwrapping it and to his subsequent questioning of Tony Devereux by phone. In his affidavit of 5 January 1995 he had also described her as witnessing him dictating as Anne wrote their forgery into the photo album. Anne, too, had described Caroline witnessing a physical fight between her parents, in which Anne tried to throw the Diary into the fire. The day before we were to meet Anne, Caroline celebrated her twenty-first birthday and we had been told she might accompany her mother, whose birthday it was this day, to the meeting. But it was not to be and Caroline subsequently turned down another invitation to talk to us by phone. Her reticence, she explained, was due to the deep emotional upheaval of recalling a very traumatic period of her life, and the fact that her memory of the Diary was anyway vague.

Anne tells us that this will be the last time she talks in any depth about the Diary and has only agreed to answer our questions because of her long professional association with Keith Skinner. Earlier that day, before meeting Anne, we had traced the route from the Barretts' tiny terraced house at the bottom of Goldie Street, over the dual carriageway, through a small estate of council houses, past Kelly's Wine Cellar and on to Fountains Road, where Tony Devereux had lived. It was a brisk walk of no more than six or seven minutes that would have taken Anne, and the Diary, to Devereux's doorstep that day in 1991. It was, Anne recalls, at night, because she would have been working in the day; still light, she thinks, and summerish, but she can be no more precise. She had told Barrett that she was going to pick something up at the corner shop (there are several nearby). The Diary was wrapped in brown paper from drawer lining (possibly from the sideboard behind which it was stored, Anne thinks) and tied with string. She had chosen Devereux 'because he was the only friend Mike had'. Barrett had maintained that in all the weeks he spent harassing him, Devereux never once let his guard slip, so what could Anne possibly have said to ensure his silence, in what was no more than a brief exchange of words? 'I asked him to give it to Mike, to do something with it because all I wanted was to get him focused on something.' She did ask him 'not to say it came from me. I didn't know the man . . . I must have been convincing but I wasn't there very long. He probably saw the way Michael was. I'm not sure that he [Devereux] ever opened the Diary. . . . I must have been bloody desperate to do a thing like that.'

There had been some confusion too as to where the Diary was kept after her father had given it to her, among other possessions, when he moved into sheltered accommodation. Immediately on receipt, she now confirms, she hid it in the middle bedroom upstairs, used most of the time they lived there by Caroline, lodged behind a heavy dresser that stood in a small alcove between the chimney-breast and the window. A £2 buy from the Salvation Army ('it had been quite posh donkeys years ago'), the dresser, which she has sometimes described as a sideboard or even a cupboard, had been full of Caroline's toys and games. In the narrow gap created by the skirting board between the wall and the edge of the dresser, perhaps 3 inches wide, Anne says she squeezed the Diary, standing on its side. Barrett had decorated the room before she received the Diary from her father, she says, but normally would have had no occasion to look behind the dresser.

(Before tracing the route from Goldie Street to Tony Devereux's house, we had been kindly shown around 12 Goldie Street by its current owners. This middle bedroom was as described by Anne. The alcove, between the chimney-breast and the window, is 5 feet long and about 14 inches deep. The owners, who bought the house after the bank had repossessed it from Michael Barrett, recall the living room walls daubed with the slogans 'Kill the Whore' and 'Kill All Prostitutes', a sad indication of Barrett's mental disintegration during this period. Also revealing were the double bolts on the downstairs doors which still exist – Barrett had told Alan Gray on several occasions that he lived in fear of his life.)

Her father, Billy Graham, Anne says, had no interest in the Diary or the subsequent book. His reaction when she told him she had given it to Barrett, she says, was typical. 'He said something like, "You stupid cow". He didn't carry on, he was like that, he didn't say an awful lot about anything . . . but he wasn't that bothered.'

Her ex-husband never once asked her if she had anything to do with the Diary, she insists, but once he started researching it he never stopped talking about it. Her rashly thought-out plan, she claims, soon misfired. 'It made Mike worse, he was drinking much more than I realised.' But why, having acknowledged her mistake and having lost the physical fight to destroy the Diary, which she says came after he announced he was going to get it published, had she not called Doreen Montgomery and told her the truth? 'I couldn't have coped with it. You've no idea what the atmosphere was like in that house. There was nothing left to do but step back and let him get on with it. . . . I look at it now and it's so stupid, but I'd gone through a lot of verbal abuse, then the physical abuse starts. After that you lose confidence in yourself. The woman I am now is not the woman I was ten years ago. I literally had no confidence in anything.'

Anne says she tried to block out what was happening, but the pressure would only grow more intense. Having endured the nightmare of the book launch – 'I felt so embarrassed, hating everything about it' – she soon experienced the pressure of the visit from the two Scotland Yard officers, whom she confirms she and Barrett believed at the time were investigating him. Towards the end of the investigation, she says, her father turned up and, so as not to worry him, she told him 'they were from the insurance'.

Then came Paul Feldman to turn the Barretts' life upside down with his theories that Anne was descended from James Maybrick and no one was who they said they were. Anne laughs. 'It got so confusing. Caroline wasn't her, Michael wasn't him. He convinced Michael so much with all of this . . . that Michael said to me, "Your mother died in 1945". I said, "Michael, I was born in 1950!"' She was also able to resolve another worrying piece of speculation from that period. The discovery that Anne's medical records had been destroyed seemed to fit perfectly into Feldman's vista of state cover-ups and identity switches. Anne has learnt since, she tells us, that her records were routinely destroyed some time after she left the country for Australia, something she believes was normal practice.

While Barrett himself dates his drinking problem to the arrival of the Diary in his life, Anne has always maintained it began earlier, when they bought Goldie Street, she tells us now. She recalls the final straw as being a holiday trip to Oxford, where his drinking had been 'horrendous'. On their return on 2 January 1994, she left him, taking Caroline with her, after being on the end of a physical beating. She and Caroline moved into a flat two weeks later. He promised to give her £100 a week, she says, but she received only a one-off payment of £1,000. 'I didn't want anything. It was Paul Feldman who said, "You're entitled to this [royalties]".' In June 1994 Barrett confessed to forging the Diary. Since then, he had twice claimed (and would do so again to us) that the confession was triggered directly by a letter from Anne accusing him of having a physical relationship with a friend. Anne says this is nonsense and that although she did write angry letters to him at this point such a relationship would not have concerned her in the slightest. She could offer no reason for the confession, except that Barrett was trying to 'get control again. I was getting control over my own life.'

According to Shirley Harrison, Michael Barrett's sister Lynn spoke of a meeting, at which Anne, Barrett, Billy Graham and herself were present, when Anne told them that Paul Feldman had offered to make her a millionaire if she would say that she had given the Diary to Tony Devereux and was descended from James Maybrick. Anne believes this was an 'off-the-cuff remark' that has been taken out of context and is adamant there was no such meeting, just a conversation between herself and Lynn, replicating Feldman's own explanation, that he was, in effect, saying that she would make a lot of money by telling the truth. Indeed, Anne says, Feldman never gave her any money, though he did once offer to send her and Caroline to America to escape the publicity.

Feldman, she says, was 'a hell of a strength to her', giving her research to do on the Maybricks when her father didn't need her. 'He was there for me and I have a lot of respect for that.' She does not, though, appear to share Feldman's conviction about her link to Florence Maybrick. 'We talked about the family connection, the Florence thing. I don't think he [her father] really believed it. He just put two and two together . . . it sounded convincing at the time. I think it was a hypothesis he had already formed. There was vague evidence it was possible. I never gave it a lot of credence.' She believes the possible Alice Yapp connection was a much more likely explanation for how the Diary eventually found its way to her father.

From the outset Anne has steadfastly denied any interest in the contents of the Diary or in Jack the Ripper. Nor, until Doreen Montgomery's intervention, did she receive a regular share of royalty payments from Shirley Harrison's book. Ownership of the physical Diary is another matter. Like Doreen Montgomery and Shirley Harrison, she believes it should not now be owned by Robert Smith. She recalls with anger the day in March 1993 when Barrett and she relinquished ownership. She, Smith and Barrett had emerged from a meeting at Barrett's solicitors, Morecrofts, at which they had advised him not to sign the transference of ownership deed for a nominal sum of £1. She says that when the three went to Rigby's pub on the other side of Dale Street, Smith convinced Barrett, who had been drinking all morning, to sign. 'I begged him [Barrett], I said don't sign, but, with Michael, I had to sign. I just had to get out. I didn't want him to sign at all.' (While broadly agreeing with Anne's account, Smith himself says that it was Anne who led him to Rigby's, where she rightly assumed Barrett had gone after storming out of the solicitors. At this stage Smith believed his visit had been fruitless. Once in the pub, Smith says, Anne and Barrett had an intense discussion on their own, while he walked away to give them privacy. 'I put no pressure on them, and, indeed, had given up hope of them signing,' he says. 'But then Mike beckoned me over and he and Anne signed three copies of the transfer of ownership.' Smith believes that Anne's fury with him can only indicate that she believes the Diary to be genuine.)

Doreen Montgomery had inserted a clause preventing Smith from selling the Diary without the permission of Graham and Barrett. However, the clause was not in the agreement transferring ownership from Smith Gryphon to Keychoice, a holding company owned by Robert Smith, in 1994. At the time of our interview (October 2002) Anne Graham, who does not want anyone to make money out of it, appears unaware of this and believes she can prevent Smith selling the Diary on. 'I will never give him the permission ever and I will put that in my will.' However, on 29 November 2002 Doreen Montgomery wrote to Anne, 'very concerned to learn' that she apparently still believed she had 'a contractual say in what happens to the Maybrick diary'. Referring to a letter she had written to Anne back in May 2000, with which a cheque for £237.52 was enclosed, Montgomery wrote: 'My letter then made it absolutely clear how Robert Smith had managed to acquire the journal.' (When presented with Anne's accusation, Robert Smith responded by saying he had always dealt fairly with the Barretts and taken his duties as custodian of the Diary responsibly. He quotes a letter from Michael Barrett to him, written in October 2002 to support this: 'I had considered at that time, as I consider it now, that I sold the diary for £1.0.0. [*sic*] for it's [*sic*] safe keeping. . . . Thank you for keeping the diary in a safe place, which suggests my wishes.' Smith also says that, 'if I felt it were no longer appropriate for me to own the diary, I would wish to consult the original owners, Mike and Anne Barrett and also Shirley Harrison, on what should happen to it, even though there is no legal obligation on me to do so'.)

Modern hoax theorists who point to Anne as a potential forger cite her biography of Florence Maybrick as proving she had the literary ability to have done so. It is an argument that incenses her. 'What am I going to do, hide in a cupboard for the rest of my life so people don't make connections? I can't do that and I'm not going to do that. Let them think what they want to think.' As to the accusations made by Steve Powell in a series of wildly fluctuating emails, that she had forged the Diary while in Australia, she reacts with amusement. He had placed the English nurse who stayed in a nursing home as being in Sydney between 1967 and 1971. According to Anne, she arrived in Sydney in November 1970 and worked in market research while sharing a flat with her friend Caroline for six months, before beginning a one-year nursing course in Canberra in 1971. She only worked for four weeks as a nurse in Sydney, in 1974, and she stayed in rented accommodation.

Like so many others whose lives have become intricately tangled up in the Diary story, Anne now wants to put the whole episode behind her. 'It's something that happened. I never wanted to hurt anybody ever. I've never hurt anybody intentionally over that but it happened.' Is it in the past? 'Oh God, yeah. If I wasn't over it I would crack up.' Anne was not the only person we would meet who wanted to put the Diary out of their life forever.

As the train pulls into Southport station on a rainy winter's day, Michael Barrett is waiting to greet us. Smartly dressed in jacket and slacks, he appears to have weathered the storms of the last decade remarkably well. He is welcoming and hospitable, anxious, he tells us, to reveal the truth. Chauffeured back by his partner of six years, who wishes not to be named (she has no interest in Jack the Ripper), we enter the neat, homely basement flat where Barrett has been living alone for some years. He was once reported as saying that all he wanted from the Diary was enough money to buy a greenhouse, and at the back of the building is a small well-nurtured garden which he says he will miss deeply when he moves in the next few weeks. Clearly sober, he says he has been winning the battle against the drink, for which he blames the Diary, for some time now. It is one of the reasons he will talk to us. 'I know what serious damage has been done by drink and I want it to stop.' He is fearful that our book will rekindle his anger about the Diary and that will lead to him drinking again. It is essential, he says, that we tell the truth.

It should be said that Barrett is most anxious to discuss what he claims is the true provenance of the Diary, that it came not via Anne's family but his own. It is, he tells us, only now, after his parents' deaths, that this can be revealed. However, some weeks later he asked us not to write in any detail on this subject or to identify the elderly relative whom we would meet the next day, who Barrett claimed could corroborate his story (though this was not the case). Without considerable further research, which we had neither the time nor the budget to embark on, we were not able, or inclined, to pursue the matter further. However, this new account immediately restricted some of the questions we had planned. We could not, obviously, press for details on how he went about the forgery he once claimed. Nor could we question him on his original claim, that Tony Devereux gave him the Diary.

Barrett's current stand is that the Diary is genuine ('If I drop dead tomorrow,' he says, 'the first question I will ask is "Was it Maybrick?"')' but that Anne Graham's account is not true. Later he promises to provide a breakdown of why this is the case, but will change his mind. However, he does tell us why he believes the Diary couldn't have been hidden from him in Goldie Street. 'I'm home all day, taking Caroline to school, doing the washing, cleaning, ironing, all the decorating . . . the Diary was hidden down a wardrobe, come off it!' It would have been impossible, he says, for him not to have come across it, doing the daily domestic chores in such a small house (Anne had given us a more modest estimate of his contribution to cleaning the house).

There is another subject we need to dispense with. On a visit some months previously, in March 2002, Barrett had given Keith Skinner ten handwritten pages, which he said he had transcribed from some of the missing pages from the Diary. He said he had removed the pages from the Diary when he first received it and had been holding out to write his own book on the subject. Now he tells us they were created by him at the outset, before he believed the Diary was genuine, to see if he could match what was written in the Diary. The content, in truth, bore no resemblance to that of the Diary. We do not dwell on the subject.

However, there are areas we want and are able to ask Barrett about. He now says that he found the 'O costly intercourse of death' quote in Liverpool Library, where he had become a familiar face

271

after months of research into the Maybricks. Shirley Harrison had planted the seed in his mind, he says, and it took him weeks to find it. A student he had been chatting to during a cigarette break had suggested that it might be old English. Eventually, on finding the Sphere volume, he now says, it did open up at the Crashaw quote and he would later recall this volume had been one of several from the Sphere collection sent for an auction he was organising in aid of the Hillsborough families in 1989. These copies were with his friend Jenny Morrison, whose son he thought might find them useful. Despite the lack of confirmation from Morecrofts' records, he does vaguely recall collecting the Sphere volume, with Alan Gray, from his solicitors. He doesn't remember lodging it, though presumes he did, after being told of its importance by Shirley Harrison.

Sometime in mid-June 1994, Barrett claims, he received a letter from his estranged wife, falsely accusing him of having a physical relationship with a new friend in his life. That letter, Barrett says, 'cost everybody a fortune'. Already angry with Anne for keeping their daughter from him, and drinking very heavily (he describes this as a terrible, lost, drunken period), Barrett says, 'She was just a friend, and a bloody good one too. I'm not being accused of something I have not done, drunk or not.' Describing the letter as 'the final straw', he claims it triggered his call to Harold Brough on 24 June 1994. Brough would later confirm to us that Barrett rang him, promising an important story and asking him to bring a bottle of Scotch. Brough did go, though without the Scotch. It didn't matter, Barrett says, because he soon discovered he had enough money to buy another bottle himself. Brough reported the confession in the next day's *Post*. Though his recollections of the details are now vague, Brough is fairly sure he left Barrett lying on the floor drunk.

Concerned at Barrett's state of health, Brough recalls ringing him back that Sunday to check how he was. This resulted in a further visit, the same day, with Barrett telling Brough he would show him the various places which he claimed had been instrumental in supplying the tools of his forgery. Brough, his daughter (who was interested in the Diary story) and Barrett now drove in Brough's car to the art shop at Bluecoat Chambers where Barrett claimed he bought the ink and to the auctioneers Outhwaite & Litherland, where he said he bought the journal (Brough thinks that, being a Sunday, they stayed in the car as all the premises would have been closed). Brough went home to file the story for the next day's *Liverpool Post*. He would later check with Outhwaite & Litherland and was told there was no record of the job lot Barrett described (this was borne out by our own visit to the auctioneers where we discovered that all prospective bidders have to complete a registration form in the office, and that this has always been the case – a fact omitted from Barrett's detailed confession in his affidavit of 5 January 1995). The following Wednesday Barrett was admitted to the Windsor Unit of the Fazakerley Hospital for treatment for alcoholism and Richard Bark-Jones issued his statement retracting the confession.

Barrett tells us that in his sober moments he intentionally led Alan Gray a 'merry dance'. It was Gray, he says, who was constantly pushing him to provide evidence of his forgery and produce a proper account of it, hence the 5 January 1995 affidavit. But his accounts were lies, he claims, and nor were they good ones because 'I kept on slipping up'. To the people who believe his forgery claim, he would say, 'More fools them, more fools them. They believe this drunken story. Just pain, misery . . . and I can say anything.'

Since Shirley Harrison's book was first published in October 1993, Michael Barrett has received in excess of £70,000 in royalty payments. There has been precious little to show for it. Much of it disappeared during the lost years of his heaviest drinking. There had been allegations, though, that some had made its way to an unidentified organiser, a 'Mr Big', of a forgery conspiracy. At one point details of Barrett's bank statements had even made their way on to the internet, revealing regular payments of £1,000 to an unidentified source. Given the dates in 1994, Barrett is convinced these were cash withdrawals (his withdrawal limit was £1,000) to pay for occasional parties, a car he bought for Jenny for £4,000, a wardrobe of clothes, etc. 'It went,' he said, 'here, there and everywhere.'

Michael Barrett's involvement with the Diary has not been a happy one, though he appears now to be getting his life back together again. But the story of the Diary is not fully told yet. Despite the many tests by experts in ink, handwriting and paper, for all the weighty opinions of historians, psychologists and authorities on the Ripper, not to mention the best efforts of Scotland Yard detectives, journalists and private investigators, over the last decade, we are no nearer knowing the true origins of this most controversial of documents than on that day in March 1992 when Barrett's telephone call to Doreen Montgomery catapulted it into the public domain. Of one thing, Michael Barrett tells us as we are leaving, he is certain. 'I want a future. I want to walk away from the Diary, forever.'

Index

Figures in bold refer to illustrations within the text.